GOVERNMENT
ZERO

Also by Michael Savage

Stop the Coming Civil War

GOVERNMENT ZERO

ZERO

NO BORDERS, NO LANGUAGE, NO CULTURE

MICHAEL SAVAGE

CENTER STREET

NEW YORK • NASHVILLE

Center Street
Hachette Book Group
1290 Avenue of the Americas, New York, NY 10104
centerstreet.com
twitter.com/centerstreet

Originally published in hardcover and ebook by Center Street in October 2015.
First Trade Paperback Edition: October 2016

Center Street is a division of Hachette Book Group, Inc. The Center Street name and logo are trademarks of Hachette Book Group, Inc.

The publisher is not responsible for websites (or their content) that are not owned by the publisher.

The Hachette Speakers Bureau provides a wide range of authors for speaking events. To find out more, go to www.HachetteSpeakersBureau.com or call (866) 376-6591.

LCCN: 2015949768

ISBNs: 978-1-4555-3609-2 (trade paperback), 978-1-4555-3610-8 (ebook)

Printed in the United States of America

LSC-C

10 9 8 7 6 5 4 3 2 1

Contents

GOVERNMENT ZERO

CHAPTER 1

Government Zero

What Is Government Zero?

There is a dance of death in the West and actual death in the Middle East, courtesy of the Islamofascists. Meanwhile, the Caesar in the White House entertains himself with a thousand sycophants, partying on behind closed doors as if the Islamofascist hand will not touch him. He thinks he's protected from this new plague, the Black Death of radical Islam.

We're facing something the West hasn't had to deal with since the wars of religion in the sixteenth and seventeenth centuries. When those religious wars ended in one place, they began in another. They lasted for over one hundred years.

The same thing is happening right now. The radical Muslims are on the warpath and they are against everyone else. They are against Muslims who are not as fanatical. They are against the members of all other religions. They think they are going to take us back to some pristine religious period in human history that never actually occurred.

It's all complete rubbish. These "faith warriors" live lower than the pigs they despise. They kidnap and rape eight-year-old girls and say the Quran authorizes it. They're not purists. They're killers. They're Nazis in head scarfs. They aren't leading a religious revival. They're trying to take us back to a state of barbarism that has been extinct for 1,200 years.

This is a barbaric revolution, and we have a man in the White House who denies its existence. But whether he chooses to acknowledge it or not, it's going to continue until someone puts a stop to it.

Jonathan Sacks called the fight against radical Islam the "defining conflict of the next generation."[1] He likened radical Islam to a starfish. When you cut off a spider's head, it dies. But when you cut off the leg of a starfish, the starfish can regenerate it. Radical political Islam is a starfish. If you defeat ISIS or al-Qaeda, they will merely come back under another name.[2]

Why would any government bring in unvetted Muslim immigrants at a time like this? It would seem that only an insane prince would do this to his country. But Obama is not insane. He's stoned. He's stoned on the orthodoxy of the progressive left. Obama and his supporters are drunk on their ideology. They think they're going to create a progressive utopia by continuing their attack on all Western values.

This is precisely how great civilizations of the past declined and eventually fell. They rejected the values that made them great and degenerated into narcissism and selfishness. They kept on partying until they were too weak to defend themselves. Then, the unthinkable happened. They fell.

We've all seen documentary evidence of the Islamofascist thugs in ISIS swinging sledgehammers at priceless artifacts they deem offensive to Islam. For one thousand years, these treasures of antiquity survived wars, earthquakes, and other man-made disasters, but not the current disaster of fundamentalist

Islam. As the columns of ancient ruins fall and the faces of ancient kings and queens are slammed with sledgehammers, we watch in horror, our advanced military technology apparently powerless to stop these Islamic vandals.

But it is not our technology or our military that has failed to thwart this destruction of priceless treasures. No. Just as we stand idly by as young girls are kidnapped, raped, and sold into slavery, we are paralyzed not by a lack of technology, but by a lack of will. We have either zero leadership or a leadership secretly enabling these crimes against humanity.

Closer to home, we are similarly paralyzed as this most evil of administrations swings its sledgehammers at our most revered institutions. A climate of fear grips the people as the sneaks in high places spy on us, sell us out to Red China in a secret trade deal, decimate our medical system, eviscerate our military leadership, evaporate our borders, erase our culture, and attack religion's basic tenets. Meanwhile, millions of illegal aliens pour over our southern border, bringing with them an unwillingness to assimilate into American culture, refusing even to speak English.

This is what I call Government Zero. We are supposed to be a nation where the government is "of the people, by the people, and for the people." Yet every poll shows this rogue government of sneaks and traitors seems to relish doing the opposite of the will of the people. It is a government of itself, by itself, and for itself, run by lobbyists.

In short, Government Zero is absolute, unchecked government power and zero representation of the people. It doesn't exist to promote conservative or liberal principles. It is not pro-immigration or anti-immigration. It is not capitalist or socialist. It is not religious or atheist. Those are all just means to its end.

Its end is its own preservation and growth. This is by no means a new concept. Most governments throughout history have exploited those they ruled for the benefit of those who controlled them. Before the birth of the American republic, Government Zero was the rule, not the exception.

That was what made the United States a great experiment. When the founders wrote the words "We the People," they flipped the distribution of power that had existed for thousands of years upside down. They put most of the power in the hands of the people and reserved very little for the government. The government was heavily regulated, and the people were largely free. The government was servant and the people its master.

It was no coincidence that the American people flourished under this scenario. The free society allowed them to pursue their happiness in a largely free market and realize exponential economic and cultural growth. The government served the interests of the people, not because it was good in and of itself, but because it was restrained and ruled by the people.

After over one hundred years of progressive assault, that relationship has reversed. Government has become the master and the people its servant. The people are restrained and the government is free to do anything it wants. The government is all-powerful and the people are powerless. The government is secret and the people have no privacy.

It's a watershed moment in American history, but again, it's nothing new. It's America reverting back to the bondage that has defined most of human history.

If that sounds somewhat abstract, I'll bring it home for you. The government can act in its own interests only by acting against yours. It can grow richer only by making you poorer.

It can expand its activity only by limiting your freedom. It can ensure its own safety only by threatening yours.

That's why the government is attacking everything that makes the world livable for the rest of us. It is attacking free enterprise, because it needs higher taxes and more regulation to expand its wealth and power. It is promoting open borders, because immigrants from socialist or Islamic countries don't share our traditions of individual liberty and limited government. It wages a war on police, because civil unrest allows it to exercise more centralized power or even martial law, eventually with a federal police force answering only to the kings and queens of government. It attacks freedom of speech, because dissent is like kryptonite to an all-powerful government.

It attacks religion, perverting its very meaning, in order to replace what Karl Marx called "the opium of the masses" with an all-powerful central government becoming the new heroin of the masses. We are well on the road to replacing the former Soviet system with an emerging USSA, the United Soviet States of America.

Thomas Paine wrote,

> *Society in every state is a blessing, but government even in its best state is but a necessary evil; in its worst state an intolerable one; for when we suffer, or are exposed to the same miseries by a government, which we might expect in a country without government, our calamity is heightened by reflecting that we furnish the means by which we suffer.*[3]

That couldn't be truer today, when we fund not only the government itself through our taxes, but also the government employee unions which continue to make the government itself bigger and more oppressive. AFSCME, the largest trade union for public employees in the United States, gave over $65 million "to politicians, lobbyists and activist groups, according to 2014 federal reports obtained by Watchdog.org."[4]

If your intuition tells you most of this money went to Democratic politicians or left-wing advocacy groups and lobbyists, your intuition is correct. It's just one more way Government Zero feeds itself by draining our economic lifeblood.

Out of the Frying Pan

The good news is this disastrous presidency will finally come to an end in a little over a year. The bad news is we could jump out of the frying pan and into the fire, with the Arsonist in charge of the whole country. President Hillary Clinton would be even worse than Barack Obama. She has all of the anti-American, socialist credentials Obama has, along with a strength and toughness he lacks. That means she'd be even more effective for the wrong side.

Meanwhile, Clinton's Democratic rivals are gaining traction with the loser segment of the electorate, preaching a message identical to that delivered by the 1930s street-corner communists on New York's Lower East Side. Unfortunately, they can't be dismissed, because the loser segment is growing rapidly in a rigged economic system, with massive welfare and an unlimited immigration of have-nots.

New York's Leninist mayor Bill de Blasio has released a thirteen-point national "Progressive Agenda" that some call the liberal answer to the 1990s Republican Contract with America. The agenda is virtually indistinguishable from the policy platforms of the Socialist Party USA and Communist Party USA, both of which have nearly identical versions of the points on their websites.

Even if Clinton survives her primary challenges, she will have been dragged even further left than she was to start with. She's already changed her position on gay marriage and joined Obama's war on police, along with rejecting the tough immigration policies implemented during her own husband's presidency.[5] She's counting on the same voter coalition that put Obama in the White House twice to sweep her to victory, meaning no position she takes can be too far left.

The vast majority of Americans completely oppose this emerging Sovietization. If the 2014 midterm elections were any indication, more and more Americans are waking up to the very real threat posed by this demonic progressive movement. If you are reading this book, you are probably one of those American patriots desperate to save this nation from ruin.

Unfortunately, elections may not be enough. With an imperial presidency on one side and no real opposition party on the other, there is little use in throwing out the Democrats and replacing them with progressives from another party. We gave Republicans control of the White House, Senate, and House of Representatives for six years in the last decade. What did we get?

I'll tell you what we didn't get. We didn't get an iota of protection of our borders, language, or culture. We didn't get smaller government or freer markets. We didn't get less federal spending. We didn't get a sensible foreign policy that places the interests of the American people first. We didn't get any improvement in immigration policy or even a good-faith effort to stem the tide of illegal immigration. At best, we got less rapidly progressive progressivism.

Can 2016 be different? It's hard to make that case. The very real prospect of a liberal Republican president, Senate Majority Leader Mitch McConnell, and Speaker of the House John Boehner will maintain one-party rule.

Jeb Bush couldn't be clearer on his noncommitment to our borders, language, and culture. He's pro–Common Core. He's not only come out publicly for amnesty for illegals, he's *rebuked* fellow Republicans, including Donald Trump, for respecting the wishes of their supporters and opposing it.[6] In his opinion, Republican presidential candidates should instead try to educate us poor rubes on how mistaken we are to ask the federal government to fulfill its primary objective: to defend America's borders.

Just to ensure there is no mistaking where he stands, Bush released a video on May 5 in which he commemorated Cinco de Mayo and extolled the great contributions of Mexican-Americans to the United States. He delivered the message personally on camera, *in Spanish.*[7]

Meanwhile, big-government conservatives McConnell and Boehner both defeated conservative movements to oust them from leadership in their respective houses in Congress. Upon retaining his Speakership, Boehner gave Nancy Pelosi an awkward bear hug and a kiss.[8] He then purged the newly elected, authentic conservatives by removing them from key committees and cutting off their funding! This was a tactic right out of the Soviet government master plan.

Supreme Zero

As we found out this past summer, we can't count on the Supreme Court to represent us, either. The Court is supposed to uphold the Constitution as the will of the people in the long-term, even when the people's representatives make mistakes in the short-term.

Instead, the Court trampled on the Constitution, the will of the people, and basic logic in its two landmark decisions in June. It decided it could rewrite legislation in upholding Obamacare,[9] just ignoring the very intentional stipulation that subsidies for health insurance premiums be paid only to recipients who purchased their insurance from an exchange "established by the state." Thirty-six states had refused to establish such exchanges. The Court ruled the subsidies should be paid in those states anyway.

Don't let the media convince you this was all over a simple legislative oversight. That's a lie. The designers of Obamacare intentionally put that stipulation in to coerce the states into setting up the exchanges.[10] They believed the states could be bought off with the subsidies. They were wrong.

Refusing to establish exchanges was a clear rejection of Obamacare by the overwhelming majority of state governments. That was their only recourse in rejecting a terrible law that had passed Congress without a single Republican vote.

So Justice Roberts was not defending democracy when he threw the rule of law and basic logic out the window in upholding the Obamacare subsidies in states that had intentionally rejected them. It was just more of the same Government Zero we get from the president and Congress.

Just a day later, the Court ruled state laws prohibiting gay marriage were unconstitutional, again overriding the wishes of the people and trampling upon the principle of constitutional government. Justice Kennedy issued what Justice Scalia called in dissent "an opinion lacking even a thin veneer of law."[11] Somehow, Kennedy imagined the ratifiers of the Fourteenth Amendment to the Constitution extended equal protection of the law to homosexuals seeking to get married, even though homosexuality was illegal in every state at the time.

This is where we are. We have three branches of government that are not only supposed to check each other with their separate powers, but limit themselves to the powers delegated to them in the Constitution. They do neither. Instead, they join together in looting our wealth, trampling our liberty, and destroying our culture at the behests of special interests and their lobbyists.

The Progressive-Islamist Takeover

Progressives have long waged a war on religion as part of their Marxist agenda for an atheist, socialist state. To get there, they believe they have to tear down and destroy everything that defines Western Civilization as it is. They share that vision with the unlikeliest of conceivable allies: the radical Islamists.

What is happening in America right now can only be described as a Progressive-Islamist takeover. It may be hard for most people to imagine how committed atheists could possibly be working with committed religious fanatics. Both groups would mercilessly exterminate the other under the right circumstances. We've seen how communist countries have treated religious people in the past, and we can see how the Islamofascists treat the subgroups who make up the progressive movement today. Those who don't swear allegiance to their brand of extremist Islam are killed or exiled. Homosexuals are thrown off rooftops. Opponents are beheaded or burned alive.

Yet, everywhere we look, we see American progressives defending Islam. They make excuses for radical Islam's atrocities while branding anyone who criticizes them as bigots. They hold conferences on terrorism and exclude anyone who might talk about the threat of radical Islamist sleeper cells within our borders, while focusing on the "threat" from American Christians, conservatives, and patriots instead.

They support Obama in bringing in hundreds of thousands of Muslims as refugees with no way of screening them as potential members of ISIS or al-Qaeda, even as those groups boast of infiltrating us in this very manner.

I'm not talking about a conscious conspiracy between the two groups, per se. They are more like kindred spirits. They may not have the same vision for what society should look like when they're finished with it, but they share the belief that American society as it is today must be destroyed. That's the linkage. Remember, the driving principle of the 1960s radicals was, "Bring it all down, man!"

Both groups also believe in absolute, autocratic rule over the people. They both want to run every aspect of your life. The progressives may be atheists and the Islamofascists religious fanatics, but they both want to take away your *freedom* of religion. They also want to take away your economic freedom. If you haven't noticed, every Islamic nation has a socialist economy. That's because socialism and autocracy are one and the same.

If a Progressive-Islamic takeover sounds unbelievable to you, I'm not surprised. The media continues to bend over backward to support a president who will not even say the word "Islamic" when he talks about the Islamic State of Iraq and Syria. They call themselves Islamic, but the president says they aren't.

The progressives claim the president avoids saying "Islamic" so as not to offend his Muslim allies in fighting the extremists. That's very convenient. It also just happens to obscure the truth in every public statement he makes about what the Islamofascists are doing. Those not keenly aware of what is going on would never suspect that we are fighting maniacs who commit their atrocities in the name of Islam.

The president's newspeak fits neatly into a much larger pattern. In every conceivable space, from immigration policy, to law enforcement, to education, to social policy, to the military, Islam is accommodated and defended.

Left-wing magazines print completely false stories about university campus rapes, while ISIS forces eight-year-old girls to marry if they're Muslim and become sex slaves if they aren't. Where is the feminist outrage over these atrocities? Why aren't gay activists marching in the streets over ISIS throwing homosexuals off rooftops?

They're too busy trying to put Christian bakeries and pizzerias out of business for not wanting to participate in their weddings.

President Obama has refused to curb illegal immigration through our southern border or to deport illegals once they're caught, in violation of his oath of office. But illegal immigrants from Central and South America are not the biggest immigration threat facing us. Much more dangerous are the hundreds of thousands of Muslims this administration has brought in through its refugee program from war-torn Muslim countries like Somalia and Syria.

What possible reason could there be for admitting more Muslim refugees than Christian, when Christians are being slaughtered by the thousands in the new Holocaust in the Middle East and elsewhere? Why bring in people among whom are those sworn to kill us and leave those being killed to fend for themselves?

One reason nothing is being done about this new Holocaust is that the government-media complex won't admit it exists. Time and again, the president has ignored or downplayed the atrocities committed by the Islamofascists, referring to them as "zealots" adhering to some unknown ideology. The media virtually never calls him on this, but they are quick to yell "Islamophobia" the minute anyone criticizes even the most brutal violence perpetrated in the name of that religion.

At the same time, the president has pursued a disastrous deal with Iran that both Israel and our traditional Sunni Arab allies have condemned. When Israeli prime minister Benjamin Netanyahu heroically spoke out against it to the U.S. Congress, Obama snubbed his visit under the pretense of neutrality toward the Israeli elections, while sending hundreds of operatives to Israel to try to thwart Netanyahu's reelection.

The administration not only claims it is committed to defeating ISIS, but that its alliance with Iranian-backed Shiite militias is winning the war and has the Islamic State contained and on the defensive. Yet, the day after the administration tried to intimidate the media into reporting more favorably about the war, ISIS captured the strategically important city of Ramadi. After the vermin in ISIS blew up portions of the magnificent ancient temples of Palmyra, what happened? Did you ever read about this atrocity against world civilization?

Just a few days after that, the president gave a commencement speech at the U.S. Coast Guard Academy in Connecticut, during which he told them the greatest security threat they'll face is climate change![12]

Is it all coincidence? I'll let you be the judge of that. All I can do is present the facts and the most objective interpretation of them I can give you. But I'm going to challenge you to look a little deeper than the talking points Obama's sorority or the Republican nonopposition leadership throw at you. What might have seemed like isolated news events the first time you heard them form an unmistakable pattern.

Vain and Aspiring Men and Women

Samuel Adams once wrote, "If ever the Time should come, when vain & aspiring Men shall possess the highest Seats in Government, our Country will stand in Need of its experienced Patriots to prevent its Ruin."[13]

I believe that time has come. We are going to need every patriot taking a stand to stop the relentless attack on our nation, both from within and without.

Recent polls show a leftward shift in America,[14] with more people identifying as liberal. Why is this happening? Because not a single Establishment Republican has articulated what a nationalist is and why a nationalist movement is necessary to save our identity as a nation. Those moving leftward are following George Orwell's satirical adage, "Freedom is Slavery."

Nationalism vs. National Socialism

As soon as anyone says the word *nationalism*, people immediately think of Adolf Hitler. That's because nationalism has been successfully denigrated by the left since the end of World War II. If you are a nationalist, you must be a Nazi, as far as the left is concerned. A lot of well-meaning people believe them.

What the progressives conveniently fail to mention is that the Nazis weren't just nationalists, they were socialists, too. The word "Nazi" is merely a shortened version of their party name: Nationalsozialistische Deutsche Arbeiterpartei or National-*Socialist* German Workers' Party. The party sought to implement socialism within a nationalist framework, meaning it put the needs of the nation before any international socialist movement.

Their nationalism made them fierce rivals of the internationalist communists, but they were *socialists* all the same. Before the Holocaust got under way, Hitler became internationally famous for his implementation of a command economy. Hitler allowed private business owners to retain titles to their businesses, but he regulated them so heavily that decisions on what to produce and how much were really made by the state. They were state-owned enterprises in all but name.

At one point, Hitler's control over the economy was so authoritarian that people were forbidden from quitting their jobs.

Hitler even got the government into the automobile business, just like another dictator we know. You may not know this yourself, but the Volkswagen, literally "the people's car," was originally produced by a state-owned factory and marketed to people who would purchase with a strange, government savings plan that never had a chance of solvency.

In short, it wasn't nationalism that made the Nazis so horrible, it was Hitler's brand of socialism. Socialism is by nature an authoritarian political system. The state seizes forcible command of the means of production and the fruits of each individual's labor. That's the definition of the word *socialism*.

Hitler's gross abuse of civil liberties was the natural result of his dictatorial command of the economy. The former were necessitated by the latter, just as civil liberties are being attacked here in support of Obama's policies. Had I told you ten years ago that someday soon you could face legal penalties for not buying a product from a private company, would you have believed me? That's just what Obamacare legally requires you to do. This is the true nature of socialism.

The nationalism I propose is obviously not national socialism. We want a strong military that projects power but is used only in defense of American interests, not to conquer the world. We wish to preserve our borders, language, and culture because they are the foundation of our liberty, not because we believe we belong to any "master race." We promote truly free markets within a regulatory structure that seeks to preserve a free and fair environment, not institute a command economy. We insist upon tariffs on goods manufactured in countries where tariffs are imposed on imported American goods or where their currency is manipulated to rig the import-export scales.

I have the intellectual honesty to grant that Obama is not an absolute dictator. However, you'll see he is an authoritarian when you look at the similarities between his authoritarian policies and those of other dictatorial regimes.

- He claims authority to spy on every American, collecting their phone and e-mail records without a judicial warrant.
- He claimed the authority to kill an American citizen on American soil without due process. He had to back up on this after Rand Paul's 2013 filibuster.
- He seized control of an automobile manufacturer and violated contract and bankruptcy laws by distributing assets to unions, rather than to the company's creditors.
- He has given tacit support to street gangs, who could be compared to Brownshirts, undermining the uniformed, local police.
- He may intend to institute a national police force.
- He has essentially erased our border with Mexico, not permitting our Border Patrol to do its job.
- He has purged the military of many patriotic and talented leaders.
- He has antagonized Russia, alienated Israel, cozied up to communist China, and reopened an embassy in Cuba without demanding any advancement of human rights.

These are all the natural outgrowths of socialism, a political and economic system that assigns too much power to the government. It is impossible to separate absolute economic power and absolute power over all aspects of life, as every nation which has experimented with socialism has learned.

Nationalism without socialism and racism has nothing to

do with the Nazis or any other authoritarian society. It is simply love of one's country and its national identity. America's national identity is built around personal freedom. Its borders, language, and culture are the elements out of which that national identity is formed. A nationalist approach toward preserving our borders, language, and culture is the only way to preserve our freedom. We must organize and create a vigorous nationalist movement.

Critics may argue I can't call for a nationalist movement and still claim to be a small-government conservative who supports limits on federal power. That isn't true. Our federal government today is an internationalist one. It aspires to rule the whole world and is willing to act against the interests of its own constituents to achieve that goal.

A nationalist government in Washington, DC, would actually be smaller government with a more limited scope than the one operating there now. It would represent the will of its own people, returning to its founding principles, including forgoing powers not delegated to it and left with the states or the people. As Abraham Lincoln so eloquently put it, it would be "a government of the people, by the people, and for the people," not a government of the New World Order controlled by a secretive group of unelected plutocrats.

CHAPTER 2

Zero Leadership

One of the consequences of Government Zero is Zero Leadership. We're already there. We have a rogue president, a sleeping Congress, a supine media, a docile, narcotized populace, and a barely functioning Supreme Court.

The rogue president tramples every institution, divides the people by race, sex, religion, and political orientation. He set out to transform the beautiful nation, and in so doing, he's causing irreparable damage.

Like a stoned plastic surgeon, he botched the operation and created a mutilated face and an ugly body politic. The anesthesia he used when he applied his scalpel forever rotted the body politic within. His toxic mixture of race and class warfare has been injected so deeply and so often and in such high dosages that the once beautiful nation will soon be unrecognizable.

The American presidency reached a new low point when Barack Obama gave his speech in Selma, Alabama. On the fiftieth anniversary of Bloody Sunday, when true victims of racism bravely marched in protest of their oppression, the president did what he always does: He divided instead of united. He reopened wounds that were healing, instead of helping them to heal further. This president takes demagoguery to a whole new level.

He was doing just what he wanted to do, which was to divide black against white, straight against gay, Asian against Hispanic, Hispanic against black. This is what the president spends every waking moment thinking about how to do.

I can refute his demagogic speech point by point, but first I want to share something completely different with you. I want to tell you about two dreams I had, both on the same night, that are both very important to what I'm trying to tell you.

The White Owl

In the first dream, I was on a trail in the woods, with my son and another person. I used to walk in the woods with my son quite often when he was a kid. As I walked in the woods in my dream, I came upon a woman. She seemed to be walking a dog on a long leash, perhaps a thirty-foot lead. I stopped for a moment, because I didn't recognize the breed of her dog. But it wasn't a dog.

As the animal turned toward me, I realized it was a white owl with one eye. It had one eye, hollowed out. I asked the woman, "Do you often come to this place in the woods?"

"Yes," she said, "we will know each other."

Immediately afterward, in my dream, I was giving a lecture in a seminar room, in a private facility. I was talking to my audience on the meaning of rain. Then, I gave a seminar to another small group on the meaning of hunger. I told them:

"Most of you understand by now that you can eat the most expensive meal in New York City, or the most expensive meal in Los Angeles, but not enjoy one bite of it. Do you know why? Because you're hungry. I am going to teach you today how to truly be hungry, so you can taste your food again."

Now comes the most important part. In the next dream, there was a black woman in a black van. She was middle-aged and heavyset. Around her were a group of black teenagers, with bandanas on. She spoke to them quietly, saying:

"America is a deep country. You must find forgiveness in yourselves in order to know that deepness."

This is what I had prayed the first black president would teach America. Instead, this president teaches the opposite. He teaches division. He teaches hatred. He teaches envy. He teaches the antithesis of his alleged Christian beliefs. We constantly hear he's not a Muslim; he's a Christian. It doesn't matter. He isn't practicing either religion.

Divisive Demagoguery

He is instead practicing the religion of demagoguery. The black woman in my dream was a healer. She told her young audience about the healing power of forgiveness. But Obama is unable to forgive. He does not have forgiveness in his heart, as Jesus taught us to have.

Let's not forget that Barack Obama has no wrongs for which to forgive anyone. He wasn't beaten by cops for demanding his rights. He wasn't denied the right to vote or go to school. He was a spoiled white kid with a black father, who decided to pretend to be a downtrodden black man.

He talks like he experienced racism himself, when he never did. Obama grew up in Honolulu, Hawaii, in a multiethnic society where there is almost no racial discrimination. If anything, whites are the minority discriminated against in Honolulu. Barack Obama has no experience with racism. Yet, he wraps himself in all the rhetoric of those who did.

Even worse, he incites hatred in black Americans for racism where it doesn't exist, all for political gain. That is how cynically and bitterly this man hates America.

I'm not saying there is no racism in the world today. Of course there is. But Obama talks as if it's still 1964 and he is Martin Luther King. He talks to black voters as if they aren't voters, as if they hadn't won that right fifty years ago. He talks to them as if Darren Wilson is one of those cops beating protestors on Bloody Sunday fifty years ago, even though two separate investigations concluded Wilson was telling the truth and found no case against him.

This is the kind of leadership you get when the people have no representation and the government exists of itself, by itself, and for itself. You get lies instead of the truth. You get division instead of unity. You get hatred instead of healing. That's Zero Leadership.

I shared my dreams with you for a reason. My soul spirit came to me that night. Those of you who are intuitive, who know there is something beyond the one-dimensional world of politics, know what the dreams meant. They are telling us that the only thing that can save this nation is spiritual, not political.

We have a void of spirituality in this nation today. It is hollowing us out and destroying us from top to bottom. Regardless of your religion, only by finding your spiritual center can you overcome the division and hatred being forced upon you by Obama and his allies.

Of course, the propagandists in the media aren't talking about him this way. They loved his speech at Selma. They called it "one of his best."[1] The *Missouri Democrat* tweeted, "I dare anyone to listen to the speech the President gave today and then say he doesn't love America."[2]

Can you believe that? That is classic Soviet propaganda, right out of *Pravda*. It is the opposite of the truth. Every line of that speech seethed with resentment for America and all the wrongs Obama believes America continues to perpetrate.

In a way, Bloomberg was right. It was one of his best speeches, in terms of accomplishing his goals. He was able to mix lies with the truth to foster division and enmity, under the pretense of honoring real heroes of the civil rights movement who overcame real racism.

In that way, Obama is a genius. He is a genius at dividing people and dismantling this great nation. He is a genius at dismantling our military. He is a genius at wrecking our economy with zero interest rates, courtesy of "Grandma" Janet Yellen, allowing him to borrow trillions. You'll soon need a wheelbarrow full of currency to buy a loaf of bread, just like they did in the Weimar Republic.

Think back to my second dream. One would assume, a century and a half after the abolition of slavery, after the Great Society, affirmative action, and trillions of dollars in welfare, after the first black president, the first black attorney general, and black CEOs running major corporations, there would be forgiveness. But there is no forgiveness in this man's heart.

Maybe I have to have forgiveness in my heart for this man who is destroying the great nation my grandfather immigrated to over a hundred years ago.

So, Obama gives a speech in Selma at the site where racial

persecution occurred fifty years ago and takes the opportunity to remind us of how terrible he believes America really is. He didn't just talk about racial discrimination. He reminded us that women didn't always have the right to vote, and about the "gay Americans whose blood ran on the streets of San Francisco and New York."[3]

Blood ran in the streets? Did I miss something? Was there a war in the streets against gays in San Francisco and New York? Yes, there has been violence against gays in America in the past, as there has been in every country in the world. I wish the president was more concerned about the Muslims who throw gay people off rooftops and then stone them to death if they survive the fall. No, Obama is only concerned with how to make America look bad.

This is American history for our president. All he knows about the history of this nation is racism, oppression, and exploitation. Nothing positive happened, except for the work done by slaves or oppressed women. His history book doesn't have the chapter where those supposedly evil white men created the freest country that has ever existed.

It doesn't contain those pages documenting the invention of the telephone, penicillin, the steam engine, motion pictures, the airplane, the suspension bridge, radio, or dozens of other life-changing, history-making inventions, by those supposedly evil, white entrepreneurs seeking profits. It certainly doesn't contain the millions of white American males who fought against slavery, much less southern plantation owners like Robert E. Lee, who freed their slaves voluntarily the minute they were legally allowed to do so.

Like everything else that comes out of his mouth, Barack Obama's version of American history is a lie.

Not only did he use the Selma event to stimulate anger, resentment, jealousy, and revenge, he actually invited the race-baiting huckster Al Sharpton to stand with him. Meanwhile, the *New York Times*, in true Soviet *Pravda* style, airbrushed out the attendance of George W. Bush and his family in their picture of the speech.[4]

That's right, the Bushes marched with the president at Selma, but as in Orwell's *1984*, the *New York Times* tried to convince you it never happened. Instead, they showed that street vermin, Al Sharpton. It's chilling.

Along with his resentful, passive-aggressive missives, Obama also peddled his usual catalog of socialist canards. One of my favorites was, "We are the slaves who built the White House and the economy of the South."

This is another half truth. The manual labor provided by the slaves was good, honest work, and it was horrible they were not doing it voluntarily or with compensation. But Obama pretends there were no architects, no engineers, no management, and no capital investment for the raw materials that also went into building the White House.

This is the same fallacy leftists since Karl Marx have pushed about laborers providing all of the value of production. I respect laborers, bricklayers, and carpenters for doing honest work, without which there would be no building. But Obama and the left talk as if the building would exist without capitalists, whose labor in the past produced the savings needed to buy the raw materials and pay the bricklayers and carpenters. He talks as if it would exist without architects, engineers, or management.

If that's true, then why don't carpenters and bricklayers just build the building without the capitalist? Why don't they do what the capitalist has done themselves, instead of working for him? I don't have to answer these questions for you. The twentieth century answered them when tens of millions starved to death trying to put Marx's ideas into practice.

Zero Truth in Leadership

It wasn't so long ago that no one in America would have disagreed with what I just said. But when you have Government Zero, the truth itself dies. A government that exists by itself, of itself, and for itself must destroy the truth, because the truth sets people free.

I recently visited a Chinese antiquities store in San Francisco. An unusually colorful pair of wooden "Foo dogs" in the window stopped me in my walk up Grant Avenue. They were ugly and colorful. Created to ward off evil spirits, they were placed at the entrance of the homes of the rich. These temple "lion dogs" date from the early seventeenth century of the Ming dynasty.

I learned that during the Communist "cultural revolution," the Red Guards roamed China and destroyed these Foo dogs as symbols of a "decadent, bourgeois" culture. Mao believed they were, in Obama's terms, symbols of "unfairness." People tried to remove and hide these treasures of China's vast cultural heritage. Some even removed ceramic roof tiles on which these lion dogs were mounted to save them from Mao's rapacious young thugs of political correctness. Mao named the thugs "Red Guards." Sound familiar?

Today, our rogue president's red guards are rapidly destroying every vestige of America's cultural heritage. From the schools to universities, young brains are being washed of history and logic. Science is being replaced by rote repetition of big lies. Children are being taught that a better, more fair world is being created when, in fact, it is a totalitarian monstrosity.

It is a world of conformist beliefs, not critical thought. It's a world where centralized authority replaces individualism; where conformity and nihilism trump creativity and faith. It is a world where the red guards of America, once independent media and academic establishments, now seek out, remove, and attempt to destroy any symbol of American distinction and greatness.

Obama is great at leading America in the wrong direction. He certainly has the audacity to spew hatred for America with a smile and the whispering intensity of a preacher. All the while he's leading us backward instead of forward.

For the rogue president, it is still 1963 and there is still Jim Crow. Socialism is still cool; it hasn't been fully discredited yet. America is still divided racially. Gays are still beaten in the streets. Women still don't have the right to vote.

He wants to lead us backward, because it divides us and keeps us fighting with one another. That is the foundation of his party's success. And he's good at it. That's what makes him so dangerous.

When I say "dangerous," I'm not exaggerating. Leadership has consequences, whether it's good leadership in the right direction or terrible leadership in the wrong direction. We've just seen civilization completely break down in Ferguson, Missouri, over what turned out to be a tragic but justified use of lethal force by a policeman defending himself. The big lie, "Hands up, don't shoot," was an invention.

Had the president and his attorney general condemned the looters and rioters unequivocally, or even just stayed out of it altogether, it might not have gone so far. But they both had to weigh in and condemn Darren Wilson before any conclusive evidence of his guilt was available. Then it turned out there was no evidence. He was innocent. By then, it was too late. The city was already burning.

I'm not saying there is no racism anywhere in police departments or that people don't have a right to peacefully protest it where it really exists. But rioting, burning the private property of innocent bystanders, and using protest as an excuse for mayhem is not peaceful protest. It is not a right. It is a crime.

Safeguarding life and property is the first duty of any public official. That's why we have government in the first place. As the Roman consul Cicero said over two thousand years ago, "Although it was by Nature's guidance that men were drawn together into communities, it was in the hope of safeguarding their possessions that they sought the protection of cities."[5]

Incidentally, Cicero also warned us about the demagoguery of "income inequality." His friend Lucius Marcius Philippus introduced a bill to redistribute property and suggested in one of his speeches that all property should be equal. Cicero condemned the speech, saying, "What more ruinous policy than that could be conceived?"[6]

Wise men like Cicero have been warning us for thousands of years about demagogues preaching income inequality and subverting respect for private property. Aristotle warned us about it, too. So Obama is nothing new. He's just another Philippus. But he goes a step further in inciting a war on cops. He's not just threatening private property with his calls to "spread the wealth around." He's endangering everyone's lives by encouraging a war on cops.

It's not just in Ferguson. Obama's socialist ally, Mayor de

Bloodio of New York City, has been just as culpable as Obama and Holder in encouraging this violence. When two cops were killed, execution style, last December, the head of the police officer's union said the mayor had "blood on his hands."[7]

He was right. Leadership has consequences. I disagreed with the nonindictment of Eric Garner's killers. I said so unequivocally on my show, *The Savage Nation*. However, like any rational person, I blamed the killing on the individuals who perpetrated it, not every cop in New York.

Mayor de Bloodio did exactly the opposite. In rhetoric worthy of his socialist idol, Obama, he said he was afraid his son wasn't safe walking the streets anymore, "and not just from some of the painful realities of crime and violence in some of our neighborhoods, but safe from the very people they want to have faith in as their protectors."[8]

Do you see what is happening? These demagogues are not just inciting people's emotions to win elections. They are breaking down the pillars of civilized society. When that common bar thug dressed up as a cop killed Eric Garner, he should have been indicted. That he wasn't was injustice for Eric Garner and his family. But when you indict all cops everywhere and express sympathy for people who murder them, none of us are safe anymore.

This is where Obama and the progressives have led us. They have incited contempt for the protectors of life and property. They have encouraged hatred of everything great about America. They have convinced a lot of gullible young people that the freest, richest, greatest nation on earth is actually a prison where white privilege reigns, women and minorities are oppressed, workers are exploited, and the environment is destroyed.

Obama is the same kind of pedantic, academic socialist as the professors who tried to have the American flag banned on the campus of the University of California, Irvine. They sided with a bunch of useless, idiotic left-wing students who drafted the petition because the American flag "contributes to racism." Does this sound familiar? These ideas start with our leadership.

Universities have become hotbeds of anti-Americanism, bent on attacking the nation's honor itself. It was from this environment that the current president emerged, and his fellow socialists in academia are feeling brave.

Do you want to know how bad this poison can get? One hundred eighty Americans have actually attempted to join ISIS.[9] That's right. Their minds are so warped by progressive hatred for America that they've actually decided the ninth-century throwbacks who burn people alive might be better.

Certainly, 180 people is like a dust speck in a nation of over three hundred million. But you should be alarmed that even one American kid could actually reject the freedom this country offers for the murderous tyranny of the Islamofascists. This is what happens when your leadership wages nonstop, demagogic war on freedom of religion, free speech, private property, and free markets. Hatred of freedom and civilization drives people toward the antithesis of freedom and civilization.

Of course, some of these are not American kids at all. They weren't U.S. citizens and they never did believe in American principles. They were radical Muslims living in Obama's America, where there are no borders. Tuberculosis, measles, and EV-D68 are not the only things this administration's irresponsible immigration policies have imported. It has also imported some of the Islamofascists themselves.

Zero Leadership for the World

That brings us to Obama's leadership on the world stage. In the face of the real oppressors of women, homosexuals, and other minorities, oppressors who are beheading people and burning them alive, he is a complete pushover. Where is his audacity in dealing with ISIS? Where is his audacity in dealing with Iran? Instead of dealing with these real threats, he is provoking a war with Russia that America cannot afford and may very well lose.

Let me tell you about another speech that was given just a few days before Obama's Selma address. It wasn't given by a Republican. It wasn't even given by an American. It was given by a foreign head of state, but, ironically, it was the first time in a long time I felt proud to be an American again.

I'm talking about Israeli prime minister Bibi Netanyahu's speech to Congress on March 3, 2015.[10] It was a mirror image of Obama's speech, just as that leader is a mirror image of Obama. Here is a real leader, stating facts and showing pride in his country's history and heritage. His speech united instead of divided. Republicans and Democrats, who broke ranks with the president for the first time since his inauguration, were on their feet cheering on dozens of occasions.

I go back in history and compare this speech to something Winston Churchill did. He also addressed Congress, during World War II. Speaking just three weeks after Pearl Harbor, he said:

Sure I am that this day, now, we are the masters of our fate. That the task which has been set us is not above our strength.

That its pangs and toils are not beyond our endurance. As long as we have faith in our cause, and an unconquerable willpower, salvation will not be denied us. In the words of the Psalmist: "He shall not be afraid of evil tidings. His heart is fixed, trusting in the Lord."[11]

Can you imagine the comparison between Winston Churchill and the duplicitous community organizer we have in the White House today? Churchill's speech also united American Republicans and Democrats. It united the United States and Great Britain against the Axis powers. This is what real leaders do. They unite.

Real leaders are also stand-up people. Despite a long history of passive-aggressive sniping from the Obama administration, Netanyahu took considerable time to thank Obama personally for those times when the president *did* do his duty to support our ally. He was gracious and deferential to a man who has constantly tried to undermine him and his fight to protect Israel from enemies who want to destroy her.

In a way, he was talking to himself during that part of the speech. Obama did not attend, citing the American custom of not meeting with foreign heads of state so close to an election.

What hypocrisy. Weeks before the story broke, I warned my radio listeners on *The Savage Nation* that Obama had sent hundreds of operatives to Israel to try to undermine Netanyahu and the Likud Party in the Israeli election. We're supposed to believe it was a mere coincidence that tens of thousands of Israelis organized and called for Netanyahu's replacement just four days after his speech.[12]

Sure enough, barely a week after the protest, Fox News broke the story that a bipartisan commission was investigating whether the Obama administration was funding efforts to oust Netanyahu.[13]

He did more than fund those efforts. The president of the United States sent approximately two hundred fanatical left-wing street operatives, including one Jeremy Bird, who ran Obama's 2008 campaign with an iron fist, to try to overthrow Netanyahu. They failed.

This election was almost as significant for Americans as it was for Israel. If you analyze it, several things jump out at you.

First, the bias of the media was so overwhelming against Netanyahu that it was beyond an embarrassment. It was a joke, a laugh line. We know the media is all anti-American, all anti-Israel, all of the time. We know they're antinationalists. The media is comprised of overeducated and underlearned people who believe they're not citizens of America, or any other nation, but citizens of the world.

Barack Hussein Obama thinks the same way. Before he became president, he went to Berlin, and in that memorable, meaningless speech, the president of the United States called himself a "citizen of the world." Boy, did he ever mean it. It may have been the one and only thing he said that day that he truly meant. He certainly isn't at heart a citizen of the United States.

So, the Israeli election was to some extent about Obama. People ask me, "Are you happy that Netanyahu won?" I say, "Well, the real story is that Obama lost." He spent all of his powers trying to defeat Netanyahu short of going to war with Israel and he lost.

Those of you who are religious were celebrating and saying it was God's hand that gave Netanyahu victory. That's one way to look at it.

I'm more of a pragmatist than I am a religionist. Pragmatically speaking, the Jews in Israel know their backs are against the wall. They know what an existential threat to their survival means. Americans don't really know what it means because they live in a dream world.

I don't blame them for that. Who wants to walk around agitated twenty-four hours a day over what might be tomorrow when they can enjoy today? Very few. Those of us who do it for a living have to do it. We are hired to do it. We are hired to be the seers, and we see what's coming in this country.

Obama's attempt to manipulate the Israeli elections failed, but it was par for the course. He consistently attacks our allies and panders to our enemies, always leading the world toward greater instability. Obama wanted more socialist leadership in Israel. That would have made Israel easier to manipulate into accepting a Palestinian state, based on indefensible Israeli borders.

That would have furthered the progressive dream of one multicultural, socialist world order, but it is not in the best interests of the American people, any more than for the Israeli people. America's interests are best served by a strong Israel, as the bulwark of democracy and freedom in a region increasingly dominated by tyranny and ninth-century theocracy.

Obama's meddling in the Israeli elections was the Arab Spring strategy all over again. Remember how that started, with those "spontaneous" protests in the streets? Do you remember Hillary Clinton cackling "We came, we saw, he died," after Mu'ammar Gadhafi was killed by an Islamist mob? She was quite self-satisfied with her "Arab Spring," wasn't she? What do you think of the results now?

Take a look at the Middle East after this administration

toppled secular governments, allowed radical jihadists like the Muslim Brotherhood to seize power, and abandoned the Iraqi government instead of leaving a stabilizing force behind, as so many advised. It's more radically Islamist than it's been in a thousand years. ISIS has established a caliphate and threatens to take over all of Iraq and then move on to Syria.

Does this benefit the American citizens whose interests Obama is supposed to represent? No. This administration's foreign policy has worked in direct opposition to the interests of the American people, almost without exception.

That's just what it was doing when trying to bring about regime change in Israel. The president and his sorority want a leftist government in Israel that will not speak up, as Netanyahu did, when the United States makes the wrong deal with Iran. They want a government that will not, as Netanyahu said, stand alone and go to war, if it must, to safeguard the Israeli people.

Netanyahu was like Gary Cooper in *High Noon* during that speech. He said to the American people, "The bad guys want to kill me and my townsfolk. We would love for you to join us, but if you don't we're willing to fight alone."

That's not to say Netanyahu wants a war. He is a war hero and knows what war is. War is hell. It's the worst thing that can happen to a society. Neither Netanyahu nor the Israeli people want war with anyone. He said himself, "Now we're being told that the only alternative to this bad deal is war. That's just not true. The alternative to this bad deal is a much better deal."

The Democrats ignored these very clear statements and claim he's fearmongering, implying he does want a war.

Do you think it is fearmongering to explain what the throwbacks in Iran are? The mullahs of Iran have said they are going to wipe out the State of Israel and then kill all the Jews in the world. That should put the fear of God in your heart. It's not fearmongering to face reality.

It was actually Kentucky Democrat John Yarmouth who was doing the fearmongering when he implied Netanyahu wants war. He said Netanyahu's speech was "right out of Dick Cheney's playbook" and that "Netanyahu basically said that the only acceptable deal was a perfect deal or an ideal deal."[14] That's a lie.

The Israeli prime minister actually gave some good advice on how to both avoid a war and make a better deal with Iran, if only Obama and the Democrats were listening.

Unfortunately, the president claimed he didn't even watch the speech, which I find extremely hard to believe. Can you actually believe any leader in the world wasn't watching that speech? As I listened to the address, I saw the leaders of every nation on earth taking time out of their busy schedules to listen to what has to be one of the most important speeches of our lifetime.

Obama said he didn't, but that he read the transcript. He said Netanyahu "didn't offer any viable alternatives" to the deal Obama was working on. That's not true. Here is what the prime minister said:

> Now, if Iran threatens to walk away from the table—and this often happens in a Persian bazaar—call their bluff. They'll be back, because they need the deal a lot more than you do. And by maintaining the pressure on Iran and on those who do business with Iran, you have the power to make them need it even more.[15]

That is what any honest person would call an alternative. To what? To the accommodating approach to negotiations the president is taking. Prime Minister Netanyahu understands the region. He understands the Iranians and their negotiating tactics. He understands that you have to be strong, the way buyers are strong in the Persian rug markets.

Taking a strong position in negotiations is not the same as provoking a war. "Peace through strength" is what won the cold war. Back when we had real leadership in this country, we faced down an empire with over thirty thousand nuclear weapons and brought it to its knees without firing a shot. We were able to do that not only because of what Ronald Reagan did, but what he didn't do.

One thing he didn't do was make threats he wasn't ready to back up. He didn't go around the world drawing red lines, only to make this country a laughingstock when adversaries crossed them with impunity. Instead, he strengthened our military to a point where the Soviets couldn't hope to keep up. He picked his battles, deploying troops only when communists attempted coups in the Western Hemisphere.

Reagan constantly won the public relations battles with Mikhail Gorbachev. He famously said, "Mr. Gorbachev, tear down this wall," while speaking to a cheering crowd in what was then West Berlin. I've often imagined him flashing that winning smile and saying, "You should have listened to me," when the German people tore down the Berlin Wall themselves, marking the beginning of the end of the USSR.

Ironically, Russian president Vladimir Putin has acted a lot more like Reagan than our own president has over the past several years. When Obama drew another of his red lines for

Bashar al-Assad in Syria over chemical weapons, it was Putin who prevented war and solved the problem with diplomacy. He worked with his ally, instead of undermining her, and persuaded the Syrian government to hand over all of its chemical weapons.

Whether you like him or not, Putin is another example of a real leader who puts the interests of his people first and leads with strength and restraint. He's shown the most restraint in dealing with the Obama administration, which has done nothing but provoke him.

Russia's interests don't always coincide with America's, but Putin understands his primary function as president. Is he a politician? Of course he is. But he never sells out his own people just to keep himself or his party in power. Maybe that's one reason the Obama administration demonizes him so much. Just as Obama probably resents the comparison to Netanyahu, he may very well resent comparisons to the Russian president who has outclassed him so many times. Obama should be building a partnership with noncommunist Russia and taking a hard line with Iran and ISIS. Instead, he's soft on Iran and ISIS and risking a disastrous war with Russia, which the United States could lose.

Maybe it's better that he's ineffective at leading, since he's trying to take America in completely the wrong direction. He doesn't care about the best interests of the American people. He cares about destroying borders, language, and culture, and building his progressive utopia.

Not acting in the interests of the people is really a problem with both parties. Sure, they disagree on a lot of things. But there is one thing more important to both parties than anything they disagree on with each other: staying in power. They love living high on our dime, and they try to do what they're elected to do only when it doesn't jeopardize their chances of keeping their cushy jobs.

I'll never forget a picture that appeared on the top of the *Drudge Report* back in early January. The Republicans had won the Senate the previous November and had just taken office that day. As of that day they controlled both houses of Congress, but do you know what picture Matt Drudge ran? It was John "Man-Tan" Boehner bear-hugging none other than the most despicable woman in American politics, Nancy Pelosi. It couldn't have been more appropriate.

What does this bear hug symbolize other than he did their bidding? He went to her, gave her a hug, and showed us all how much opposition there really is in Washington. I'm sure you can find this picture without too much effort. Boehner looks like a satisfied little boy being hugged by the mama bear, Nancy Pelosi, who really runs the show.

Twenty-five representatives had opposed Boehner's reelection as Speaker. That was the opposition out of hundreds of Republican representatives who hold a majority in the House. Those were the only people out of over five hundred elected representatives who thought anything should change at all.

So, you can expect more of the same rather than less of the same. You can recognize the election was for naught. It had no meaning whatsoever. You can brace for taxation without representation to continue. You can expect the oligarchy to answer to the Wall Street powers who truly run the country.

As I've said, we can't even count on the Supreme Court to act in our interests most of the time. Obama's appointees Elena Kagan and Sonia Sotomayor are bad enough, but what about supposedly conservative justices? Obamacare could have been struck down even with Kagan and Sotomayor on the Court if that fool John Roberts hadn't sold us out, calling Obamacare a tax.

So, there's no leadership and there is no opposition party, neither in the Congress nor in the Supreme Court. If that sounds hopeless, believe me, that's how I feel sometimes, too. But it's not hopeless. Later in this book, I'm going to tell you exactly how we solve these problems in the long term and restore the America we loved.

In the meantime, we have to hold on to as much of our freedom as we can. The good news is that Obama's administration is almost over. What a celebration we should have when the most divisive presidency in American history comes to an end. The bad news is we can't be sure that what follows it won't be worse.

Leadership Post-Obama

We don't know who the Republican nominee is going to be yet, but it still doesn't look like any of the candidates can beat the Limber Leopard, Hillary Clinton. I called her that in my 2005 book, *The Political Zoo*, because, in addition to being willing and able to change her spots at any time, she has a strength the current president lacks. Unfortunately, she's on the wrong side. She could bring stronger leadership in the wrong direction than we have right now.

She may not have attended school in an Indonesian madrasa, but she's been making friendly with Muslim groups since the mid-1990s. The president is supposed to be responsible for the actions of his Cabinet, but do you really believe the academic in chief had any control over the Limber Leopard?

Clinton has been siding with the Muslims since before Obama was even a community organizer. It's a good thing she's not associating with those intolerant, bigoted conservatives. Her husband shares her affinity for the throwbacks. "Wolf Boy" Bill Clinton actually called for the arrests of the *cartoonists* at *Jyllands-Posten* after the riots over their satires of Muhammad and Muslims. Never mind punishing the rioters and murderers—Wolf Boy wants to arrest the cartoonists for exercising their right to free speech.

This is still what passes for progressive or liberal today. Remember the Pope's answer to the murders at *Charlie Hebdo*? Those who insult someone's religion should expect a "punch in the nose." Neofascism is alive and well, and the Clintons could step right in to lead the wolf pack again.

The Limber Leopard also seems to share her husband's ability to sidestep any controversy, no matter how egregiously she's behaved. Forget E-mailgate. Nobody cared, even when the progressive jackals at the *New York Times* and the Associated Press seemed to turn against her. She gave a press conference that would have gotten Richard Nixon hanged instead of just impeached, but she just brushed it off. The rules don't apply to her.

That really didn't surprise me. If she could get a U.S. ambassador killed due to her dereliction of duty as secretary of state and not be held accountable, who's going to care about her e-mail server? It's not as if cybersecurity for the top foreign policy official in the country is important when ISIS is hacking into databases containing the home addresses of active-duty soldiers. No, all the liberals care about is that she'd be the first female president.

While E-mailgate should be important, the bigger issue is really her legacy as secretary of state. It was the worst tenure in the history of that Cabinet position. She has literally destroyed the world order and not for the better. She has wrecked the Arab Crescent. She has started a new cold war with Russia. How much worse can it get? World War III? This is what we should be talking about when considering her candidacy for president.

Hillary's even worse than Obama on health care, too. Remember, the Limber Leopard was pushing a completely government-run, single-payer health-care plan when she was the First Lady back in the 1990s. Fortunately, we did have some semblance of an opposition party at that time, and her efforts at socializing medicine gave her party a landslide midterm election defeat, giving control of the House and Senate to the Republicans.

How times have changed. After eight years of nonstop, anticapitalist rhetoric from the current Marxist in chief, there may not be enough clear-thinking Americans left to resist. She just might be able to pull off as president what she failed to do as "co-president."

Even so, we may want to be careful about how vigorously we oppose her. Elizabeth Warren is even worse.

She is a woman who could be elected only in Massachusetts. She has at least one thing in common with the president, which is claiming to be someone she is not. As I said before, Obama was a spoiled white kid with a black father who decided to become a downtrodden black man. Elizabeth Warren is a blond-haired, blue-eyed white woman who claims to be Native American.

That was how she got into Harvard and how she ruled in Harvard. That's how she got over on whitey, by playing the ethnic race card as a Native American. Sound familiar?

However, "Elizabeth Warren is not a citizen of the Cherokee Nation. Elizabeth Warren is not enrolled in the Eastern Band of Cherokee Indians. And Elizabeth Warren is not one of the United Keetoowah Band of Cherokee. Nor could she become one, even if she wanted to," according to the *Atlantic*.[16] She's even less a Native American woman than Obama is a downtrodden black man. Yet, she "described herself as a minority in a law school directory and was touted as a Native American faculty member while tenured at Harvard Law School in the mid-1990s,"[17] based on what is reported as an unsubstantiated claim of having one-thirty-second Cherokee blood.

You don't think she used her phony Native American ties for political gain, don't you? You don't if you're a 1960s liberal anachronism who thinks Chairman Mao was a great leader.

Remember Obama's speech when he told business owners, "You didn't build that"? Guess what? He didn't come up with that piece of socialist sophistry on his own. He didn't even get it from his own speechwriters. Elizabeth Warren actually said it first.[18]

So we could have another presidential candidate claiming to be someone she's not, who's even more socialist than Obama. Let's see how the progressive jackals behave as the campaigns really get into full gear. I wouldn't be at all surprised if the Associated Press takes down Hillary with their lawsuit, so

Fauxcahontas can step into the void. The AP is suing the State Department for access to Clinton's records.[19]

That was why I was warning my listeners not to be too anxious to get rid of the Limber Leopard when the E-mailgate story broke back in March. As terrible and truly vicious as she is, Fauxcahontas really would be worse. She says she's not running, and maybe she won't this time around, but she's not going away. Nor are her poisonous, socialist ideas.

Meanwhile, the prospects on the Republican side aren't much better. Can you imagine making a choice between Jeb Bush and Hillary Clinton? Have we not had enough Bushes and Clintons for sixteen out of the past twenty-two years? Can anyone possibly say with a straight face the American people are represented by either of these insiders?

Jeb Bush thinks Common Core is just a wonderful idea. He thinks we need more immigrants, because they have stronger families and are more entrepreneurial. I'm not kidding. With conservatives like him, what do we need liberals for?

Who else is there? Marco Rubio certainly isn't ready for prime time. I might vote for him out of default, but he has no, as they used to say ten years ago, gravitas. He's not a president. He's not a leader. More important, he, too, would sign his party's death warrant by flooding the nation with immigrants. But the Republicans are so desperate they might make him a candidate just because his last name ends in a vowel.

The important question to ask here is, "Where will any of these Republican candidates lead this nation?" We can see where the progressives have led us. It does no good if we elect a Republican who's not a conservative and just continues leading us down the same road, with a few prettier words.

This is why I said the Israeli election was important for

America. If you analyze the election, you understand what needs to happen here.

Netanyahu was behind in the polls just before the election. He then made a dramatic move to the right, toward his base. The number one subject in his rhetoric during the last few days before the votes were cast was the left wing. He kept mentioning the left wing in Israel. He set himself apart by running on an authentic conservative platform: a nationalist conservative one.

A Bird Needs Two Wings

They're not ashamed in Israel to admit there's a left wing and a right wing. Here in America, we have only a left wing and a far-left wing. A bird needs two wings to fly. This country is going in circles because it has two left wings, flapping around the clock. A bird needs a left wing *and* a right wing to fly.

There actually is a right wing in America, but it isn't the Republican Party. You see some semblance of it in the Tea Party. You see it here and there in politics. But do you know where the right wing really is? It's in the hearts of the people.

This nation is primarily a center-right nation. I'm not talking about Hollywood. I'm not talking about Manhattan. I'm talking about the rest of America, affectionately known as "flyover country." That's where the people who actually work for a living reside. They are the ones who know, for example, the cops are the real victims in this country, not the criminals. Those are the kinds of people you find in flyover country.

Netanyahu turned the election around and won because he said the things the Israeli people needed to hear. I'm not talking about the phony Israeli protest manufactured by Obama's operatives to try to topple Netanyahu. I'm talking about the real Israeli people, their equivalent to our people in flyover country. They understand the dangers they face. They know they need strong, conservative leadership.

You might assume relations with Israel would improve now that the people have spoken, but don't count on it. Our passive-aggressive, academic president was so childish he neglected to call Netanyahu to congratulate him for several days after the election, breaking with all precedent. Obama cares as little for the Israeli electorate as he does for our own.

Israel's in for a bumpy ride for the next two years. Make no mistake about it: Obama's true colors have come out on Israel. He is going to continue to disrupt our ally and pander to our enemies, regardless of elections or national security.

Despite what he said in his speech, Netanyahu is not really free to act on his own against Iran, no matter how much he'd like to. Israel is a client state of the United States with regards to military hardware. He's dependent upon the cooperation of the American government, and it doesn't look like he's going to get a lot of that.

Yes, Israel has a hard army of men and women. The conscription in Israel is a requirement, unlike here. It's not an all-volunteer army. Everybody in Israel has to go into the military. The ultrareligious were previously exempt, but this has changed recently, for the betterment of Israel. No one should get a free ride there.

The United States is a different country, but there is a lesson for true American conservatives from the Israeli elections. The Republican Party has to run candidates who appeal to the center-right sentiments of the American voter and stop trying to pretend they appeal to everyone. They need to stop pandering to the left wing, stop pandering to the illegal aliens by talking about a bistate solution for America, meaning flooding America with 40 million illegal aliens.

If someone stood up and said, "No, if I'm elected I am going to turn back the flood of illegal aliens. I don't care what the president did with his pen. I am going to overturn him. I am going to save America. I'm going to preserve America's borders, language, and culture because I am an American. I am not an internationalist."

If someone gave a nationalist speech like that, I can assure you the election would be a landslide victory for the nationalist candidate, just as it was in Israel.

Americans have been sold down the river by the media, tricked into believing most people are liberals who don't really care about the country and consider themselves "citizens of the world." They've come to believe it. Joseph Goebbels said a long time ago when he worked for Hitler, "If you tell a big lie often enough, it becomes the truth."

Well, guess what? The truth will set us free. If you tell the truth often enough, it will set a nation free.

The Chicken and the Egg

Leadership is both an influence on and a reflection of society. There's a chicken-and-the-egg kind of question: Do we have corrupt leadership because the people are corrupt, or do we have corrupt people because the leadership is corrupt?

The answer is yes. One feeds upon the other. Only a corrupt people could elect a government like the one we have, which in turn leads the people into further corruption. After a while, the government takes on a life of its own, existing merely to perpetuate and grow itself, rather than benefit the people it governs. And the people become its slaves, fighting with each other over the handouts the government distributes from an increasingly smaller group of producers, whom the government both depends upon for its existence and holds up to contempt.

This is how a mighty nation can rot from within and become weakened in the face of its enemies. Remember what I told you about the Roman Republic? The same thing happened there. They didn't listen to Cicero. They eventually had internal division, demagoguery, and a large welfare state. They had Government Zero. They were weakened and overrun by barbarians. The same could happen to us if we continue down this road.

CHAPTER 3

Zero Strategy Against ISIS

Islam Woven into the Fabric of America?

In 2015, Obama held an extremism conference, at which he said things that are not only delusional, but frightening. If he actually believes what he said, he's insane. He knows better. Consider this statement by the Marxist in chief:

> *Here in America, Islam has been woven into the fabric of our country since its founding generations.*

Really? Islam has been woven into the fabric of our country since its founding? I had no idea! I didn't know that George Washington was secretly a Muslim and got on his knees on a prayer rug and prayed to Mecca at Valley Forge.

I had no idea Ben Franklin did his experiment with the kite for Allah. I didn't know he was secretly praying to Mecca every day and just didn't want to shock those cracker colonists with their weird behaviors and worship of Jesus. So he kept it hidden.

Even Betsy Ross, who made the American flag, had a burka hidden underneath the floorboards. Did you know that? She must have. Obama said Islam has been woven into the fabric of our country since its founding, so Betsy Ross must have had a burka somewhere in that old cottage of hers. She just couldn't shock those cracker colonists by coming out and wearing it.

I didn't know any of this. I didn't know the founders were secretly Muslim. It must be a product of my racist upbringing. I never learned in history class that Islam was woven into the fabric of America.

Of course, I'm being sarcastic. All we have left is ridicule, scorn, and sarcasm, because we have no electoral power whatsoever. We've lost it. That's Government Zero. We have zero representation.

We elected an opposition party last November, which Obama nullified the next day with, as he put it, "my pen and my phone." His arrogance and deceit have been upheld by Boehner and McConnell, who are nothing but turncoats. They're wearing the red coats right now. They are the British. They are not American patriots.

I agree 1,000 percent with Rudolph Giuliani that Obama does not love America the way we love America. The America he loves is a socialist, Islamist America, one that has had Islam woven into its fabric since its founding generations. Since that America doesn't exist, he's trying to remake the real America into it. Rewriting American history is just part of his plan.

No matter how much damage this devious hater of America does to the nation, when I can't take another minute of it, I go out on my deck and look at the birds. I feel better because I know we and the world will survive him. We will survive him because we have survived other evils. We will survive the evil emanating out of this man's brain and the horrible people he brought with him to Washington, many of them worse than he is. We will survive it all.

No matter how they hate America, no matter how they connive to put these boll weevils into every aspect of our lives, they will fail. They will fail because this country and its people are greater than those left-wing, communist, socialist Islamic fanatics. At least, that's what I believe. I'm perennially optimistic about America in the long run.

Showing Our Hand

I'm optimistic despite news stories like one breaking at the time of this writing. It was titled, "Showing Our Hand? US Military Official Outlines Plan to Retake Iraqi City of Mosul."[1] Did you hear this story? Or didn't it make it to the local newspaper covering homophobia or the wonders of global warming? Read this story from earlier this year:

> *A U.S. military official on Thursday outlined plans to retake the vital Iraq city of Mosul from Islamic State terrorists as early as April—an unusual move that swiftly drew criticism that the Pentagon was revealing too much information to the enemy.*[2]

This was before plans to attack Mosul were eventually scrapped. Now, why would they have done this? Why would they have signaled to the enemy when they were going to do it and how many Iraqi brigades would be involved? Imagine if Dwight Eisenhower leaked a story telling Hitler, "D-Day's coming June 6. Hey, Adolf, we're going to have X number of boats, X number of planes, X number of gliders, and we're going to be landing at this part of Normandy. Forget about that diversion on the coast of Belgium. We're landing in Normandy. Okay, Adolf? Message received?"

A U.S. military official told ISIS when and how he would attack them and which of our allies would participate, including three brigades of Kurdish Peshmerga and five Iraqi Army brigades. In the past, this man would have been arrested and tried for treason for making these statements. What possible reason could Obama have for allowing this?

I know. "Savage, you don't understand. This is all fake. They're feigning this attack to conceal the real one. They're not really going to do it that way with that number of brigades. They're going to attack but not from that side. They're not actually going to take Mosul. They're going to attack another city. Savage, you took it hook, line, and sinker."

Did I? Do you believe Obama is that smart? Is he the new Eisenhower? Ask yourself if that was the new Eisenhower in Libya or Egypt. Was that the new Eisenhower letting our people die in Benghazi? Not a chance.

So why did Obama approve this? I don't know. The same man who says Islam has been woven into the fabric of our country since its founding might have said, "Tell them what we're going to do. We want them to be hit a little bit, but not too hard."

Or maybe the sorority girls running his administration told him, "Tell them that we're coming, and maybe they'll lay down their arms and start a business." Yes, Marie Harf knows what she's talking about. She went to a great university.

Obama's coalition of Iranian-backed Shiite militia eventually did attack and successfully recapture the lightly defended city of Tikrit. ISIS committed very little to it. But in case anyone actually believed this was some masterful strategic move by the Obama sorority, they didn't have to wait long to be disabused. ISIS recaptured the much more important city of Ramadi.[3]

The America Obama Loves

Yes, Barack Obama does love America. There's no question about it. Rudy Giuliani is under fire for saying he doesn't and some pundits on Fox News are siding with the leftists. They're running scared, saying, "Of course Obama loves America!" I think Martha Washington herself said it. Fox's Blondie, Megyn Kelly, took that side. She didn't want to be accused of hating the president.

Barack Obama loves America and Western culture just like his father, Barack Hussein Obama Sr., who was jailed in 1949 by the British while working in the Kenyan independence movement. That gave his son a hatred for Great Britain he still shows today.[4]

Senior Obama wrote an eight-page essay, "The Problem with Our Socialism," which asked, "How are we going to remove the disparities in our country, such as the concentration of economic power in Asian and European hands?" That was Daddy Obama.

Obama loves America like his mother, Stanley Ann Dunham, who taught him in Indonesia to "disdain the blend of ignorance and arrogance that too often characterized Americans abroad." That's straight from Mama Obama's lips. Her friends claim she was an atheist, a woman who challenged her son's school curriculum with questions like, "What's so good about democracy? What's so good about capitalism? What's wrong with communism?"

These are the kinds of things he learned from his parents.

He loves America like the people in his madrasa in Indonesia, where pro-American teachings are extremely hard to find. In an Indonesian madrasa, everything is taught according to how it will honor Islam. Now you understand why his extremism conference bent over backward to not say "Muslim." The only prayer said at the conference was offered by an imam. No rabbis, priests, or Buddhist monks were allowed to pray.

He loves America like his grandparents, who moved their daughter and grandson, Barack, to Seattle, specifically to attend Mercer Island High School. Maybe that was because the chairman of the Mercer Island School Board, John Stenhouse, testified before the House Un-American Activities Subcommittee that he had been a member of the Communist Party. I kid you not. Look it up.

Obama loves America like mentor and father figure Frank Marshal Davis, member of the Communist Party USA, whom Obama described as "being a decisive influence in helping him to find his present identity as an African American," the most left-leaning and least anticommunist demographic group of any in this nation.

He loves America like his preacher of twenty years and the inspiration for his book, *The Audacity of Hope*, the Reverend

Jeremiah Wright. Wright married the Obamas. He also infamously asked that "God damn America," saying the attack on 9/11 was America's chickens coming home to roost.

Yes, he loves America like his good friends Bill Ayers and Bernardine Dohrn, who built bombs to attack federal buildings and police stations, killing innocent Americans.

He loves America like his wife, Michelle, who was never proud of her country until 2008, when her husband won the presidency.

Barack Obama loves America; it's just not an America you or I are remotely familiar with. It's the America founded on socialist, communist, Islamic, atheist, black liberation theology, and radical anarchist values. The real America's enemies would also love the America Obama loves.

What's in a Name?

There are actually a few representatives in Congress who recognize this. House Homeland Security Committee chairman Michael McCaul called Obama's early 2015 extremism summit "a psychotherapy session without any substance." He said the president continues to be politically correct by insisting the United States is not at war with Islam, but that ISIS not only says it is at war with the United States, it is fighting for religious reasons. "I think we are at war with Radical Islamists," said McCaul. "I think it is important to define the enemy to defeat the enemy. But Obama's trying not to offend the Muslim world."

Representative McCaul is right, but he's only half-right. Obama may refuse to call ISIS an Islamic group, but that was not what the three-day conference was really about. It was really about what Obama and his leftist true believers consider "domestic terrorism." In other words, it was about you, because you decided to read this book or listen to *The Savage Nation.*

It was about those of you who attend church and believe in God, those of you who are willing to fight abortion, and those of you who believe in traditional family values. You are the enemy this group of characters who have taken over America are really concerned about.

Perhaps you didn't know the FBI Director James Comey was not invited to the White House summit on extremism. Maybe that didn't make it to your local paper, either. This was the FBI director who said there are sleeper cells in every state of the Union except Alaska. That's why Obama didn't invite him. He can't control him. The FBI director actually knows what's going on and doesn't fall in line like Jeh Johnson.

Who is Jeh Johnson, anyway? Where did he come from? He's supposed to be the secretary of Homeland Security. It was his department that broke our borders. They won't acknowledge that Islamists are among us. That's some homeland security. It sounds like they're working for the other side.

There's a militant group running America. We know the enemy is ISIS, but they don't even invite the FBI chief to a summit on extremism. Isn't anyone else as concerned about this as I am?

They did invite the FBI's Russian counterpart, Alexander Bortnikov, to the meeting. That makes some sense, as the Russians are already fighting Islamist militants within their own borders. But it's absolutely bizarre considering our own FBI chief wasn't invited.

Obama's new Goebbels, Josh Earnest, says they didn't invite

FBI chief Comey to the summit because his boss, Attorney General Eric Holder, was invited. You know how American Holder is. You know how much he loves America. It was like inviting Al Sharpton to the meeting. Yes, he and Obama love America. It's just Central America, not North America.

So they put Holder there, a man who has been thrown out of office because of his extremist behavior, but not the head of the FBI.

They did invite some FBI officials. I have their names. If you knew who they were, your hair would stand up. You would immediately understand why Obama permitted them to attend the meeting, which was largely attended by Muslims. And the band played on.

"We wanted to make sure that there wasn't a perception that this conference was overly focused on law enforcement tactics," said the new Goebbels.

One day there should be war crimes trials, like the Nuremberg trials, where the administration's sorority girls are tried. They should be forced to wear sackcloth and answer as to why they agreed to go along with undermining the pillars of our safety and freedom.

The spokesgirl Earnest said the administration's efforts to counter violent extremists are premised on the notion that local officials and communities can be an effective bulwark against violent extremism. But they won't be looking for the Islamist terrorists FBI Director Comey said have already infiltrated those local communities. No, they will be looking for you, who are a "right-wing extremist" because you are Christian, believe in God, oppose abortion, or simply "talk about the Constitution."

Undermining Intelligence

There has been a virtual coup in the intelligence communities. One of the first shots was fired by the queen of military contracting herself, Dianne Feinstein, when she undermined the CIA.

I can't tell. But it continues. Now, we hold summits on extremism and don't invite the director of the FBI. We'd rather focus on local communities than the maniacs lopping off people's heads and setting them on fire while they're still alive.

In the worst example of man's inhumanity to man since Hitler, ISIS burned a Jordanian pilot alive. What a sad day it was for the human race. ISIS took that poor Jordanian pilot, put him in a cage, and burned him alive. And the best that our president could say is, "Our thoughts and prayers continue to be with Lt. Kasasbeh and the Jordanian people."

It gets more depressing every day that we have such a weak president, who would permit ISIS to rage like this across the Middle East. They perpetrate a blitzkrieg on innocent civilians with little more than a wrist slap via our F-18s and a few missiles. Ask yourself how long can this go on? Is this Hitler taking the Sudetenland? Is this Hitler taking the Rhineland? Or is this ISIS wanting to conquer the entire world and convert it to fundamentalist Islam?

A Hobson's Choice

What should the United States do? We understand that you can't kill everyone on Earth in order to get at the bad guys.

However, there will come a time when a decision is going to have to be made that is a Hobson's choice.

I'll remind you of what Harry Truman had to decide in World War II. The American people were exhausted with war. They had defeated Germany, but the war in the Pacific raged on. The American military estimated it would cost the deaths of one million American men to conquer the Japanese mainland. The Japanese would not surrender, even though their air force and navy had been decimated. In fact, they issued bamboo knives and told every resident, even old women, who were taught to make knives out of sticks, that when the Americans came, they would have a duty to kill them.

So Truman knew the enormous cost of a land invasion. What did he decide? Better them than us. He knew that if he dropped experimental weapons on Hiroshima and Nagasaki, thousands, if not hundreds of thousands, of innocent Japanese men, women, and children would die. He knew it was horrible and tragic, but better them than us.

That was what Truman decided. Now here we are in a world where there is moral equivalency, not only in the universities but in the academic running America, a man who spends all of his viciousness attacking Republicans and the American people themselves rather than ISIS.

What would you do? The more I think about burning a man alive, the sicker I get. I ask myself, who was worse, Hitler or the Islamofascists? Even Hitler would not publicize what he was doing to people in the concentration camps. He hid it. So why are these monsters publishing it on the Internet?

They are publicizing their atrocities to induce terror in the world's population. They are doing what their antecedents did in the seventh century, when Islam first broke out of Mecca and conquered a good portion of the Middle East. They did it through burning, killing, raping, and even burning libraries. That's how they did it then, the good old-fashioned way the Mongols did it.

We have the weapons to stop them, but not the leadership. We have young men in F-18s who could take them off the map in seventy-two hours. But we have a woman running the air force who has never flown a Piper Cub and who answers directly to the sorority running America.

The more I think about not only burning a man alive in a cage for all the world to see, but the world doing little about it, the more disgusted I get. People today are so apathetic. They'd rather watch laugh-a-thons on television or the perversion in the movies than say, "Enough is enough. Do something to stop them before they kill all of us."

The people don't demand it, so the government does nothing. Instead, it attacks the Tea Party.

The Enemies Within

Meanwhile, the destroyers of America have formed a domestic fifth column that *is* doing something. It's just doing all the wrong things. Code Pink's leadership met in Iran with Holocaust deniers, putting headscarves on. These leftist, feminist troublemakers hate America so much they actually prefer the monsters in Iran who consider them half a person in courts of law.

That's just one example of the enemy within, but they represent an awful lot of others. Just turn on MSNBC, for as long as you can stand it. I was doing just that one day and it hit me.

The Holocaust deniers are the ISIS deniers. It was like a bulb went on in my head. The very same leftists and Islamists who deny the Holocaust deny ISIS's monstrosities. Am I wrong or am I right? Listen to these people yourself and tell me if I'm wrong.

Watch the laugh-a-thons tonight on television. Watch all of the government jesters, like Bill Maher, Stephen Colbert, or Jon Stewart. Oh, that's right, Jon Stewart quit. What a loss. Watch the rest of them cover up for Obama. Watch them spend more time attacking Republicans, conservatives, Tea Party members, the military, football players—everybody but ISIS. Ask yourself how we can win a war when we have so many enemies within.

So what did Obama say when ISIS published a video of themselves burning a Jordanian pilot alive?

> *But should in fact this video be authentic, it's just one more indication of the viciousness and barbarity of this organization... And it also just indicates the degree to which whatever, uh, ideology they're operating off of, uh, it's bankrupt. We're here to talk about how to make people healthier and make their lives better.*

He talked about vaccines. Instead of vaccinating America against Islamofascism, he talks about measles. Notice also the president said, "Whatever ideology they're operating off of." He won't even say Islamic State. That's propaganda. It's doubletalk. Listening to the president, you'd think some unknown organization, practicing a mysterious, unknown ideology, burned a man alive. Don't we know exactly who they are and precisely what ideology they're following?

The acronym ISIS stands for Islamic State. It's not the Christian State; it's not CRISIS. It's not the Buddhist State; it's not BISIS. It's not the Jewish State; it's not JISIS. It's not the Hindu State; it's not HISIS. Mr. President, wake the hell up! The people will only take so much. We are in danger.

Incidentally, where are the gays? Why aren't gay activists lining up against ISIS, given the atrocities ISIS commits against homosexuals? They're too busy attacking the Tea Party. They're attacking Republicans. They're attacking conservatives. Just like the feminists, they'd rather attack everything good about America than stand with Americans against the monsters who'd persecute or kill them if they had the chance.

Anyone with an IQ above 90 knows that we have worse than a quisling in the White House. Some might say he's a fellow traveler. I don't agree with that at all. I don't believe he's a sympathizer with Islamic terrorism. I think he's an ostrich who puts his head in the sand. He sees what is actually happening and wants to say it's not happening. How else can you explain his refusal to recognize ISIS as Islamic terrorism?

I know. He doesn't want to ignite a war against all of Islam. That's what his spokesgirls tell us. His supporters say the academics running America are afraid to ignite a religious war.

I have news for them. The Jordanian king says this is already WWIII.[5] The religious war already started a thousand years ago. The Muslims started it when they began wars of conquest to establish their world caliphate. The religious war is simply reaching a higher temperature because there is no effective opposition.

Don't forget that Obama caused the rise of ISIS. He was warned by the military not to remove all American troops from Iraq, was he not? Was he not told to keep a force of one hundred thousand there to prevent this from happening? And what did he do?

He gave them the middle finger. He said, "Screw you. I know more than you. I am Obama the Great. I know everything. I know better than doctors about medical care. I know better than the military about the military. I know everything about climate. I'm an expert at everything." So, he pulled all American troops out of Iraq and created a vacuum.

The Iraqi Army fled and left our Abrams tanks and other heavy weapons in the Islamic State's hands. The Iraqi soldiers have probably joined ISIS by now, since they know how to use the tanks. Thanks to the ostrich's arrogance, we have Islamofascism on a blitzkrieg rampage throughout the Middle East.

We have a vicious, pedantic, academic cadre running America. They are technocrats, without any emotion except hatred for their political enemies. They do not consider ISIS their political enemy. They don't even care about ISIS. It's nothing to them. They all think like a community organizer, who cares about nothing but fighting the domestic opposition party. There is no such thing as a foreign power to them. Their only foreign power is the Republican Party.

I was lying on the rug with my dog, trying to find some comfort, when I saw the story about the Jordanian pilot. I started to play with my dog. He smiled and I said to him, "Teddy, you know, animals don't do this to other animals."

The human animal is the most vicious animal on the planet. Now take a vicious animal and give him a religion to cloak himself in, and what you have is ISIS. It's just like when Hitler brainwashed the German people to believe in National Socialism, or Nazism. This is what's going on now. Man's inhumanity to man.

As a little kid, six years old, I would watch movies with my father up in the mountains, during the summer. They'd bring movies into the casino for the kids. Imagine that. No TV, videos on phones, or Xbox.

There was a movie I loved called *Bring 'Em Back Alive*, with Frank Buck. He would go into the jungles of Africa with his pith helmet and bring back animals for the zoos. When I would see a tiger that looked ferocious to me, or a lion, my father would say, "Well, they're not really vicious. They just hunt." He said, "Man is a more vicious animal than any animal on Earth." As a little boy, I didn't quite understand what he meant.

Do you understand what he meant now? My father, now deceased, told me man is more vicious than any animal on Earth. "Only man kills for pleasure. Only man kills for sport. And some men kill for religion," he said. He was right.

We're not supposed to acknowledge that today. As I said, the monsters setting people on fire don't call themselves CRISIS; they're not a Christian group. They *call themselves* the *Islamic* State of Iraq and Syria. That's who burned a Jordanian pilot alive without any anesthesia. But you won't hear the word *Islamic* from the humanitarians on the left. The Holocaust deniers and the ISIS deniers are now one and the same.

We didn't even hear it at the time from any of the Republican candidates for president, except one. I don't have a lot of respect for Lindsey Graham. I think he's a snake. But at least now that he's pretending to be a contender, he actually said something against radical Islam. It must have been news to Obama, who doesn't know who did it. He doesn't know why they did it or who they are. They're masked men. We don't know what their unknown ideology is. They're just some zealots.

The academic running America would rather talk about measles, after he brought in at least one hundred thousand infected people. They didn't all have measles, of course. Some had a flu we had no resistance to. Some had tuberculosis, previously eradicated in America but now resurging in Massachusetts. Some did have measles, because measles is endemic in Mexico and Central America, as is the flu they brought with them.

So, the president doesn't want to talk about ISIS. He'd rather lecture you about getting vaccinated. He opens up the door to the infected and then tells you to go get vaccinated. Why didn't he vaccinate the illegals in Honduras before he brought them in? Why didn't he send that moron from the CDC down to Honduras to see if they were healthy enough to be brought in by the trainload last summer, before he dumped them on our cities and put them in our schools?

Where Is the Media?

Everything these pedantic academics do is wrong. It will lead to a greater disaster than you could ever imagine unless the opposition increases its voice. Remember something: My job in the media is to remain an opponent of any government not doing the bidding of the people. My job is to remain a strong opponent of policies that I believe endanger the American people. That's what the media is supposed to be doing.

We're supposed to be a thorn in the side of the government.

When the media becomes a mouthpiece for the government, like Fareed Zakaria of CNN, permitting Obama to get away with one gigantic lie after another without questioning him, they are in essence *Pravda* or *Izvestia*. Do you remember how that ended?

ISIS burns people alive, throws homosexuals off rooftops, rapes and enslaves women, but we don't hear one word from the progressive media. They'll scream to high heaven if a Christian baker refuses to bake a cake for a homosexual wedding, but don't say a word when ISIS throws a homosexual off a roof and then stones him to death. They'll cry a river if a man makes an inappropriate remark to a female senator, but they'll say nothing when ISIS enslaves all women under their control, prohibits them from driving, holding a job, or being educated beyond the seventh grade. This is how much they hate America.

The New Good Germans

They've succeeded at one thing. They've anesthetized the American people. No wonder every other channel I click is running a program about a vampire or a zombie. The American people are zombies and vampires. The liberal media and academia have turned America into a dead world, a world of zombies and vampires. The average man doesn't care anymore. He says, "Why do I care what they do to each other? Let 'em kill each other."

Go and stop the average man walking in Manhattan today with a microphone and a camera and say, "Uh, sir, excuse me.

We've just heard that the Islamic State has burned a pilot alive in a cage. Do you have any comments?"

"Eh, don't bother me. I'm in the garment center. I have business. I don't care. It's nothing to do with me. Let them all go to hell. It doesn't bother me."

Stop the next woman. "Madame, how do you feel about the ISIS throwing the gay man from a roof and the Muslim crowd stoning him to death afterward?"

"Don't bother me. That's their problem. It's a civil war. What do you want? To drag us into another world war? We like our president. He's smart. He knows what he's doing. He's keeping us out of that mess. Okay? Now, get out of my way. What, are you a member of the Tea Party?"

Do you think I don't know the average American? They're the new good Germans. That lady and that man I just mentioned are the Germans who smelled the smoke of burning flesh in Auschwitz and Dachau and said they didn't smell it. "Ah, don't bother me. Please. There's nothing like that going on in the ovens. Go away. What, do you work for the Jews?"

That's what the good Germans said. They didn't know there was a Holocaust. They didn't know there were concentration camps. They went about their business. They made the strudel. They pressed their white tablecloths. They put the girl in a communion dress. They brushed her teeth in the morning and sent her to church. They didn't want to be bothered with the smell of human flesh a mile down the road any more than the man working in the garment center or the woman on the Upper East Side stepping into a limo or an Uber.

The president is even worse. Not only does he deny the thousand-year-old religious war, he wants to blame you for what ISIS is doing. It's all Christians' fault, or at least Christians are just as bad. Here's what he said at the 2015 National Prayer Breakfast:

> *Lest we get on our high horse and think this is unique to some other place, remember that during the Crusades and the Inquisition, people committed terrible deeds in the name of Christ. In our home country, slavery and Jim Crow all too often was justified in the name of Christ...So it is not unique to one group or one religion. There is a tendency in us, a simple tendency that can pervert and distort our faith.*

Can you believe the audacity of this man? Covering up Islamist genocide by bringing up atrocities committed seven hundred years ago by Christian crusaders? This is the rhetoric of the Islamists themselves!

Besides, the Crusades were in reality countercrusades. They were the Christian *reaction* to hundreds of years of Muslim aggression, atrocities, and land grabs. Which side is this president on?

Any other nation would have impeached him a long time ago. After having let the entire world down by not attending the march for free speech in France, following the *Charlie Hebdo* murders, any other nation would have impeached him. He didn't even send Joe Biden or John Kerry, who speaks French. There was a message sent by this administration to the Islamists, to the Muslim Brotherhood, saying something. What was he saying to them?

For that matter, why didn't Boehner attend the rally? We can criticize the president, as we should. He skips intelligence briefings. He will not engage with Congress. He ignores his Cabinet. But there's enough blame to go around. Boehner should have stepped up to show what the leader of an opposition party does when a president embarrasses the nation and lets down the entire world. We don't have an opposition party.

We have a crippled, passive, cowardly government at every level. All of the Pentagon social media accounts have been hacked by ISIS. ISIS has posted the names and addresses of the U.S. generals, their families, and their children. They've said, "American soldiers, we're coming. Watch your backs." Why can ISIS, a ragtag army that Obama called "the JV team," penetrate the Pentagon's cybersecurity?

Maybe it's because the Pentagon has been watching the Tea Party instead of ISIS. Along with Dianne Feinstein, they've been monitoring *you*, the American patriot, instead of the real enemy. Meanwhile, the zombies all around us don't even know there was a rally in France. It was larger than the victory celebration after WWII. Do you remember the pictures of the French people celebrating in the streets after the Americans and British had liberated Paris from the Nazis? This event was bigger.

It was an historic day, but our president didn't go. I don't buy the story that security was the issue. Didn't Netanyahu need security? Didn't Angela Merkel need security? Didn't Mahmoud Abbas need security? Jordanian King Abdullah?

It's rubbish to believe that. Obama told the world to drop dead. Maybe it was narcissism. After all, he would have had to hold hands with other leaders and be just one among many, instead of the king of the heap. He couldn't link arms with François Hollande and David Cameron and Merkel and Netanyahu and Abbas. He would have been just another leader, instead of the Supreme Leader of the Universe.

So, maybe he didn't attend for a couple of reasons. One, to watch a basketball game. Two, out of narcissism. But the third reason is what bothers me: to send a signal to the Islamists. Even I don't want to let my thinking go there, but how can I avoid it? Even the liberal *Daily News* said, "He let the world down."

This is a breach that no American should ever forget. But the 47 percent who do nothing, who sit on their behinds and collect government checks, couldn't care less whether this doofus went to Paris or not. Do you think they care?

If you were to confront even a college-educated woman who worships Obama, like the average, self-satisfied woman on New York's Upper East Side, and say to her, "You're a liberal. How do you feel about your president not going to Paris when four million people were there marching for free speech?" Do you know what she'd say? "Drop dead. He has his reasons." That's the zombie world we're living in.

Finally, Obama's spokesmouth, a man who will go down in history as the second coming of Joseph Goebbels, finally comes out with this:

> *Some have asked whether or not the United States should have sent someone with a higher profile than the ambassador to France. And I think it's fair to say we should have sent someone with a higher profile to be there.*

That was very nice, Josh. Where did you get that? Which sorority girl gave you that one?

Islam's Thousand-Year War on the West

What does it all mean? I'll tell you. We're living in very dangerous times. It's clear as a bell to many of us who actually studied the Crusades, which, contrary to what the imam in chief told you, were initiated by Muslims trying to dominate the Christian world. You didn't learn that in public school. You learned exactly the opposite. You learned the Christian crusaders were the villains and the poor Muslims were only defending themselves.

Were the Muslims defending themselves at Vienna? Were they defending themselves in medieval Spain? Maybe Islam was woven into the fabric of Spain since its founding generations, just like in America. It must have been woven into Italy's fabric, because the poor Muslims in Sicily had to defend themselves from those awful, oppressive, Christian Sicilians.

Islam has been at war with the world for 1,400 years. That's a fact. I didn't make it up. It's not racist; it's not sexist; it's not homophobic; it's not fattening. It's true. It is the most intolerant of all the world's religions, especially the virulent, Salafist version of Islam that is currently plaguing the earth.

The Muslims were eventually defeated and thrown out of Europe. They were stopped at Vienna in 1529. They were defeated and expelled from Spain and Italy. They were driven back into the Middle East and northern Africa. It was these victories that made the West safe for the Renaissance, out of which all of modern civilization sprang. Religious and political freedom, private property, free enterprise, and free trade all flourished in the West after the defeat of the Muslims in Europe.

Now they're marching against civilization again, and the West seems to want to let them overturn the West's previous victories. The Obama administration is in denial just as Neville Chamberlain was at Munich, refusing to recognize the forces of evil for what they are.

For the president to not even understand the history of his own religion, or at least his father's religion, is very worrisome. This is the man who told us during his presidential campaign in 2007 that his "intimate understanding of the Muslim world [would] make us safer." How'd that work out in Iraq? How about in Libya or Egypt?

A wise man said, "Those who do not know history are doomed to repeat it." I certainly don't want to see history repeating itself. The Muslims were already defeated by the West once. We shouldn't have to fight them again. Had Obama not left a vacuum in Iraq, there would be no ISIS. If he recognized them for what they are now and did what any other president would have done to them, they would no longer be a threat.

Instead, he gets up there at his extremism summit and talks about terrorism in these minimalist, academic phrases that I thought went out of style a long time ago. When I heard him give that speech, I was relieved in one sense. I realized then that he was not a Muslim Brotherhood double agent. He couldn't be. They wouldn't let him in. He isn't smart enough.

No, he's not a double agent. Maybe he's just a stupid, liberal college teacher who was pushed ahead and became president. I don't know if that means we're in more trouble or less. They say the road to hell is paved with good intentions. It could be that Obama is just a good liberal who is dragging the world to hell through sheer stupidity.

Then again, maybe he's not so stupid. It's hard to believe even an academic could be making the strategic mistakes Obama is making with Iran. This crazy, dictatorial, narcissistic, anti-American maniac has threatened all of Congress, including most of the Democratic Party that's sane, that if they should dare put sanctions on Iran, he will veto the bill.

Take a guess who was standing alongside him, saying "Amen," with this dictator. It was none other than the reincarnation of King George III, David Cameron. How do you feel living in America and having a British prime minister dictating American policy? President Obummer, joined by British dictator King David Cameron III, sharply *warned* Congress not to dare pursue sanctions on Iran.

Does anyone believe that Obama is not owned lock, stock, and barrel by Iran? Why does Obama insist that Iran can be trusted? Even one of the leading Democrats, Sen. Bob Menendez of New Jersey, has said that if Obama waited as he wants to, sanctions will not be able to be imposed quickly enough if the talks collapse.

Direct Action for a Nuclear Iran

So you have to ask yourself, why does Obama want Iran to get a nuclear weapon? I'll tell you. I've studied this man's behavior for all the years he's been in office and I understand what he does. He's an extremist. He's an activist. He's using a technique known as direct action. The radical left uses direct action to make their policies faits accomplis. The opposition is nullified before they can even respond.

For example, he violated the Constitution by flooding

America with illegal aliens over the summer. What happened? Nothing. They're here. They're near. They're everywhere. The illiterates do not even read or write in their own language. He flooded America with them, many of whom were diseased.

That's why we had TB breaking out in Lynn, Massachusetts. That's where the killer flu is coming from. If you don't believe me, investigate for yourself how many children have become paralyzed or have died from this virulent flu strain and this virus, brought in with these so-called "Obama's kids" on the trains last summer from Mexico, Guatemala, and Honduras. We had an election in which we said, "We want the borders protected." Obama responded, "Okay, yeah, right, work it out because I'm letting them in anyway."

That's direct action. He goes ahead and does what he wants first, then says, "It's too late to stop me. I've done it. Now, what are you going to do about it?" It leaves the opposition with no choice but to make the best of things afterward, instead of preventing a bad situation in the first place. It's a known radical tactic, which is why the radical community organizer in the White House keeps using it.

Now, he wants Iran to have the bomb, so he's saying, "Delay on the sanctions and we'll talk to them and blah, blah, blah, then we'll come back to you." Meanwhile, they'll have the bomb and he'll say, "Oh, well, now we can't stop them. The cat is out of the bag."

It's just more direct action, directly opposite the wishes of the American people. This is what he's doing.

So, why does Obama want Iran to have the bomb, if they're so bad? The answer is Israel. It always comes back to Israel and the Jews. Israel is the bad boy to Obama and the anti-Semitic sorority girls. Once Iran has the bomb, he can blackmail Israel into giving up Judea and Samaria for a Palestinian state. This is one of his top agenda items, on his mind from the day he left Punahou High School.

It's one of the radical leftist dreams to cut Israel in half and make it indefensible. Obama wants to destroy it as a Jewish state, just as he's destroying this nation as a fundamentally Christian nation. He wants to turn America into a multiculturalist hodgepodge, even if it means flooding us with as many unproductive Mexicans, Hondurans, or even Muslims as he can.

He would also like to see Israel turned into something other than a Jewish state. That's the goal of the new world order. They do not want any nations built upon a single religion, unless, of course, they're Muslim. Muslims can do as they wish, at least while they're useful in bringing down Judaism and Christianity. But as far as any state in their new world order, there can be no borders, culture, or language. The whole world must be transformed into a multicultural, polyglot state.

So Obama wants Iran to have the bomb. That's why he threatened Congress with a veto. Once Iran has the bomb, he'll blackmail Israel into giving up Judea and Samaria, allowing them to be absorbed into a Palestinian state. That will be one more step toward Israel not being Jewish and, eventually, the United States not being Christian.

Not only do they hate the traditional, Judeo-Christian values that Israel and America were founded upon, but to liberals like Obama, the anti-Zionist, anti-Jew Jimmy Carter, and his fellow travelers in the universities of America and Europe, Israel is the reason the Muslims are on the warpath. This is one of the great lies you'd expect from Adolf Hitler's ministry of propaganda.

Denying the Global Threat

There are Muslim wars around the world right now, including in Afghanistan, Burma, Pakistan, the Philippines, Bangladesh, India, China, Kazakhstan, Kyrgyzstan, Tajikistan, Libya, Mali, Nigeria, Somalia, Algeria, Cameroon, Uganda, Chechnya, Dagestan, Russia, Iraq, Syria, Israel, and Yemen. Around the world, wherever you look, there are Muslims at war with their neighbors.

Some people say they're not a threat to the United States, so why should we care? They're forgetting quite a bit of history. The Muslims weren't a threat to Italy and Spain when they were still fighting other tribes around Mecca. They weren't a threat to Austria until they laid siege to Vienna and almost broke through to conquer the rest of Europe.

The Mongols were nobodies once, too. Do you remember learning about the Mongols in high school history class? They are a pretty good model for the modern variety of Islamic murderers. A very good comparison can be made to the Mongol conquests of the 1300s under Genghis Khan and his successors.

Wherever the Mongols went, they either assimilated or massacred the local population. That's exactly what ISIS is doing now. That's what they will do in France. That's what they will do *here*.

The *Charlie Hebdo* murderers were the advance team. They were like cockroaches sent out on a test case to see how far they could go. They got into that hall of journalism and slaughtered at will. The test went very well indeed. Despite all the braying by the sheeple in Paris, the antigun liberals who attack conservatives who would defend them, it looks like the sheeple are just waiting for the slaughter. They're just like the sheeple slaughtered throughout history, by the Mongols and other barbarians.

Just like in Nazi Germany, the Jews are the canary in the coal mine. Oh, I'm sorry. You probably didn't know that the people murdered in the Paris delicatessen were Jews. How would you know? The president described them as just some "folks in a deli" shot in a random act of violence by some "zealots." Thank goodness for Jonathan Karl, one of the rare journalists in the media who actually does his job. He called Josh Goebbels Earnest on the big lie:

"This was not a random shooting of a bunch of folks in a deli in Paris. This was an attack on a kosher deli. Does the president have any doubt that those terrorists attacked that deli because there would be Jews in that deli?"[6]

No, the president didn't see the perpetrators as Muslims or the victims as Jews. The victims were "folks," Obama's word for anyone who doesn't have an identity. When a black man is shot by a police officer, whether justified or not, he's a black man. When a Jew is murdered by an Islamic terrorist specifically because he's Jewish, he's just one of the folks, the nobodies, the people who don't matter.

Islam is at war with the rest of the world, including any moderate Muslims who won't bow to the caliphate. ISIS has declared war against the United States, just as the Pasha of Tripoli did when Thomas Jefferson took office. They have captured and killed American citizens, just as the Muslim Barbary pirates did in 1800. Jefferson sent in the Marines, and that war ended in victory for America.

But we don't have Jefferson in the White House. We have a pedantic, academic socialist who was educated in an Islamic madrasa, mentored by a black American communist leader, and married by a black liberation theology preacher who wants God to "damn America." He is a president who won't even say the words *Islamic* or *Muslim* and pretends he doesn't know who ISIS is. He has a worshipful media that lets him get away with it.

This is why we live in dangerous times. Civilization itself is under attack and we don't have the knowledge, the will, or the leadership to defend it. We have progressive idiots running the country who would risk letting ISIS continue to rampage unchecked to further their own war against American values. We have a compliant media who supports them, feeding propaganda to a nation of zombies who can't do more than bay like sheep waiting for the slaughter.

We need to replace a nation of zombies led by a pedantic, academic socialist with a nation of patriots led by a warrior king. It's our only hope.

CHAPTER 4

Zero Military

The Purges Continue

Joseph Stalin executed his generals in the 1940s out of fear they were plotting a coup against him, which they were not. As a result, the Soviet military was unable to operate effectively. Similarly, other dictators have purged the military in paranoid fits. Today, we are witnessing a similar purge, carried out not with bullets but with smears, innuendo, and spurious legal charges. But it is a purge of senior military officers nevertheless.

In my last book, *Stop the Coming Civil War*, I told you about the hundreds of high-ranking officers dismissed from the military for failing to comply with the Progressive-Islamist takeover. Gen. David Petraeus, Maj. Gen. Michael Carey, Vice Adm. Timothy Giardina, and Gen. Stanley Allen McChrystal were just a few of the heroes purged from the new progressive military.

This was by no means the end. The administration has continued from right where my last book left off, with each attack upon our military even more outrageous than the last.

Lt. Comm. Wes Modder is a nineteen-year veteran of the U.S. military. He is a highly decorated former Marine who did tours with the Eleventh Marine Expeditionary Unit and Naval Special Warfare Command. He was a force chaplain for the Navy SEALS.[1] He served in Desert Shield and Desert Storm. At any other time in American history, he would be considered a hero.

He's about to be kicked out of the Navy.

No, Chaplain Modder is not accused of dereliction of duty. He didn't walk off his post and join the enemy, nor was he involved in any type of scandal. The same commanding officer who last reviewed Modder as "the best of the best," and a "consummate professional leader worthy of an early promotion" has now written him up for discrimination "against students who were of different faiths and backgrounds."[2]

That doesn't mean he actually discriminated against anyone. Chaplain Modder did not recommend anyone not be promoted or in any other way affect the lives or careers of his accusers. All he did was answer questions honestly about his Christian faith. He accurately represented the Bible's teaching on extramarital sex and homosexuality. For that, he's been cashiered.

Chaplain Modder was the victim of the same kind of ambush perpetrated against the owners of Memories Pizza in Indiana. Unbeknownst to Modder, his assistant chaplain was a homosexual man, married to another man. This assistant relentlessly plied Chaplain Modder with questions about homosexuality in a deliberate attempt to entrap him into saying something objectionable by progressive standards. That wasn't particularly difficult. All the chaplain had to do was quote the Bible.

This is just another wrinkle in the ongoing purge and reconstruction of the military. The Obama administration continues its quest to transform the military from an institution of patriotic warriors, largely inspired by Christian principles, into an atheist, multicultural, progressive bureaucracy.

Not only do they purge competent, battle-hardened officers and replace them with progressive academics, they also purge chaplains committed to their faith and replace them with pseudochaplains who are willing to accept the progressive worldview, regardless of their faith. They are expected to be enthusiastic about Islam, even though it's the ideology inspiring the maniacs our military is fighting.

It's all part of the Progressive-Islamic takeover of America. In the private sector, they relentlessly attack small businesses run by Christians. In the military, they attack patriotic warriors and Christian chaplains. In both cases, anyone who resists their agenda must be destroyed.

What never ceases to amaze me is the lead role played by gay activists. One would think they would be the first to oppose the Islamofascists, as homosexuals are among the first tortured and executed under Islamic rule. These are the maniacs who throw homosexuals off rooftops, stone them to death, and commit all manner of atrocities against them.

Yet, here they are, participating in Obama's purge of the military, at least in the case of Chaplain Modder. You would think they would be seeking to strengthen our military against the barbarians who would kill them first, but they don't. They will launch an all-out war against a Christian restaurant that refuses to cater a gay wedding, but not a word of protest against those who would behead the couple if they had them under their power.

It's a tragic irony that gay activists would participate in a military purge, because they have been the victims of precisely the same tactics in the past. For all of the left's characterizing conservatives as "Nazis," it is this progressive administration that is actually acting like them. Since public schools don't teach history anymore, you may not have ever learned about "the Night of the Long Knives." It was a purge conducted by Hitler against his own Brownshirts.

The Brownshirts, or SA, were Hitler's unofficial, paramilitary thugs. They were the equivalent of the street gangs that Al Sharpton was riling up in Ferguson and elsewhere. Sharpton's thugs aren't as organized or well-armed, nor in uniform. But they play roughly the same role in Obama's dictatorship as the Brownshirts did in Hitler's.

The leader of the SA was a man named Ernst Röhm, a street brawler who happened to be a homosexual, as were most of the leaders of the SA. Hitler and the Nazis abhorred homosexuality as much as their modern-day counterparts, the Islamofascists. But they tolerated it in the Brownshirts while they were useful. Once they were no longer useful, Hitler turned on them and murdered them.

I can't help but see the parallel to gay activists supporting the Progressive-Islamist alliance. They may be useful to the alliance in destroying Western Civilization as we know it. But at least one side of that partnership would treat them the same way Hitler treated the homosexual Brownshirts. Moreover, the Islamofascists would kill the homosexuals in far more brutal fashion.

Along with his prime targets, social democrats and communists, Hitler also disposed of loyal conservatives. Anyone who did not conform to his vision of the "new Germany" was killed, arrested, or intimidated into silence. On why he acted outside of the court system and without due process for the victims, Hitler said that because of the threat to the German people, he had declared himself "the Supreme Judge of the German People."

Does this sound vaguely familiar to you? Did Hitler not effectively place himself above the law and the German constitution, ignoring the courts and the legislature? Today, we have a president who boasts he will do the same thing with his pen and his phone. Sometimes, history repeats itself.

Of course, our pedantic academic president would never have the fortitude to perpetrate such brutal acts. Thank goodness he's much too passive-aggressive for anything like that. He may cut you loose if you're serving your country overseas in a dangerous region, but he won't do anything directly attributable to himself. His breed would rather send operatives like the weasel who set up Chaplain Modder and then pontificate about diversity and "white privilege" in the military.

He has shown he will go after people in his own party if they stand in the way of his foreign policy agenda. That's just what Sen. Robert Menendez believes Obama did with the administration's prosecution of Menendez over corruption charges.[3] Menendez was an outspoken critic of the decision to ease the trade embargo on Cuba and of the nuclear deal with Iran. Menendez stated unambiguously that the prosecution was intended "to silence me."

I don't know if Menendez is guilty or not. Charging a New Jersey politician with corruption is a little like handing out speeding tickets at the Indianapolis 500. That the administration decided to focus on a Democratic critic of its anti-American policies seems a little too convenient to me. If it wanted to fight corruption in politics, it could have started with the equally corrupt Chicago political machine that helped put Obama in the White House or the California Democrats raking in fortunes on contracts steered toward friends and family.

Not only has the administration purged people from the military for political reasons, they've actually gone after people for being too effective at fighting the enemy. Maj. Mathew Golsteyn has already been stripped of the Silver Star he earned for heroism during the Battle of Marja in Afghanistan. He was actually in line for the medal to be upgraded to Distinguished Service Cross, second only to the Congressional Medal of Honor, when he ran afoul of one of Obama's appointees.[4]

Secretary of the Army John McHugh, who has never served in the military, decided to revoke his Silver Star because of unsubstantiated accusations of wrongful conduct in killing an enemy bomb maker in Afghanistan in 2010. The Army investigated him in relation to these charges and did not find sufficient evidence to charge him with a crime.[5]

Nevertheless, Golsteyn is now fighting a less-than-honorable discharge from the Army, on top of having his medal revoked and being kicked out of the Special Forces.

Forget whether the accusations against this hero are true or false. Why is the government even investigating a war hero for killing an IED bomb maker in the first place? IEDs are the number one killer of American soldiers deployed in the Middle East. Why is the administration overly concerned with how this enemy combatant might have met his end?

The name George Witton comes to my mind. You have probably never heard that name. George Witton was a soldier in the British army at the turn of the twentieth century. He was also the subject of a politically motivated witch hunt regarding his treatment of the enemy during the Boer War. He wrote a book about it called *Scapegoats of the Empire*, which was the basis for the 1980 movie *Breaker Morant*.

Witton and his brothers-in-arms were accused of shooting prisoners, an arguably more egregious offense than whatever Golsteyn may have done in eliminating an enemy bomb maker who was still in the field. Yet no one who read the book or watched the movie would consider Witton anything other than the victim of politically motivated injustice.

The Progressive-Islamic alliance is doing the same thing to our soldiers today. While ISIS rapes, kills, beheads, and sets people on fire, our rogue progressives persecute our warriors on slim evidence trumped up by the enemy.

Maj. Gen. Michael Keltz joined the ranks of the purged last May when he was forced to resign over a racially charged comment he made during the disciplinary hearing for a lower-ranking officer.[6] And what was this horrifying comment that cost a two-star general his career?

He told the officer being disciplined that he appeared "drunker than 10,000 Indians" in a photo.[7]

Seriously, that's it. That's what cost this general his entire career. I'm not saying the comment wasn't inappropriate. But wouldn't a public apology for the remark have been more appropriate? Can anyone seriously argue this remark did so much harm that a two-star general's career had to be sacrificed?

Incidentally, I can't help wondering if the reaction would have been the same if the general had said "drunker than 10,000 Irishmen." I think we both know he'd still be on the job.

In another questionable prosecution, the four Blackwater security guards convicted of first-degree murder for killing the enemy were sentenced earlier this year to decades in prison. Despite their own testimony that they were under fire and killed only in self-defense, they've been mercilessly prosecuted by the Islamophilic, anti-U.S. military administration.[8]

The prosecution of the Blackwater guards and attempted purge of Golsteyn are even more outrageous when you consider the administration's support for a man we now know likely deserted his post in Afghanistan and joined the enemy. At the same time the Army concluded it could not charge Golsteyn with a crime, it filed formal charges against Sgt. Bowe Bergdahl for desertion and misbehavior before the enemy.

I am not going to convict Bergdahl in my book before he has received due process. I won't lower myself to the anti-American standards of progressive jackals. But at the time of this writing, two things are true: The Army found enough evidence to charge Bergdahl with desertion. It did not find evidence to charge Golsteyn.

Yet Golsteyn's persecution continues, while the Obama administration continues to stand by Bergdahl, at least passively. As of this writing, it has issued no formal statements on the military charges against Bergdahl or how they relate to the administration's strong support for him prior. The most we've heard is it's inappropriate for the White House to comment "on what's obviously an ongoing investigation by the military."[9]

That's very convenient. What will Obama say if he's found guilty? What does he tell the parents of those who died trying to rescue this man, especially after it's come to light that the administration knew he likely deserted six years ago?

That's right. We also now know that the Naval Criminal Investigative Service (NCIS) investigated Bergdahl's disappearance and found substantial evidence that he planned his desertion back in 2009. That means the White House knew Bergdahl likely deserted six years ago, before sending six men to their deaths attempting to rescue him from captivity.

Susan Rice must have known about the 2009 NCIS findings in June 2014 when she infamously described Bergdahl as having "served with honor and distinction." Just like Obama, she sounded like a guilty child caught in a lie when she followed with "And we'll have the opportunity eventually to learn what has transpired in the past years." How can this woman still be employed as national security advisor?

As I tell my listeners on *The Savage Nation*, follow the bouncing ball. When you step back and look at who the administration has purged and who it has defended, there is an unmistakable pattern. Effective leaders in the war for Western civilization, like General Petraeus, Major General Carey, or Vice Admiral Giardina, are purged based on spurious, trumped-up charges. War heroes like Maj. Mathew Golsteyn are purged, despite no charges being brought against them at all.

If you are too critical of Islam or too devoted to Christianity, like Lt. Comm. Wes Modder, you are a target. The Progressive-Islamist alliance will bend over backward to attack you, including using gay activists to entrap you.

Contrast that with the treatment of an accused deserter. The White House has stood by Bowe Bergdahl, promoting him from private to sergeant during his absence, despite knowing he was likely a deserter since the day he walked off his post five years ago. President Obama literally stood next to Bergdahl's father, who appeared on the White House lawn in the beard of a Muslim cleric, sending Bergdahl coded messages in Arabic.[10]

And by the way, Nidal Malik Hasan, a devout Islamist and perpetrator of the Fort Hood massacre in 2009, who killed thirteen people, including a pregnant woman and her unborn child, while wounding over thirty others, has still not been executed for his crime in 2015. How is that for military justice?

This is how transparent the Progressive-Islamist alliance has become. It is openly flaunting its sympathies, while actively weakening the only institution that stands between us and the maniacs overrunning the Middle East.

From Soldiers to Social Workers

As egregious as the military purges is the administration's appointment of wholly unqualified civilian leadership in the cabinet. I have yet to find any evidence that Secretary of the Air Force Deborah Lee James has ever piloted a plane. There is no mention in any bio I can find of her having a pilot's license or having ever taken lessons. As far as I can tell, she's never even flown a Piper Cub.

We do know she got violently ill while riding along on the USAF's Thunderbirds last year.[11] Granted, flying an F-16 isn't a requirement of her job as air force secretary, but what qualifications *does* she have relevant to this job? She has no military experience whatsoever. According to her official bio, she has held staffer jobs in Congress and executive positions for a defense contractor. She was an assistant secretary of defense for reserve affairs under Clinton.[12]

Don't misunderstand me. I am aware that this is a civilian position, as it should be. A bedrock American principle, enshrined in our Declaration of Independence, is that the military should at all times be subordinate to the civil power. We have laws on the books prohibiting anyone from being appointed secretary of the Army, Navy, and Air Force within five years of their active duty.

Still, that doesn't mean it is a good idea to appoint a secretary of the Air Force who has never even flown a plane, even in civilian life. The combined military experience of this administration's secretaries of the Army, Navy, and Air Force is two years. Only Secretary of the Navy Ray Mabus has served at all. But as we've seen with Secretary McHugh, they are willing and able to advance the Progressive-Islamist agenda.

That may be the reason the administration picked James for her job. She has one qualification that trumps all others for the Obama administration. She's a true believer in this administration's quest to remake the military into a progressive social club.

This past March, Secretary James unveiled her "sweeping plan to increase opportunities for women, minorities and enlisted airmen."[13] In addition to lowering height requirements and other standards, her plan quite explicitly calls for quotas, *particularly in the pilot ranks.* She might call them "diversity and inclusion requirements," but they are quotas just the same. This means she will require a certain number of female and minority pilots, regardless of whether they are the best candidates for the positions.

Retired colonel Terry Stevens, who actually served thirty-five years in the Air Force, including eight years in personnel, wasn't buying it. "If you're going to do that instead of picking the best qualified of any applicant, then you're actually downgrading the quality of the force," Stevens said.[14]

This isn't just theoretical nonsense to be debated at a think tank seminar. All of this adds up to a weaker military on the battlefield. Our pilots' hands are tied trying to fight ISIS. The dearth of actual airstrikes was one of the factors contributing to the Islamic State's victory at Ramadi. This is what happens when you have a sorority running the military. According to the *Washington Times*:

A former official who is frequently in the Pentagon said, "The building is very guarded about what they say, but clearly the White House is running the campaign, which has them furious."

This source said combat pilots can loiter over a target for hours before approval comes to strike it. Sometimes approval never comes.[15]

The sorority girls decide when our air force pilots can release a rocket. I suppose it's difficult for them to manage everything, given their important work cooking the books to prove global warming, proving racism by white cops causes inner city crime, and proving homophobia is everywhere. Meanwhile, ISIS now controls Ramadi. You can watch their victory parade on YouTube.

This is just more of the same from an administration who wanted to lower the physical standards for admission into the Marine Corps. That was a reaction to the revelation that almost half of the female recruits were unable to perform the minimum requirement of three pull-ups. Never mind that their fellow soldiers might be in more danger on the battlefield if they had to depend upon soldiers physically unable to perform their functions. Diversity trumps battle readiness in the new progressive military.

This past April, the long experiment with integrating women into combat ended when the last two female recruits washed out of the Marine Corps' Infantry Officer Course, after failing to complete the Combat Endurance Test. The female recruits were already granted lower physical fitness screening standards, but had to match male performance on this phase of the test. They were unable to.[16]

One can only guess what the progressive answer to this predictable outcome will be. I suppose the Combat Endurance

Test will be waived as a requirement next. Then, maybe they can waive the requirement that Marines be able to fire a service weapon. Doesn't that offend the antigun crowd?

Now, we're going to be downgrading the skill level of pilots as well. Don't misunderstand me. I believe the jobs should go to the best pilots, whether they are women, men, black, white, Hispanic, or Native American. We need the absolute best talent available piloting our state-of-the-art aircraft and supporting our troops on the ground and ships at sea.

Secretary James sees it in completely the opposite way. She believes we need diversity in the personnel piloting our aircraft, whether the pilots represent the best talent or not. She'll sacrifice talent to fulfill race and sex quotas. That puts lives at risk. Ask any of our troops on the ground what's more important to them: the best air cover possible or the most diverse? How would they like the equivalent of a Germanwings copilot in charge of a fighter jet?

Not only are the progressives weakening the military with affirmative action, they are going on the offensive against white soldiers. Approximately one month after Secretary James's announcement about implementing racial and gender quotas for pilots, a story broke about soldiers at Fort Gordon being lectured about white privilege during a training seminar.

Among other important information disseminated to our troops that day was a Power Point slide entitled "The Luxury of Obliviousness," which had this to say:

> Race privilege gives whites little reason to pay a lot of attention to African Americans or to how white privilege affects them. "To be white in America means not having to think about it."[17]

I'm sure the pedantic academics in the White House sorority were very pleased to learn white soldiers were "educated" about their privilege. Meanwhile, back here on planet Earth, the U.S. military has been integrated for almost seventy years. Americans of all colors have been fighting together and dying for each other since before the academic in chief and most of his sorority were born.

Our troops need training, equipment, and team building that helps them survive and succeed in combat. They don't need divisive nonsense like this building tension between men and women who would otherwise put their lives on the line for each other without a second thought. Ask anyone you know who's been in combat. There is no white privilege on the battlefield. Bullets and bombs kill and maim in very equal-opportunity fashion.

The Army spokeswoman who responded to the incident said the slide in question was not authorized by any higher command and that the individual instructor had inserted it without permission. That would be a perfectly reasonable explanation if this were an isolated incident. But there is plenty of precedent for this soul-bending propaganda being foisted upon our soldiers.

The military's "train the trainer" manual, which nobody disputes is authorized by command, is even worse. Warning military men and women about a "White Male Club," the manual says,

> *Simply put, a healthy, white, heterosexual, Christian male receives many unearned advantages of social privilege, whereas a black, homosexual, atheist female in poor health receives many unearned disadvantages of social privilege.*[18]

Forget that white privilege is just another divisive, progressive canard used to sow discord among people who would
otherwise unite against them. Ask yourself this: Does subject-
ing soldiers to this kind of training build unity or divisiveness
within the unit? Does it make it more likely or less likely that
soldiers of different races or genders will trust each other with
their lives, as soldiers are required to do every day in combat?
Does it make the military stronger or weaker, and America
thereby safer or in greater danger?

I don't think I have to answer these questions for you.

Supporting Our Enemies

While the war on our military goes on with direct action like
purges and divisive policy, it also weakens it indirectly by making our enemies stronger.

It's become almost routine at this point to see a news story
about the administration losing track of weapons that eventually end up in the hands of our enemies. One of the problems
seems to be that our Islamophilic president can't make up his
mind whether he is pro-Sunni or pro-Shiite.

All we know is he's not pro-American. In any of the myriad
conflicts the administration has created in the Middle East,
you can always depend upon one constant: This administration
will do exactly the opposite of what's in the best interests of
the American people.

After some hand-wringing over whether to support Saudi
Arabia against the Iranian-backed Houthi rebels in Yemen,
Obama decided he had to support our longtime ally. But that
was only after we learned the Pentagon could not account for

over $500 million in weapons previously donated to the Yemeni government by the United States:

> *"We have to assume it's completely compromised and gone,"* *said a legislative aide on Capitol Hill who spoke on the condition of anonymity because of the sensitivity of the matter.*[19]

"Compromised" means they are in the hands of either the Houthis or al-Qaeda, both of whom are fighting Saudi Arabia in Yemen, presumably with weapons we supplied. At least in this case they're not shooting at our own soldiers with guns we provided, as they have in other cases where the administration armed our enemies.

I'm not going to spend a lot of time documenting cases of the administration's bungling resulting in weapons falling into the hands of al-Qaeda, ISIS, or other extremist groups we're supposedly fighting against. There are too many. They all relate back to the root cause of the problem, which was the disastrous Arab Spring engineered by Hillary Clinton's State Department and supported with U.S. covert and conventional military action. By the time you read this book, there will likely have been many more pictures of head-scarfed terrorists posing in front of crates of U.S. ordnance.

Much more damaging has been the administration's support of Iran. Of all of the Islamist governments in the region, Iran's has to be the worst, unless you count ISIS as a legitimate government. Yet it is the ninth-century throwback mullahs who are suddenly the U.S. government's ally of choice over our traditional Sunni allies like Saudi Arabia, Jordan, and Egypt.

Perhaps that's one explanation for why Obama refuses to

recognize ISIS as Islamist. How can he recognize the truth about the "religion of peace" while he's negotiating with the mullahs?

Every step he has taken in the Middle East has furthered Iran's dominance in the region. Progressives are still claiming ISIS wouldn't exist if George W. Bush hadn't invaded Iraq. That may or may not be true. I certainly didn't support Bush's invasion then or now. Let's just say George W. Bush wasn't his father, in my opinion.

Nevertheless, Obama still had choices when he inherited an Iraq with an elected government and relative stability within its borders. After everyone told him to leave a stabilizing force in Iraq to prevent precisely the kind of development ISIS represents, he pulled out of the country completely. That left a vacuum ISIS was only too happy to fill.

Faced with the worst radical Islamist threat since Suleiman, Obama responded weakly, refusing to commit to more than nominally effective airstrikes. This was his answer to barbarians who were annihilating Christian communities that had existed in the Middle East for thousands of years. He allowed ISIS to grow into a force that is now a credible threat to take over Iraq and Syria.

Obama's eventual solution further elevated Iran. In addition to Iranian-backed Shiite militias, there very well may have been Iranian regulars on the ground in the victory over ISIS in Tikrit.[20] That gives Iran a military presence in Iraq, made legitimate by U.S. support of its mission there.

This is something the administration will likely deny or at least try to downplay, but it really amounts to a technicality anyway. Whether the Shiite troops were wearing official Iranian military uniforms or not, it was Iranian assets our U.S.

pilots were supporting in a battle our own military could have won even more easily.

The real game changer is the administration's decision to allow Iran to develop a nuclear weapon. Obama all but admitted this while commenting on the preliminary version of his infamous deal with the mullahs. Speaking to the fifteen-year time period the agreement covers, he said,

And at that, at the end of that period, maybe they've changed, maybe they haven't. If they haven't changed, we still have the options available to me—or available to a future president that I have available to me right now.[21]

Of course, the pseudo-interviewer Steve Inskeep of National Propaganda Radio didn't challenge the president on this statement. That's because NPR is just an arm of the Obama administration. It's a wholly owned subsidiary of the Democratic Party and always has been. So Obama was allowed to tell his fairy tale about how this deal will benefit America, her allies, and world peace. But that's not what he was really saying. A real journalist would have drawn him out.

Allow me to translate what Obama really said during that interview. He admitted that his deal would allow Iran to develop nuclear weapons and future presidents would have to deal with it. During this interview he looked like a scared child who got caught lying and admits in a secret meeting with a friend, "Yeah, they're going to get nukes, but it's someone else's problem."

A real, adversarial media would have called him on the carpet for saying something this incompetent. If we lived in a rational society with a legitimate government, this one statement alone might have led to impeachment. But we don't. We have a weak anti-American in the White House and a largely nonexistent opposition party that refuses to do what they were elected to do and stop him.

Just to put the icing on the cake, Obama spent the weekend after his Iran deal went from bad to worse making friendly with Cuban president Raul Castro. That's right, while millions of Cubans suffer in a prison nation, Obama dances with another devil.[22] This time, it's a full-blown communist who continues Fidel Castro's regime of slavery over the captive island nation.

I go back and forth on this president. Sometimes I think he's a power-mad dictator. But when I listen to interviews like the one he gave NPR, I think he might just be a pie-in-the-sky, daffy, academic lunatic who has no connection to reality. Then again, he knew the real world well enough to become president.

Still, the man sounds like a typical academic nut. He talks about Iran as if it exists in a vacuum, as if we know nothing about the mullahs. We don't know they're bloodthirsty murderers who have killed our own troops, vowed to wipe Israel off the map, and sponsored terrorism and revolution all over the Middle East, including the Houthi revolt in Yemen.

Anyone who gets elected to the White House is an egomaniac by definition. When you combine that with academic obliviousness, a pretty face, and a gift for oratory like Obama's, you have someone very dangerous in your midst. That's why we have a separation of powers, like the requirement that treaties have the advice *and consent* of the Senate. That's supposed to prevent wrongheaded, disastrous, and dangerous deals like this one with the throwbacks in Iran.

Nevertheless, he goes on unopposed promoting the

Progressive-Islamist takeover, knowingly or not. He has Libya in flames, Egypt on the verge of civil war, ISIS rampaging in Iraq, Iran gaining influence throughout the Middle East, and Israel in a corner with its back to a wall of Islamic hate.

Alienating Our Allies

As I said, when you understand what is in the best interests of the American people, you can count on this administration to do exactly the opposite. It weakens our military from within and strengthens our enemies. It's no surprise that it also alienates our allies.

Whether he's incompetent, crazy, or crazy like a fox, Obama has obviously allied himself with the mullahs in Iran. That he's fighting their proxies in Yemen at the same time is either the incompetent or crazy side of his policy. But you have to wonder what he meant when he made this statement:

> *I think the biggest threats that they face may not be coming from Iran invading. It's going to be from dissatisfaction inside their own countries.*[23]

Obviously, he's talking about the kind of "dissatisfaction" characteristic of the Arab Spring he and his secretary of state, Hillary Clinton, helped engineer. He specifically addressed these comments to "our friends in the region, our traditional Sunni states." That means Saudi Arabia, among others. What is he saying? Is this a veiled threat to incite the same kind of revolt in Saudi Arabia or just more pie-in-the-sky, academic naïveté?

Saudi Arabia can't take it as anything other than a threat,

whether intentional or not. It's as if Obama were saying, "Oppose me in my dealings with Iran and you'll end up just like Gadhafi." Of course, he says it all with a smile, in his usual passive-aggressive manner. Just like the racial incitements during his speech at Selma, he pretends he is acting in friendship. But if you were the Saudi king, how would you take it?

Then, just when you think you have this man figured out, he comes out with this in the same interview:

> *How can we strengthen the body politic in these countries, so that Sunni youth feel that they've got something other than [ISIS] to choose from?*[24]

Now he's back to the idiotic idea that radical Islam can be defeated by getting the throwbacks jobs or inspiring them to "start a business," as one of his sorority girls said at a press conference earlier in the year. He's like a raving lunatic, threatening revolution and regicide in one breath and talking about social programs and reform for the maniacs in the next.

Maybe he's a Marxist revolutionary suffering from a messianic complex. He clearly wants to turn the world upside down and remake it in his own image. He issued a veiled threat to our ally Saudi Arabia about a possible uprising against their oppression, but when asked why the brutal theocrats in Iran shouldn't fear the same fate, he says his nuclear deal will encourage "science, technology, and job creation." Then, in the breath after that, he says his deal won't necessarily lead to regime change or stop Iran from developing nuclear weapons, but that's a future president's problem!

Whether he's evil or just unbalanced, this man clearly cannot be trusted by America's allies. The options are not great in forming alliances with any of the Muslim nations, but the United States has traditionally partnered with more stable Sunni nations like Saudi Arabia, Jordan, and Egypt. Now, Obama has clearly sided with the Shiites in Iran, over the objections of Israel and our other allies.

No one trusts the Iranians. Israel obviously doesn't trust them, but neither do most of our European allies, whose reaction was lukewarm at best. Most important, the American people do not trust them.

While the progressive *Washington Post* gleefully reported that a poll taken just before the preliminary deal showed a majority of Americans supported a deal with Iran, it also showed something else. Nearly 60 percent of those polled didn't believe a deal would prevent Iran getting a nuclear weapon.

Whether that was a reflection of their faith in Obama or mistrust of the Iranians is unclear, but they have little reason to trust either party to these negotiations. One burns our flag literally, while the other does so figuratively with every speech, policy, and executive action.

The American people did not have to wait long to have their suspicions of Iran's untrustworthiness confirmed. On the same day the preliminary deal was announced, Iran was already backing away from the terms the Obama administration claimed Iran had agreed to.

The administration's fact sheet said "Iran will be required to grant access to the IAEA to investigate suspicious sites or allegations of a covert enrichment facility, conversion facility, centrifuge production facility, or yellowcake production facility *anywhere in the country*" (emphasis added). It also claimed, "All 6,104 centrifuges will be IR-1s, Iran's first-generation centrifuge."[25]

Immediately after this release, Iran's defense minister denied that the agreement included inspection of military sites. He then told the Iranian parliament that Iran would begin using its much faster IR-8 centrifuges the day a permanent deal takes effect.[26]

A few days later, the supreme leader, Ayatollah Ali Khamenei, made a speech that ostensibly accused the United States of lying about what the Iranians had agreed to and said that all sanctions on Iran must be lifted immediately upon enactment of a formal agreement. Khamenei also said he neither supports nor opposes the negotiations until the details are spelled out, saying "the deceptive other side wants to restrict us in the details."[27]

Do you understand what he did? For all intents and purposes, he walked away from the negotiations, just as Netanyahu warned they would. There is no way the United States can agree to lift sanctions immediately upon signing a formal agreement, before Iran has demonstrated its compliance with any of its own responsibilities. Khamenei knows this. He's just maneuvering for even more concessions out of a deal that already conceded too much to this murderous regime.

Netanyahu told Congress this would happen six weeks before it did. He told Congress on March 3 the Iranians would negotiate just as they do in the Persian rug markets. He advised the U.S. to walk away from them first, because Iran needs the deal more than the U.S. does.

Obama said he didn't listen to the speech but had read the transcript. Apparently, he didn't read it very carefully, or he was just too arrogant to take some good advice, because it appears the administration was completely blindsided by this predictable and predicted move by Iran.

At least one of three things is true. Either Iran began reneging on the preliminary deal before the ink was dry, the U.S. government was lying about what terms they really secured, or the U.S. government was just incompetent in negotiations. Maybe all three things are true. It really doesn't matter; it was a bad deal for America and its allies from the start.

Our best and closest ally in the region is Israel, the only Western democracy there. The United States has strategic alliances with Muslim nations like Saudi Arabia, Jordan, the UAE, and Egypt, but Israel is the only nation in that region that is built upon values similar to the United States'. Unsurprisingly, it is this nation the Progressive-Islamist alliance attacks the most vehemently.

Obama failed in his attempt to foment a coup d'état in Israel during the last election. He sent hundreds of left-wing agitators to the country in the months leading up to the elections in an attempt to replace Netanyahu with someone who would not oppose the Progressive-Islamist agenda. When that failed, the administration continued its propaganda attacks on the Israeli government.

In an astounding example of misinformation, the White House tweeted a diagram mocking one used by Netanyahu during his historic speech to Congress. The administration's diagram, a cartoon created by one of Obama's sorority girls, no doubt, attempted to show that Iran would have a faster path to a nuclear weapon without the infamous nuclear deal, just one day after it admitted the deal would not actually prevent Iran from getting a nuke.[28] It's not only antagonistic toward Israel, but it insults the intelligence of the American people.

While Obama has alienated allies we already had, his worst strategic blunder may have been in turning a potential ally into an enemy. I'm talking about Russian president Vladimir Putin, whom the administration has constantly gone out of its way to antagonize and demonize.

Postcommunist Russia's interests don't always align with the United States', but Russia would certainly be a better fit than Iran. Russia is a large, powerful, First World nation that faces the same kinds of threats from radical Islam we face, only much closer to home. From an economic and political perspective, it is in the interests of the American people to foster closer ties with Russia.

Unfortunately, Russia and her nationalist, conservative president do not fit in with the Progressive-Islamist agenda. Putin's domestic policies are not "gay friendly" enough for the progressives. He signed a law in 2013 that made it illegal to promote propaganda of nontraditional sexual relations to minors. It subjects anyone who promotes homosexuality to minors to a fine.

The liberal media went apoplectic. If you believe what they've said about it, you'd think Russian police were rounding up homosexuals. The law doesn't make homosexuality illegal. As Putin himself said, "This should not look as if we intend to persecute people of some non-traditional orientation. One does not preclude the other. I believe that such balanced approach is absolutely the right one."[29]

Personally, I would oppose such a law here in the United States, but let's put things in perspective. If you promote homosexuality to children in Russia, you may be fined. Compare that to what happens to you just for *being a homosexual* in a radical Islamist country. There, you get thrown off a rooftop and stoned to death. Where is the progressive outrage over that?

Just as they looked the other way while Stalin and Mao

killed a hundred million people in the twentieth century, progressives can look the other way when the Islamofascists burn people alive, rape them, enslave them, and cut off their heads. Where are the so-called radical feminists on the wholesale enslavement and rape of non-Muslim girls as young as eight years of age?

Putin offends the other half of the Progressive-Islamist Alliance with his policies against radical Islam. From listening to the progressive media, you might believe he crushed a peaceful, separatist movement in the idyllic Republic of Chechnya. Just as they provided cover for Stalin and Mao, the progressive media constantly made excuses for the Islamic International Brigade, which in reality was just another brutal group of ninth-century throwbacks seeking to enslave an entire region.

Putin vowed to wipe them out in 1999 and was uncompromising in his treatment of the separatists. He wasn't there to win hearts and minds or convince the throwbacks to start a business. He was there to protect the Russian people from barbarians. That he succeeded is more galling to the Progressive-Islamists than anything else.

Now the Obama administration has joined with its fellow progressives in Europe to help instigate the revolution in Ukraine. Just like the Arab Spring, the Ukraine revolution had foreign fingerprints all over it, including support from Obama, who admitted to CNN his administration "brokered a deal to transition power in Ukraine."[30] That's Obamaspeak for ousting the democratically elected president, Viktor Yanukovych.

I believe there was even more involvement by the U.S. government and its progressive allies in Europe in fomenting that revolution. We already know the Obama administration sent hundreds of leftist operatives to Israel in an attempt to defeat Netanyahu. We know about the administration's involvement in the so-called Arab Spring. It's hard to see the revolution in Ukraine as anything other than another chapter in the Progressive-Islamist destruction of the world order.

I'm not implying Obama is the first president to use covert action. International politics is a rough business. My problem is with where and why he has employed these tools. What possible U.S. interest was advanced by regime change in Ukraine? What is to be gained by openly antagonizing Russia? Russia should be a close ally of the United States against the Islamists by now. Instead, this maniac is actually risking a war with her. That's a war the U.S. could very well lose, especially with a military made weaker every day under his command.

It's just more evidence that this man has no place in the office he's in. More and more people are asking the question I've been asking about him for years. Is he playing for the other side, or is he just a clueless, pedantic academic who is incompetent leading a nation in the real world?

I was also the first to give you the answer. It doesn't matter. Either way, he's flying this country and the world into a mountain, just like that unbalanced pilot on the German plane. More importantly, he's executing the Progressive-Islamist agenda to perfection, intentionally or not, preparing the way for his successor to complete the transformation of America into a socialist prison nation.

Where Is Our Warrior King?

Thanks to the mess the progressives have made of the world order, we have to change our tactics. We need to do more than speak softly and carry a big stick. We have to start swinging that stick if we're going to survive.

The Progressive-Islamist alliance accused George W. Bush of being a crusader. They believed the myth that the Crusades were Christian aggression against Islam. The truth is the Crusades were a response to hundreds of years of Muslim aggression.

Here's the problem. The West stopped fighting the Crusades when the Muslims were thrown out of Europe, but the Muslims didn't. They've continued their thousand-year war against civilization right up to the present. They were contained for a time by Western economic, social, and military superiority. Now they're loose again, thanks to the Progressive-Islamist Arab Spring.

We need a new Richard the Lionheart. We're facing worldwide jihad, just as Richard and his successors faced during the Middle Ages. It's going to take a real leader commanding a refocused military to defeat it.

The American public is dying for a warrior king crusader. That explains why *American Sniper* is the most popular movie of modern times. Why do you think it grossed $100 million over a single weekend? Because we'd like a sniper to run for president, to be our warrior king crusader, to save this country before it's too late.

Right now, we have a sorority running the military as a social services organization. That's not what a military establishment is supposed to do. I have no problem with women, homosexuals, minorities, or anyone else voicing grievances, as long as their opponents are free to disagree when those grievances are unfounded.

But the military is not the proper forum for this. It is not a town hall. It is a martial institution with one purpose and one purpose only: to destroy the enemy before it destroys us.

The military must be run by people who have the strength to take decisive action when it is needed and the restraint to avoid action when it is not in the interests of the people. We have exactly the opposite in charge now.

We have a group of progressive academics who won't say the word *Islamic* when describing the real enemy. As ISIS rampages through the Middle East, they are more concerned with not offending Muslims than protecting Western Civilization from its greatest threat since Hitler and Stalin.

At the same time, they treated the military like a new toy they got for Christmas when overthrowing governments during the Arab Spring. They were like a two-year-old with a machine gun, shooting in all directions because he doesn't know any better. They destroyed stable, relatively secular governments and replaced them with radical Islamist ones, almost without exception.

It's hard to believe it all wasn't intentional. Both the progressives and the Islamofascists have an interest in destroying the world order. Intentional or not, that's just what both groups are doing. They are truly fellow travelers.

The world order wasn't perfect before the Progressive-Islamist onslaught. Nothing constructed by human beings ever is. But it did keep America safe for seventy years. Whether you like it or not, that's the truth.

Did America support some oppressive governments? Yes. There isn't really another kind in the Middle East, outside of Israel. Now we're seeing the other side of the story. We can see just what kind of people those dictators were repressing.

Whom do you prefer, the dictators or the radical Islamists? Did getting rid of Gadhafi make Libya freer and safer? Did it increase or decrease American national security? Was Egypt freer under the Muslim Brotherhood than it was under Mubarak, a U.S. ally? Hillary Clinton famously boasted after he was killed "we came, we saw, he died"—to the cackles of her feminist cadre.

The truth is there were no good choices in most of these countries before the progressives blew them up. Former administrations recognized this and did the best they could, forging partnerships with lesser evils to advance U.S. interests. That meant a strong alliance with Israel and cooperation with traditional Sunni allies like Egypt, Jordan, and Saudi Arabia.

A warrior king knows how to pick his battles. He knows when to negotiate and with whom. He risks military conflict only when it is in his country's interests, and then he commits to destroy the enemy, not win hearts and minds.

The enemies we're facing right now do not have winnable hearts or minds. They aren't going to be dissuaded by a government jobs program. We need to face reality and elect the kind of leadership that will deal with the enemy as they truly are.

As Richard Gabriel writes in *Military History* magazine:

> *It's unfortunate that in today's world the Arabic word* jihad *is most directly associated with heinous terrorist acts committed by Islamic extremists who either don't know or don't care about the word's origin and true meaning.*
>
> *The doctrine of jihad, or holy war, was Muhammad's principal military legacy. It is indisputable that divinely justified warfare became a force of major importance during*

the early Islamic period, was a significant motivator for the Muslim conquests that followed Muhammad's death in 632 and remains a primary characteristic of Islamic warfare. Pre-Islamic Arabia knew no notion of ideology of any sort, and certainly no notion of religiously sanctioned war.[31]

Do you understand what he's saying? Jihad is not an aberration within Islam by a few radical elements. It is a foundational part of the religion itself. It has underpinned Islam since Muhammad and remains a driving force within mainstream Islam today. It doesn't just inspire terrorism. It inspires the conflict Muslims have with their neighbors in all the countries I told you about in the last chapter.

We're in desperate need of a new Richard the Lionheart as president who puts aside the pantywaists who have run this country off the rails. Not tomorrow. Not after many of us are decimated. Right now. He wouldn't sit here waiting for sleeper cells to strike, even after the FBI has opened investigations of ISIS in forty-nine states.[32] He would hit them before they hit us.

This assumes we have leadership that isn't playing for the other side.

The Islamofascists are fighting a religiously sanctioned war, if you consider Islam a religion at all. Retired U.S. admiral James "Ace" Lyons doesn't. He said, "Until you recognize Islam is a political movement masquerading as a religion, you're never going to come to grips with it."[33]

How else could you describe these maniacs, who are willing to kill boys in Iraq, machine-gun them for watching soccer, in the name of Allah? No religion would teach that. These are the brutal tactics of a Jacobin political movement. That's one more thing the progressives and Islamofascists have in common.

Admiral Lyons pointed out something else I've been saying for years. We had our chance to stop the Islamofascists before it came to this. We could have stopped them when they took our hostages in Iran, but Jimmy Carter is part of the Progressive/Islamic alliance. We could have stopped them after they bombed our embassy in Lebanon, but Reagan's order to respond was disobeyed by Caspar Weinberger. There is blame to go around for both sides of our one-party system.

Now we're back to where we were in the Middle Ages, with the Islamofascists on the march toward Vienna. This is not World War I. We are not fighting European nations who recognize international rules of war. We're fighting throwback lunatics who don't realize it's 2015 and who rape, murder, and torture as their ancestors did a thousand years ago.

We don't need a jobs program. We don't need diversity in the Air Force. We don't need equal opportunity for mullahs. We need a warrior king crusader to rebuild our military and defend Western Civilization once again.

The Vikings' Fate

If you think social engineering of the U.S. military is without consequences, I invite my skeptical readers to study the Danish or Swedish military of today. After many a decade of progressiveness, the descendants of Vikings are today unable or unwilling to defend their homeland against an Islamist invasion. Witness the capitulation. Thank the progressives, the gays, the feminists, and the socialists. Is this what you want for the United States, to be a helpless giant?

CHAPTER 5

Zero Education

Contrary to what you have been told by our progressive media, the United States spends more per student on education than any other nation in the world. We spend over $15,000 per student annually. Yet, U.S. students rank twenty-fourth in literacy[1] and thirty-first in math literacy.[2] Across the board, U.S. students perform poorly compared to other countries that spend less per student on education. How can that be?

There are a lot of answers to that question. One of them is that American public schools don't spend a large percentage of their time teaching reading, writing, and arithmetic. Instead, they spend it indoctrinating children into the progressive religion. This means teaching them to hate or mistrust everything that made Western Civilization in general and America in particular the freest, most prosperous civilization in human history.

There is a direct connection between the phony economic recovery and the destruction of American education. What the government calls unemployment continues to fall even though unemployed people don't actually get jobs. They just give up looking for work and become permanent residents on the welfare rolls. Our education system is contributing significantly to this disastrous trend.

The federal government has been increasingly involved in education since Jimmy Carter created the Department of Education in 1979. It's no accident that school and student performance has plummeted almost from that moment on.

Thomas Sowell once wrote, "The most fundamental fact about the ideas of the political left is that they do not work. Therefore we should not be surprised to find the left concentrated in institutions where ideas do not have to work in order to survive."[3]

That couldn't be truer than for education, a field dominated by leftists for more than a century. From what students are taught, to how they're taught, to how it's all paid for, education is a microcosm for the epic failure of progressivism over the past one hundred years.

Lesson One: People Are Evil

One of the first things our progressive schools teach kids is to believe they're evil, to feel guilty they were ever born. Does that sound outrageous to you? It isn't.

If you don't believe me, ask your own child what he or she has learned about science in school. You may hear some basics, like photosynthesis or the order of the planets in the solar system. But before long, you'll find out that your child has also been taught that human beings are bad. Human beings upset the fictitious balance of nature and cause the extinction of animal and plant species. They're also taught the global warming lie, starting at as early an age as possible.

Much of this is driven by the increasingly centralized control over curriculum by the federal Department of Education. As I told you in my last book, *Stop the Coming Civil War*, the federal government hasn't mandated a national curriculum yet. Instead, it has bribed states into adopting its dictates through federal funding in return for adoption of national standards like Common Core.

Conservatives instinctively resist national control of education and their instincts are correct. Take a look at the first ten lesson plans that were listed on the "Science" page of Kids .gov, the federal government website providing educational resources for children to study in science class:

Air Pollution: What's the Solution?
Air Quality Index (AQI) Toolkit for Teachers
Air Quality Resources for Teachers
Conservation Central Online Curriculum
EekoWorld—Lesson Plans
Energy Education—Teach and Learn
Energy Lesson Plans and Activities
Energy Star Kids
Estuaries.Gov—Educators Page
Fossil Fuels for Younger Students[4]

Have you noticed a recurring theme? Does this look to you like a comprehensive overview of anything you'd recognize as a primary or secondary school education in science? Or does it look more like the agenda for a radical environmentalist rally?

The rest of the list is similarly skewed toward phony environmental science. There are at most three lesson plan categories representing purely scientific subjects like geology, biology, or rudimentary engineering. The rest are largely propaganda to teach children "actions students can take to protect their health and reduce air pollution" or "how you and your classmates can make big changes and help save the world."

As you might have guessed, the "Energy Education—Teach and Learn" section teaches kids about all of the wonderful green energy research being done by crony capitalists getting rich on taxpayers' money. But don't expect to find the most important thing children should learn about these rip-offs: They've all been miserable failures.

All of this is part of the larger narrative that people and the modern world we've created are inherently evil. We're a scourge that upsets the fictitious balance of nature and is killing Gaia, the earth goddess. Only our benevolent, omnipotent rulers in Washington can save the earth from people and people from themselves.

Earlier this year, the Detroit Opera House presented *The Very Last Green Thing.* The opera depicts students of the future taking a field trip outside. This is a rare occasion in the story because the air is so polluted, goggles and masks are required just to survive outdoors.[5]

It's not a very original story. There are at least a dozen similar stories in leftist twentieth-century literature, most of them more interesting than this one. What makes this noteworthy is that it was performed by the children themselves. Using the power of music is a particularly devious but effective tactic employed by radical environmentalists to indoctrinate children early on to their religion.

Most people are familiar with how Hitler used music as an emotional tool to brainwash the public. This is no different.

In Fort Campbell, Kentucky, prekindergarten students put

on a fashion show featuring clothing they made entirely out of recycled materials contributed by their parents. The kids made everything "from dresses to accessories to environmentally-friendly superhero attire."[6]

This doesn't sound so bad in a vacuum. The kids had fun and there is nothing wrong with learning to make clothing by hand nor to appreciate recycling. But listen to the rhetoric from one of the pre-K teachers involved in the project:

> *"We read books about recycling; we talked about Earth Day and how we can save the planet…At this age, they're very impressionable, and their parents are listening to what they're saying," said Emanuel.*[7]

So the teacher acknowledges the kids are impressionable and that she is instilling ideas that will stay with them into adulthood. And what is the primary lesson they're taking out of preschool, before they're in any way able to critically analyze it?

The planet must be saved. From what you ask? From people.

Ask yourself what this means to a young, impressionable child. It teaches that child to feel guilty about being a human being. It attempts to imbue him with the self-loathing at the root of progressivism. This is where it starts.

Indoctrinating children into any ideology before they are intellectually equipped to question it is evil in and of itself. But it's especially evil to teach them to feel guilty for being born. That's what the whole environmental movement is based upon. They want to convince people their very existence is evil, resulting in a debt they can never repay, no matter how much they're taxed.

They begin encouraging children to form an emotional

bond to this idea at a very young age. That makes it even harder for them to question it later in life, when they have the intellectual capacity to do so. Some people can never overcome the emotional bonds they formed as children to progressive ideas. That's why reason doesn't work in persuading them.

Lesson Two: The Free Market Is Evil

For those who think I'm exaggerating the extent to which children are brainwashed into radical environmentalism, let me issue a challenge. Show me a classroom that has children singing songs and doing art projects celebrating capitalism and free enterprise. I won't hold my breath.

Ask your child what he learned about the industrial revolution. Again, you'll hear a few basic facts. You'll hear about the emergence of mass production, the assembly line, and maybe even a few of the many inventions of those greedy, white males like Edison and Bell.

But if you talk to your child for more than a few minutes, you'll eventually hear the progressive lie about that wonderful time in human history. You'll hear the industrial revolution created child labor and monopolies run by robber barons who exploited their workers. You will hear the early progressive governments came in and saved us all from capitalism.

What is this teaching children? It teaches them the free market is inherently bad, or at least dangerous, and the government is a benevolent force that protects us from it. They are never taught the unintended negative consequences of government regulation. They are never taught that the Sherman Anti-Trust Act was lobbied for by Standard Oil's competitors so they could charge consumers higher prices for oil. I wasn't taught this in school. Were you?

Here is something else you never learned in school: The industrial revolution actually *ended* child labor by making parents productive enough to not need their children to work. It was a sad reality that children had to work in factories to ensure the family could eat, but child labor didn't start during the industrial revolution. Child labor was a fact of life for all of human history. The work children did in factories during the industrial revolution was actually much easier than the back-breaking work they did previously on the farm.

The government was only able to pass child labor laws when families *no longer needed* children to work. Had child labor laws been passed before the industrial revolution, the children would have starved. Why else would parents make their children work?

Do you actually believe parents were sadistic monsters or greedy slave drivers in the nineteenth century? It's ridiculous, but that's what government schools have taught whole generations to believe. They have taught them to believe illogical, ridiculous lies. This is only one of them.

Those so-called monopolies and robber barons are just more of the same progressive nonsense. Did you know that Standard Oil had hundreds of competitors when the Sherman Anti-Trust Act was passed? Did you know that Standard Oil had lowered its prices for decades before the government broke it up, making life for the middle class and poor a little easier? I didn't learn that in school. I'll bet you didn't, either.

I know what you must be saying: "Savage, now you've gone too far. This sounds like an implausible conspiracy theory where everyone is out to brainwash us."

That's not what I'm saying. You have to understand the history of public schooling and the progressive agenda. They've had control over public schools for over one hundred years. Most of the teachers who advance the agenda don't even realize they're doing it. Most are well-intentioned, public-spirited people who want to educate children. They were taught these progressive lies by teachers who themselves didn't know any better. Now they're passing the lies on to those who will teach your grandchildren or great-grandchildren.

The only reason there are any conservatives left in this country is progressivism is inherently unrealistic and self-contradictory. Many, many conservatives started out as liberals, but the real world showed them how horrible this life-denying philosophy really is. They cured themselves of progressivism.

Lesson 3: American Culture Is Evil

Along with junk science and phony progressive history, public schools also teach multiculturalism as a required subject. There isn't any one classroom or teacher dedicated to this. It's taught in all classes, all the time.

I should clarify: I mean *progressive* multiculturalism, which is the celebration of all cultures except one—American culture. Speaking in grammatically correct American English is not part of the agenda. Students who speak English as a second language or who actually can't speak any language properly at all are given first priority. They have to be accommodated, even if it means students who read, write, and speak English very well suffer.

Earlier this year, students at Pine Bush High School in

upstate New York catcalled and denounced their student body president for reciting the Pledge of Allegiance during the morning announcements. Some students actually sat down in protest.[8] Believe it or not, I couldn't have been happier to hear it.

I was happy because it wasn't the Pledge the students were protesting, but the language it was recited in. As part of its efforts to celebrate National Foreign Language Week, this school's administration thought it would be just wonderful to have the Pledge to our flag recited in the language of the maniacs who burn our flag. Wouldn't that show how tolerant and accepting we progressive Americans are?

These pedantic academics are constantly trying to provoke clear-thinking people with stunts like this. From depicting Jesus as black to recasting classic male heroes as women to this latest stupidity, they continually attempt to shock people into realizing how racist or sexist or close-minded they are. They just can't wait to say, "Oh, are you shocked by that? Aren't you glad I made you recognize your subconscious prejudices? Aren't I just wonderful?"

According to Fox News, "The school said the pledge was recited in Arabic as a way to honor National Foreign Language Week 'and in an effort to celebrate the many races, cultures and religions that make up this great country.'"[9]

Really? Public schools celebrate races, cultures, and religions? What week do they celebrate Caucasians, American culture, and Christianity?

They don't. Those are not allowed. To celebrate those would be racist, intolerant, and theocratic. Don't you realize how oppressive white people have been to other races? Don't you realize American culture is capitalist and built on slavery and exploitation of low-paid workers? Don't you realize we have a separation of church and state?

Guess what? The kids in this school weren't buying it. Whatever other progressive nonsense they've unknowingly accepted, that inherent common sense that eventually led Reagan away from liberalism must have kicked in and they fought back. Eventually, the school issued an apology. Score one for the good guys, at least for now.

Conservatives won that battle, but they're losing the war in public schools. The progressive narrative that Muslims are a persecuted minority and Islam a misunderstood religion of peace is too well funded and pervasive. In a school in Wisconsin, students were given an assignment to "pretend you are…Muslim."[10]

The assignment asked students to give "3 examples of what you do daily for your religion and any struggles you face."

This would be funny if it weren't so tragic. I'm wondering if any of the students had the presence of mind to say, "I have more trouble practicing my Christian religion than Muslims do practicing theirs." It would certainly be true. Referring to God as "Allah" is perfectly acceptable in public schools, while referring to God as "God" or "Jesus" is strictly prohibited.

Think about how far the school environment has deteriorated to get to the point where an assignment like this could be given to students, while any reference to the Christian religion is banned. Can you imagine the uproar if the word *Christian* were substituted for *Muslim* in this assignment? How about if the teacher asked students to imagine they were a Christian living in western Iraq right now? Which group is more persecuted, Muslims in America or Christians in Iraq?

I doubt most American schoolchildren today could answer that question correctly.

Marcuse and Fromm for Kids

In my last book, I told you about Herbert Marcuse and Erich Fromm, who were intellectual leaders in the "sexual revolution" of the 1950s and 1960s. If you didn't read it, let me sum it up for you. The sexual revolution was all about moving America toward socialism. Marcuse and Fromm believed that if Americans were liberated from sexual repression, they would give up their individual liberty and become functionaries of the state, whose only value was greater degrees of hedonism.

I'd say they were quite successful, wouldn't you? Look around you. Look at the prevalence of sexual license in all areas of American culture. From music videos to movies to the most popular websites on the Internet—porn sites—Americans are literally saturated with sex. The sexual revolution succeeded in breaking down all morality and restraint in the sexual lives of adults. Sex education and free condoms are accomplishing the same thing in schools.

I'm sure if you made that last statement to any of your liberal friends, they'd screech, "What? You don't want teenagers to have condoms? Are you against safe sex? Don't you care about the children's *health care*?"

These are the kinds of replies you get from liberals. If a conservative says anything about condoms, liberals automatically assume they want them legally banned. That's because they only understand two approaches to anything: ban it or subsidize it. That people should choose what they want to buy, pay for it with their own money, and take responsibility for the consequences just doesn't occur to progressives.

If teenagers are going to have premarital sex, it's obvious

they are better off using condoms than not using them. But what about not encouraging them to have sex in the first place? Isn't that what handing out free condoms in school does? Is it not still an accepted economic principle that when you subsidize something you get more of it?

By subsidizing condoms in schools, you are going to get more kids in schools having sex. Do I even have to ask if more teenage sex is a good thing? Are more teenage pregnancies a good thing? More teenagers with STDs?

By the way, redefining condoms as "health care" is a linguistic coup that puts Orwell's newspeak to shame. Even Goebbels would have been proud. Suddenly, condoms become the same as cancer treatments or heart surgery. Then liberals can cry, "How can you heartless conservatives deny children health care?"

I'm sure you remember Sandra Fluke making the condoms-are-health-care argument to Congress in trying to get them subsidized. It didn't end there. She's inspired a high school senior in Gainesville, Florida, to make the same argument in getting condoms provided by taxpayers in her public school.[11]

The aptly-named Kira Christmas decided taxpayers should be Santa Claus when it comes to condoms, regardless of their relatively affordable cost, even for low-income earners. She started a petition to garner support. The only problem was the school district superintendent. He objected to the idea on what has unfortunately become very unusual grounds.

"Teaching kids about birth control, disease prevention, those kinds of things but as far as actually giving out condoms, that's really a parental role, a family role, that is not something that the school district should be taking on," said spokesperson Jackie Johnson.[12]

Imagine that. Educating children and making decisions regarding their sexual activity should be left up to parents. What a novel idea. It might be too dangerous, though. If parents were allowed to make decisions regarding their children's sexual education, they might start asserting a right to make decisions regarding all aspects of their children's education. We can't have that, can we?

The school superintendent eventually caved to the pressure and reversed his decision prohibiting condom distribution in Alachua Schools.[13] The "compromise" the school board made was to allow parents to opt out of the program.

They can't opt out of paying for free condoms for school-children, but they can fill out a form and send it in to the school. The school nurses will refuse to distribute condoms to those students whose parents have dutifully filled out the government form.

One of the most disturbing aspects of this story is the extent to which local students have been brainwashed into the progressive, socialist mind-set. A foundational socialist plank since Plato has been that the government should raise and educate children, rather than parents. This is what Hillary Clinton really meant when she said, "It takes a village to raise a child."

Apparently, at least some young people in this school district believe the government does a better job as well. A freshman student at University of Florida writes in his school paper:

> *Parents, on the other hand, often live in states of euphoric ignorance. Many are unaware of their children's sex lives, and they avoid potentially awkward conversations by settling for the sexual education their kids receive in school... Changing family dynamics and facilitating conversations*

*about the importance of safe sex will take much more time,
so, until then, we need schools to help students overcome these
obstacles.*[14]

Another teenage student, presumably from the Alachua
school district, echoed Wilde's sentiments: "If your parents
don't want to talk about it, they feel awkward then it's a good
thing to have like a nurse there just willing to do it."[15]

Yes, parents are incompetent and inadequate when it comes
to raising their own children, so the government has to help
until such time as family dynamics can be changed. These
comments could have been made by Vladimir Lenin. It's horrifying that they came from American teenagers. It looks like
government schools are at least succeeding at one thing: producing good little socialists.

The Common Progressive-Islamist Core

The power-hungry maniacs out to steal the minds and souls
of our children aren't satisfied with merely taking power away
from parents. They also want power over education taken away
from your local school board and even your state. If they get
their way, only the National Ministry of Truth will decide
what children learn or don't learn in school. This is what Common Core is really about.

Last year, Wyoming prohibited adoption of the National
Academy of Social Sciences (NGSS) standards for K–12 education because they included teaching global warming as established science. They included a prohibition in their 2014–2016
budget for any use of funds to review the standards.

The progressive jackals went wild and launched an all-out campaign against the legislators. On March 2, 2015, the Wyoming governor signed a bill overturning the prohibition and allowing the state board of education to review the standards. It is only a matter of time before the board of education approves the standards and another example of grassroots resistance to the progressive agenda is crushed.

This is how it happens, one progressive lie at a time. If left unchecked, this set of standards or some other will be adopted in every state, and generations of children will grow up not knowing anyone ever questioned the climate change scam, just as they've grown up never knowing Standard Oil lowered its prices for two decades before being broken up by the government.

That was why I warned readers about Common Core in my last book, *Stop the Coming Civil War.* It's not only because it's ineffective. We've all seen Common Core's processes for doing what used to be simple math problems lampooned on the Internet. It's not only because it adopts every progressive lie ever told as established scientific or historical fact.

One of the men who actually wrote the Common Core standards admitted this at a debate at Saint Anselm's College in Manchester, New Hampshire, last year. "The reason why I helped write the standards and the reason why I am here today is that as a white male in society, I've been given a lot of privilege that I didn't earn," said David Pook.[16]

Of course, Pook is going to have a hard time determining whether the standards will truly overcome the white privilege he believe exists. That's because the exclusive New Hampshire prep school he teaches at has only seven black students currently enrolled, out of a total student body of 369.[17] This typical limousine liberal may go whole days without even seeing a black student.

What is most dangerous about Common Core is its potential to become *the* required set of educational standards for all schools, public or private. Just imagine if the list of lesson plans I provided from Kids.gov became the standard curriculum in every public school. That's what progressives really want. If they can make Common Core mandatory, no nonprogressive will ever emerge from an American school again. That's why it has to be stopped.

Over the past year, there has actually been some good news on this front. Parents across the nation and across the political spectrum are taking a stand against Common Core. Believe it or not, liberal New York State is leading the charge.

Ninety-five percent of eligible children at Brooklyn New School didn't take Common Core tests administered in April 2015. Seventy percent of their peers joined them at West Seneca Central School, outside Buffalo, New York.[18] In all, an estimated 200,000 eligible students will have opted out of these tests statewide.[19]

The opt-out movement isn't confined to New York. New Jersey, Colorado, and California now have growing opt-out movements,[20] with more expected to follow. Richard Brodsky of the liberal think tank Demos called the opt-out movement "a citizen revolt."[21] For once, I agree with him. That's just what it is.

I don't mean to imply that millions of progressives have suddenly seen the light and become conservatives. Different groups of people oppose Common Core for different reasons. Teachers unions, like all unions, don't want their members accountable to anyone, in any way.

Liberal parents who oppose any kind of grading and want everyone in sports competitions to receive a trophy oppose Common Core testing because it's just too stressful and may bruise the self-esteem of their precious little snowflakes.

Whatever their reasons, it's apparent that opposition to Common Core is not an exclusively Republican or conservative position. Conservatives and liberals are instinctively resisting it. Yet the federal government continues to shove it down our throats. That's Government Zero. The government doesn't represent conservatives. It doesn't even represent the progressives who elected it. It represents itself and pursues its agenda regardless of the will of the people.

The Biggest Bubble Yet?

I've been talking about the higher education bubble for some time now. It has continued to grow since my last book and may be nearing a breaking point. Earlier this year, the Federal Reserve reported that only "37 percent of borrowers are current on their loans and are actively paying them down, and 17 percent are in default or in delinquency."[22] That means a staggering 63 percent of student loan borrowers are behind on payments or in default.

Just to put things in perspective, the average default rate expected in most commercial markets is a little over 1 percent. According to Investopedia, "As of January 2015, the default rate for a broad swath of the credit services industry including first and second mortgages, auto loans and bank cards was 1.12%. For every $100 that was lent, $1.12 was defaulted on, or not paid back."[23]

If the federal government weren't guaranteeing the loans, which forces you to pay them back when the students default, this bubble would have exploded long ago. But that can go on for only so long. Remember, government-backed loans by Fannie Mae and Freddie Mac played the same role in the housing meltdown.

In reality, the education bubble is identical to the housing and dot-com bubbles. It has all the same symptoms resulting from all the same government interventions.

First and foremost, we have a central bank that has inflated the currency beyond any historical precedent. This is the only reason there are enough U.S. dollars in existence to lend to every single high school graduate who wants one.

When money is scarce, lenders give loans only to the most creditworthy individuals. When there is a virtually infinite supply of money, lenders will eventually make loans to all comers, regardless of creditworthiness, especially when they have nothing to lose if the borrower defaults.

So, just as in the dot-com and housing bubbles, the first culprit in this bubble is the Federal Reserve. If they hadn't created an unlimited supply of money, the rest of the problem would be academic.

Of course, it doesn't end there. Disasters like the housing meltdown require a symphony of bad policy, and we have a true maestro in that regard occupying the White House.

The next movement in the symphony is the guarantee itself. This is the same "moral hazard" everyone talked about with the "Greenspan put" in the 1990s and the Fannie and Freddie guarantees in the 2000s. It doesn't take a rocket scientist to figure out that when the government says it will pay back any loans that default, more are going to default.

The truly immoral part of this equation is their making you pay for this. Why should taxpayers be financially responsible to pay back money borrowed by people they don't even know and whose decisions they have no control over? What possible justification is there for this, other than the usual socialist mantras?

The combination of unlimited, cheap supplies of money and the moral hazard of government-backed loans is having the same effect on the education sector of the economy as it had on the housing sector. It's hard to believe so few seem to see it.

College tuitions continue to outpace inflation, just as housing prices did. This isn't hard to understand. Guaranteeing loans to everyone artificially increases demand. Remember, demand isn't just the *desire* to purchase; it's also the *ability* to purchase. When the government guarantees loans to everyone with your money, demand explodes and prices with it.

The bubble also misallocates resources. Do you remember all those people in the house-building business who lost their jobs in 2008? They shouldn't have been working in the house-building business to begin with. There wasn't enough *real* demand to support all those employees in that sector.

So, why didn't they just get jobs in another industry when the bubble popped? Because the jobs weren't there. The capital that would have created them had all flowed to housing, where profits were guaranteed while the bubble lasted. Do you see how the harmful effects of government intervention multiply geometrically?

When the education bubble pops, the same thing is going to happen to millions of people employed in the education sector. They're going to be out of work with no prospects and no skills to bring to a new job. They'll just join the record number of Americans receiving government welfare benefits, thanks to the Food Stamp President.

It couldn't work out better for the progressives bent on destroying the American economy and overwhelming the system, just as Cloward and Piven suggested. If you aren't familiar with them, I'll talk more about them in a later chapter.

Employees aren't the only resources misallocated by the bubble. It also artificially inflates the number of people who choose to go to college in the first place.

I'm going to say something that I'm sure will send liberals into apoplectic shock. Everyone should not go to college. That's right, you read that correctly. I'm sure somehow that will be interpreted as racist, sexist, or at least heartless. But it's not racist. It's not sexist. It's not heartless and it's not fattening. It's the truth.

We didn't always assume that everyone, or even most people, should go to college. College used to be a place you went if you were planning on a career in medicine, law, engineering, or other specialized professions. People planning on other lines of work didn't waste the money to go to college because their money and time was more wisely invested in apprenticeships and other, practical work experience.

The idea that people have to go to college in order to be successful is a new one. It's also complete baloney. Bill Gates, Steve Jobs, Larry Ellison, and John Paul DeJoria are just a few contemporary billionaires who didn't get a college degree. Mark Zuckerberg doesn't have one. Even our leftist propagandist David Geffen doesn't have one.

This is nothing new. A large percentage of the most successful people in American history did not earn college degrees, from Benjamin Franklin and Abraham Lincoln to

Henry Ford to Wendy's Dave Thomas. Neither Frederick Henry Royce, cofounder of Rolls-Royce, nor George Eastman, founder of Kodak, had college degrees. There are hundreds more examples.

That doesn't mean you have to be a history-making entrepreneur to be successful without a college degree, either. I know dozens of small business people making six-figure incomes doing electrical work, landscaping, plumbing, and even janitorial work. Many of these businesses are starving for quality employees while college graduates with useless degrees are working fast-food jobs or living in their parents' basements.

Don't get me wrong: I'm not saying every single individual in this country should not have an equal opportunity to attend college if he or she wants to. What I am saying is that each individual should have to take responsibility for that decision. Similarly, banks who make huge profits on student loans should also take responsibility for the money they lend. Taxpayers shouldn't be bailing out students or banks.

If that were the case, students would have to make prudent choices on whether or not to go to college and, more important, what they are going to learn there. Banks would have to consider the chances the student has of paying back the loan out of the money he or she will earn after graduation.

That is exactly the opposite of what is happening in our bubble education economy right now. According to the federal government's National Center for Education Statistics, the top five majors in terms of degrees earned in 2010–2011 were business, social sciences and history, health professions and related programs, education, and psychology.[24]

Three out of these five majors rank in the bottom twenty in terms of earning potential for graduates.[25] That means most students entering college right now are choosing the majors least likely to help them earn enough money to pay back their student loans. Those entering education in particular are setting themselves up to be sitting at ground zero when the education bubble explodes. It's tragic.

So, what does Obama suggest we do in the face of this problem that has been building up for generations? Make it worse. His "Pay As You Earn" (PAYE) program just encourages more of everything that caused the problem. There is no incentive against taking out tens or hundreds of thousands in student loans to subsidize a low-paying major when you will be required to pay only 10 percent of your income in payments, regardless of how low your income may be.

Don't get me wrong. I'm not blaming all of this on Obama. That idiot George W. Bush did exactly the same thing while the Federal Reserve blew up a housing bubble on his watch. He cheered on his "ownership society" while the bubble got bigger and bigger. He further nationalized education with No Child Left Behind, doubling the size of the Department of Education Republicans used to vow to abolish.

That doesn't make Obama's policies any better. Just as in every other area, he's doubled down on the mistakes of the past while managing to make new ones no other president would have dreamed of.

Sooner or later, the education party is going to end, just as housing did. The banks don't have to worry. The Dodd-Frank act has made them even more "too big to fail" than they were in 2008.

The losers will be the rest of us: unemployed college graduates with useless degrees in art or women's studies, small businesses that can't expand for lack of skilled workers, and society in general suffering the effects of a dumbed-down, brainwashed, unskilled, and unemployable population that is increasingly dependent on the government handouts that help the progressives keep winning elections.

Our Most Important Fight

You can begin to see why American students do so poorly compared to students in countries that spend less on education. It's also why the Democratic Party wins elections. The two phenomena are related.

The school system spends most of its time teaching kids things that aren't true and almost no time teaching them things that are. They learn a completely false version of history and junk science like global warming, while their competitors in other countries are developing advanced skills.

Meanwhile, American students can't read, write, or speak their own language properly. They're taught math in a way that even parents with graduate degrees in math can't understand. Common Core discourages reading the classics and encourages reading reports generated by the Federal Reserve. Do you think they'll be able to recognize history repeating itself reading government reports instead of the classics? Not likely.

American students are constantly brainwashed with the idea that Muslims are viciously persecuted in America, regardless of the evidence of a growing, active jihadist population in our midst. They are taught to believe the mere mention of God or Jesus on public property is discriminatory, while the murder, rape, and torture of Christians by radical Islamists is rationalized away.

Overall, the school system produces the prototypical Democratic voter. He or she is completely ignorant of real history, incompetent in critical thinking, unable to understand or express complex ideas, and unprepared to learn the specialized skills that make him or her competitive in the twenty-first-century marketplace. This student graduates with a learned suspicion of entrepreneurs and no suspicion of government.

They learn abortion is a right but private property is not. They are encouraged to have sex but are discouraged from entering the workforce, even if college isn't the best thing for them at that point in their lives. They emerge from high school feeling guilty about who they are if they are white or male, and aggrieved and victimized if they are female or a minority. They become low-information voters, even if they go on to get college degrees.

Meanwhile, the economic policies that have created and continue to expand the education bubble continue to steer students toward useless majors dominated by leftist professors who teach students no marketable skills but imbue them with Progressive-Islamist brainwashing.

Education may be the most important fight we have. Unless we can change these trends, there won't be enough clear-thinking, self-sufficient, patriotic Americans left to defeat the dark forces trying to destroy our civilization. I'll tell you what I believe we have to do at the end of this book.

CHAPTER 6

Zero Culture

First World to Third World

America's culture has gone from First World to Third World status. It's swimming in a mire of sex, drugs, base entertainment, class envy, entitlement, and apathy. Welcome to the new Progressive-Islamist America.

Today, the average American high school senior has lived his whole life being told that businessmen are evil, minorities are viciously persecuted in America, Islam is the religion of peace, and Christianity and Judaism are the religions of white privilege, ignorance, and intolerance. He is taught to loathe himself if he is white and male or to consider him- or herself persecuted if a minority or female, whether it's true or not.

Kids haven't just learned this in school. It's reaffirmed in films, on television, in the music they listen to, and by the so-called news media. From the moment children begin perceiving the world around them, they are inundated with progressivism. I doubt most parents realize it. They've been fully indoctrinated themselves.

I'm not blaming this all on Obama or even government in general. Certainly, poor leadership plays a part, but there is a cause-and-effect dimension to the decline of our culture. A corrupt government contributes to the corruption of the people, but the opposite is also true. You don't get the policy makers we have now unless the people themselves are already corrupted. It's very much a vicious circle.

Remember, politicians, entertainers, and media peddle envy politics, trashy entertainment, junk science, and substandard journalism only because there is demand for it. Some of the blame for Government Zero rests squarely on the people's shoulders.

Hollywood's War on American Culture

As I tell my listeners on *The Savage Nation*, follow the money. Late last year, Gov. Jerry Brown signed a bill tripling the tax break incentives for Hollywood.[1] As with all crony capitalism, the cover story is this will keep jobs from moving out of state or overseas.

In reality, it's just another arm of the government-media complex that is waging all-out war on American culture. Multimillionaire film moguls like Harvey Weinstein and Jeffrey Katzenberg get even richer. In return, they make movies that promote a message the progressives in the state and federal governments approve of. And what the progressives in government approve of are anticapitalist, antireligion, antimilitary, or, in short, anti-American films.

When the film *American Sniper* attracted the biggest box

office in decades and threatened to bring the people together in their love of country and the military, the harlots of Hollywood's left with their fellow travelers in the media began a campaign of hatred against the film and its hero. It was hatred and vitriol they don't express toward the Islamic barbarians who are raping, beheading, and conquering the Middle East as the Nazis did in Europe.

Muslim students at the University of Michigan were successful in getting the college to cancel a screening of the film by "claiming the film promote[d] anti-Muslim rhetoric and made them feel unsafe."[2] The college announced its plans to stimulate the students' intellects with *Paddington*, a movie based on the stuffed animal, instead.

Following news reporting of the decision, the university faced outrage on a national scale and eventually reversed its decision. But these are the kinds of tactics used to attack American culture and patriotism every day on campuses and elsewhere. As usual, Muslims teamed up with progressives to silence any voice not uttering the Progressive-Islamist narrative.

For those who actually watched the movie, it doesn't glorify war. I'm an antiwar conservative and believe war is the worst thing that can happen to any society. It should be avoided at all costs and always be a last resort. But when civilization itself is under attack by barbarians who set people on fire while they are still alive, it has to be defended by somebody.

The movie depicts war as it actually is. The whole reason soldiers are heroic is they do a job nobody wants to do but which has to be done. They do it at great personal risk to defend civilization. Some of them make the ultimate sacrifice so that we can go on writing books and making movies and enjoying the blessings of liberty.

Clint Eastwood made a film celebrating these heroes and portraying those who fight for civilization positively, and people flocked to the theaters to see it. The left could not let this verdict stand.

Just like the red guards had done in Mao's China during the so-called Cultural Revolution, America's red brigades worked tirelessly to demoralize and defeat their natural enemy: the most productive, patriotic citizens of America, who were naturally drawn toward a film that affirmed their values.

That's why you have Hollywood attacking American values with their movies. Out of one side of their hypocritical mouths, they're antigun. Out of the other, they make movies rife with gunfights, knifing, butchering, murdering, and mayhem.

Harvey Weinstein is one of the worst. Last year, he said he was going to make a movie with Meryl Streep that would make the NRA "wish they weren't alive after I'm done with them."[3] He promised in the same interview to stop making movies glamorizing guns.

Over a year later, he still hasn't made his antigun movie, but he has obviously decided to break his vow against making violent movies. He currently has *Kill Bill Vol. 3*, a remake of *The Crow*, and another Quentin Tarantino movie, *The Hateful Eight*, in production.[4] So much for no more violent movies.

Even Weinstein's claim that he's never owned a gun and doesn't want one is disingenuous. He may not own a gun personally, but he has a large cadre of armed bodyguards who provide him protection the average American can't afford. I'm not sure if that makes him more or less hypocritical than Dianne Feinstein, who actually has a concealed-carry permit herself.

Sean Penn is another Hollywood elitist peddling hypocritical antigun nonsense. Penn used to be an unrepentant gun owner until a few years ago. In 2013, he sold his gun collection to an artist to be melted down for sculpture, apparently because his new girlfriend at the time didn't like them.[5]

Of course, once Penn decided he didn't want guns, he immediately concluded no one else should have them, either, even though most people can't afford the armed bodyguards he and Weinstein can rely on when they're unarmed personally.

Penn's newest movie is called *The Gunman*. I couldn't make this up. He actually starred in a typical Hollywood shoot-them-up action film immediately after attacking the Second Amendment and calling guns "cowardly killing machines." Meanwhile, I haven't heard anything about him disarming his bodyguards.

Jeffrey Katzenberg and David Geffen are also living a life of luxury from their for-profit film and music ventures, but raise millions for leftist politicians who attack everyone else trying to make an honest living.

We'll have to see if Geffen can beat out Weinstein and Penn for Hypocrite of the Year. After raising money for Bill Clinton in the 1990s, he had a falling out with him when Clinton refused to pardon Leonard Peltier. Geffen indirectly called the Clintons liars in a 2007 interview, when he was backing Obama. He called Hillary Clinton an "incredibly polarizing figure."[6]

Let's see if he still thinks she's polarizing now that it's her or a Republican for president. One of his spokesmouths already confirmed he'll vote for her, even if he believes she's polarizing and a liar.[7]

Hollywood is awash with the usual liberal hypocrisy: capitalism and profits for me and socialism and misery for everyone else. They make billions on movies glorifying guns and have concealed-carry permits or armed bodyguards themselves, but want to ban guns and free enterprise for you and me.

Any film affirming patriotism, love of God and country, entrepreneurship, self-reliance, independent thinking, or any of the other heroic qualities inherent in the American ethos must be vilified out of existence.

The supposed evil of capitalism is another recurrent theme in almost every movie. Entrepreneurs are villains. Corporations become large and successful not by producing products that millions of people choose to buy, but by murdering people.

If a businessman is the hero in a movie, he is heroic only if by the end of the movie he rejects capitalism and the profit motive and "learns" how wrong he was to believe in free enterprise. If he is a white male, he also has to learn how inherently evil he is because of that.

You've probably been exposed to this without even realizing it. Do you like science fiction movies? The Alien franchise was popular enough to spawn several sequels. They were pretty good movies, if you like science fiction, especially the original. But they all peddled the usual socialist propaganda.

The real villain of the films was an evil corporation willing to sacrifice the lives of its employees to bring back the alien life-form for some unknown purpose. We learn during the sequel that the company was interested in selling the organism to the military. So the Hollywood Marxists manage to smear free enterprise and the military at the same time. What a bargain.

That corporations have to murder people to succeed is a fairly common theme coming out of Leninist Hollywood. *The Fugitive* and *Total Recall* are two other popular examples. These are just fictional stories, but they constantly reinforce the leftist idea that for-profit businesses can make money only by harming people in some way.

It's the tired "zero-sum game" fallacy. One economic actor can profit only if another realizes a loss. The idea of two parties trading to their mutual benefit is just beyond the comprehension of these freedom-hating subversives.

If your tastes run more to romantic comedy, rather than action or science fiction, you don't have to worry about missing out on leftist propaganda. In *Two Weeks Notice* [*sic*] with Sandra Bullock and Hugh Grant, Grant's character must learn not to act in the best interests of the company's shareholders, among other things.

In the especially awful *Sweet November*, Keanu Reeves must learn how evil he is for being hardworking and devoted to his career, in addition to learning how bad he is just for being a man. He is taught all of this by Charlize Theron's character, whom we learn over the course of the film is apparently sleeping with a different man every month, in order to save them from their evil selves, before dying of cancer at the end of the film.

Believe it or not, Hollywood wasn't always like this. Yes, liberals have always infested the arts, from filmmakers, to actors, to musicians, to painters. But just as in American politics, there was once a strong opposition party in Hollywood.

Conservative icons like John Ford, John Wayne, Gary Cooper, and Spencer Tracy once made films that affirmed American values. They celebrated capitalism, patriotism, heroism in battle, and resistance to tyranny.

Back in those days, the left wasn't so bold in coming out against movies celebrating America's heroes on the battlefield. Even the liberal *New York Times* said that 1949's *Sands of Iwo*

Jima had "so much that reflects the true glory of the Marine Corps' contribution to victory in the Pacific that the film has undeniable moments of greatness."[8] The reviewer regrets that the movie didn't portray the Marines more realistically off the battlefield, as that didn't do enough justice to the U.S. Marines.

Hollywood movies actually celebrated capitalism, too. One of my favorites was a film called *Boom Town*, with Clark Gable and Spencer Tracy. The film begins with the two legendary actors playing partners in a wildcat oil company. They eventually split and become fierce competitors, the fortunes of each rising and falling throughout the movie.

Near the end of the film, Gable's character has worked a deal to slow down production, which threatens to put Tracy's character out of business. The federal regulators try to prosecute Gable's character for restraint of trade and call Tracy's character as a witness. Rather than seek protection from competition from the government, here is what Tracy's character says on the stand:

> *He wanted these guys to produce less oil, so that their wells would flow years longer and not ruin the field. That way, they'd get all the oil there was to get out of the wells. Don't you get the idea? He was for conservation. Now, how could a guy be breaking the law when he's trying to save the natural resources of the country? Now, he didn't know he was doing anything that you might call noble, but being one of the best oil men there is, he's got the right hunch about oil.*

Wow. When was the last time you heard an argument for the free market like that in a Hollywood picture? With just a few sentences, he blows up the entire liberal complaint against free markets.

Liberals constantly talk about markets as if there is an inherent conflict between individuals pursuing profits and the "greater good of society." There isn't. Just like Spencer Tracy said, entrepreneurs pursuing profits benefit society at the same time. In fact, they benefit society *because* they are pursuing profits.

Entrepreneurs also protect the environment more than will a million government employees with a trillion of your tax dollars. By trying to maximize revenues and minimize costs, they naturally conserve resources. Raw materials cost money. An entrepreneur seeks to get every bit of value possible out of every yard, pound, or fluid ounce of raw materials, because the more value they provide for any given cost, the more profits they make. There is no conflict between profits and the environment.

Let me share one more jewel from this diamond mine of real American culture. After Tracy teaches the judge and the movie audience that capitalism is good for the environment, he asks a question we all should be asking ourselves now:

> So, now I'm wondering. Is it getting to be out of line for a man like him to make a million dollars with his brains and with his hands? Because if that's true, we'd better rewrite this "land of opportunity stuff."

That's what Obama and the progressive left want to do: rewrite this land of opportunity stuff. Instead of people feeling inspired by entrepreneurs who made a million bucks with their brains and their hands, they want people to feel aggrieved and envious. They want them to resent businessmen who offer them jobs and opportunity and revere the government that offers them handouts.

Men weren't the only heroes during Hollywood's golden age. Another of my favorites from this period was *Mildred Pierce*, starring Joan Crawford. The main plot is about Mildred Pierce's devotion to a daughter who is wholly unworthy of it and eventually betrays her mother and commits a murder. But what I love most about this film is the way heroism is portrayed.

When Mildred Pierce's unfaithful husband leaves her, she doesn't complain about a war on women or look for a government handout. She starts by baking cakes in her kitchen, which grows into a baking business, which she then grows into a successful chain of restaurants. She wins her own independence through hard work and making the most of the opportunities a free market offers her. She is heroic *because* she is a successful entrepreneur.

She is self-reliant and successful, but there is no implication that she becomes so at the price of her ethics or morality. On the contrary, her sound, moral character is one of the reasons for her success, as it is for most entrepreneurs in the real world.

The film is prescient in one way. The contrast between the faithful, hardworking Mildred Pierce and her snotty, entitled, greedy daughter is a perfect metaphor for the contrast between the greatest generation and the baby boomers. The former defeated two tyrannical empires and built the most prosperous economy in world history. The latter set out to destroy everything their parents built and create an amoral, godless, socialist sewer.

You might be wondering how things could have changed so much in Hollywood. How could the same town that produced

Sands of Iwo Jima, *Boom Town*, and *Mildred Pierce* become so uniformly leftist? What happened to the opposition party in Hollywood?

You may as well ask why there are so few climate scientists who challenge the global warming hoax in the Intergovernmental Panel on Climate Change (IPCC). The answer is the same for both questions. Anyone who dissented was purged, through propaganda and character assassination.

The False History of the McCarthy Era

Unless you were born yesterday or have been living under a rock, you probably have some knowledge of what is now called McCarthyism. While most people don't know all the details, most are aware that for a period during the late 1940s and 1950s, Sen. Joseph McCarthy of Wisconsin headed the House Un-American Activities Committee (HUAC).

As head of the committee, McCarthy accused many members of the U.S. State Department and other departments within the government of being communist spies or communist sympathizers. He and the HUAC also blacklisted a number of Hollywood movie producers, directors, scriptwriters, and actors because of their alleged communist affiliations.

If you know all of the above, I have news for you. You've fallen prey to yet another progressive mind trick. You've swallowed another liberal fairy tale hook, line and sinker.

This particular lie isn't even internally consistent. First, *Senator* Joseph McCarthy couldn't have had anything to do with a *House* Un-American Activities Committee. McCarthy was never elected to the House of Representatives. He was a U.S. senator. He chaired the Senate Committee on Government Operations, but the House Un-American Activities Committee had existed for over a decade before McCarthy's campaign against communism.

More importantly, the HUAC did not blacklist anyone from working in Hollywood. That wasn't a power any congressional committee had, then or now. The committee had the power to investigate subversive activities that threatened the form of government proscribed in the U.S. Constitution and to bring charges of real crimes, like espionage, when probable cause was established.

The committee subpoenaed various Hollywood figures to appear for questioning. When some of them refused to answer, they were charged with contempt of Congress, a misdemeanor. In response to the charges, the Motion Picture Association of America, a *voluntary association of private individuals*, issued a statement indicating they would no longer employ those people charged with contempt by Congress.

The infamous blacklist was not effected by Senator McCarthy and was only indirectly related to the HUAC. It was really just private individuals within Hollywood exercising what used to be recognized as an inherent, inalienable right: the right to associate or not associate with anyone you pleased. These Hollywood employers did not want the powerful influence of their studios used to promote communism and subvert the U.S. Constitution.

In the years that followed, many more people were blacklisted. I'm sure that some were wrongly accused. Senator McCarthy became a symbol of the supposed witch hunt nature of the investigations, even after Alger Hiss was found guilty of perjury for denying his involvement in Soviet espionage.

McCarthy had some personal foibles, alcoholism possibly being one of them. He was eventually censured by Congress after the same kind of multimedia, total war-style character assassination that liberals have used on so many others who have opposed their agenda.

What the progressive jackals have been successful in erasing from America's collective memory is the one, most important fact: McCarthy was right. For the most part, his allegations were justified, as were the suspicions of those on the HUAC who subpoenaed the actors and screenwriters.

We know this because of another bit of conveniently forgotten history called the Venona Project. Venona was a counterintelligence program run from 1943 through 1980 that decrypted Soviet intelligence communications.[9] From the decrypted messages, U.S. intelligence was able to identify the Rosenbergs, Alger Hiss, Klaus Fuchs, and many others as Soviet spies in regular communication with the KGB. Hollywood producer Stephen Laird, who was also a reporter for *Time* magazine and CBS, was also identified. Hundreds of other people are mentioned in the decrypted messages, many of whom are also justifiably suspected of having been working with the Soviets during this period.

Despite this hard evidence that his allegations of communist infiltration into government, media, and entertainment were generally true, McCarthy remains a poster child for right wing paranoia. Just like a suspect in a crime whose indictment is reported on page one of the newspaper, but whose acquittal is reported on page fifty-seven, or not at all, no one remembers McCarthy's vindication due to these decoded messages.

So effective was the vilification of McCarthy, the HUAC, and the private individuals who decided not to employ communists that a complete reversal in Hollywood occurred. It became politically incorrect to voice any opposition to communism at all, just as it is political suicide to express any concern over radical Islam today. "McCarthyism" and "reds under the bed" became in-vogue witticisms to imply paranoia in anyone who expressed a concern about communism, even though many of those concerns were justified.

Today, "Islamophobia" is used in the same way to vilify anyone who might express some concern about a well-equipped army of ninth-century throwbacks who are rapidly conquering territory in the Middle East and establishing a brutal, murderous theocracy. Suggest that this has something to do with Islam itself and you are set upon by the liberal jackals in much the same way McCarthy was all those years ago. But all of their propaganda doesn't change the truth.

Rotten Role Models

Athletes, musicians, and other entertainers have even more influence on young people than movie stars. Unfortunately, that influence is almost universally bad. When kids aren't being bombarded with song lyrics and commentary by musicians pushing the leftist worldview, they're watching their idols in professional sports committing crimes and generally acting like thugs.

In April, *Time* magazine released its list of the "100 Most Influential People."[10] Topping the list was a talentless hack married to an exhibitionist wife whose chief claim to fame is an overly large behind. He will be largely remembered himself for rude, inexcusable behavior during two Grammy Awards ceremonies where he interrupted acceptance speeches to voice his opinion that the winner didn't deserve the award.

Every boxer, regardless of skin color, goes on and on like Muhammad Ali, apparently unaware Ali did it tongue in cheek to promote his fights. What does it tell nine-, ten-, and eleven-year-old boys who idolize these athletes when they exhibit no humility in victory or grace in defeat?

The bad examples set for our children by athletes and entertainers don't stop at rudeness or poor sportsmanship. Violent crimes, including murder, sexual assault, and other offenses continue to plague professional sports and entertainment. One NFL player was convicted of murder in April of this year,[11] while another made headlines for viciously assaulting his girlfriend in an elevator.[12]

Young girls have similarly poor role models. If they learn anything from pop music stars, it's that dressing and dancing like a stripper is "empowering." Madonna's antics a few decades ago seem tame now compared to the virtual pornography of the average music video.

Even parents seem unconcerned when watching preteenage girls performing highly suggestive dance routines. The Internet is flooded with videos of eight- and ten-year-old children mimicking sexual intercourse. I'm not blaming the kids for this. They don't know any better. It's a depraved culture that bombards them with sexual images and references in all media.

A Culture of Envy

Picking up right where our current leader will leave off, Hillary Clinton is on the campaign trail inciting class warfare over income inequality. In a desperate attempt to ward off any possible challenges from even more radical socialists, Clinton actually vowed to "topple the 1 percent" at a press conference earlier this year.

It's hard to believe Clinton has the nerve to say this, being a government-subsidized member of the 1 percent herself. Her husband is not only the wealthiest former U.S. president alive, but with a net worth of $55 million, he's among the ten wealthiest of all time.[13]

Now that we know her and Bill's charity fund contributes very little to charity compared to what it takes in, it's even more hypocritical for her to criticize legitimate businesses who provide valuable products to people who know what they're purchasing when they hand over their money. According to the *New York Post*, the so-called charity "took in more than $140 million in grants and pledges in 2013 but spent just $9 million on direct aid."[14]

Hillary doesn't see anything wrong with living lavishly off the public. She believes she's provided invaluable service that we should all be eternally grateful for. Never mind that most of her service was completely disastrous, like the Arab Spring she engineered as secretary of state and the "reset" of relations with Russia she was supposed to lead.

While Hollywood peddles the "corporations kill people" story line, progressive politicians and media push another whopper: Rich people don't pay taxes.

Where does the government get the money to provide the services it provides, however incompetently? Liberals don't ever seem to know the answer to this question. Contrary to what you might read in the *New York Times*, most of the money comes from those evil, greedy, rich people.

The truth is, rich people pay *most* of the taxes in this country. Fifty-five percent of all income taxes are paid by individuals who earn over $200,000 per year. Seventy-eight percent of all income taxes are paid by individuals who earn over $100,000 per year.[15]

Yet, all we hear is "the rich don't pay their fair share." Seventy-eight percent seems more than fair, doesn't it? You would think, when listening to the Marxist in chief or his accidental speechwriter, Elizabeth Warren, that upper-income Americans are somehow finagling out of paying any taxes at all. That's all part of the progressive narrative, along with phony American history and moronic economic theories.

It's part of their all-out attack on American culture, specifically in this case the Protestant work ethic and the deeply held beliefs in private property, free enterprise, and self-reliance. These have all been bedrock American principles since the Pilgrims rejected socialistic principles in the 1620s.

These values grew out of America's Western European, Judeo-Christian heritage. That's one reason white people and religion are demonized. American culture must be ripped out by the roots. They want to transform American culture into belief in socialism, central planning, and dependency. Inciting racial tension through demonization of successful white people helps accomplish that.

Self-loathing liberals want to transform America into a self-loathing, guilt-ridden, atheist culture they can wallow in, with a tax-subsidized life of luxury to help ease their "pain." It is crony capitalism and luxury for them, socialism and misery for everyone else. Hillary Clinton is their perfect spokeswoman, a fabulously wealthy, Gulfstream liberal who condemns other wealthy people who actually earned their money.

She and the Progressive-Islamist alliance are waging war on our culture in every medium they can, including public school, movies, music, business, politics, and religion. In every conceivable space, capitalism, individual liberty, patriotism, nationalism, and religion are under attack.

Zero Reality on Race

I used to stop in at a coffee shop around the corner from my house and buy a cup of coffee for fifty cents. That was quite a few years ago. For two quarters I got a hot cup of coffee, some friendly service, and maybe a newspaper left on the counter by the last customer. If I talked to the guy behind the counter, it was about the weather or some other small talk.

Today, I walk into a Starbucks and pay four dollars for a cup of coffee. Instead of a secondhand newspaper, I'm handed a questionnaire seeking to determine just how much white privilege I'm guilty of. This is all done under the pretense of "stimulating empathy and compassion for one another," but we all know that's nonsense. It's about reminding white people how evil they are.

Consider the questions: "I have _____ friends of a different race." "My parents had _____ friends of a different race." "In the past year, someone of a different race has been in my home _____ times."[16]

Can you believe this? This is what it has come to. One of the most successful corporations in America peddling the most pedestrian liberal white-guilt trash to its paying customers. Instead of working to develop new products or cut their exorbitant costs, they want to make white people feel guilty if they haven't had a person of a different race over to their house in the past year.

For those suffering from acute liberalism, allow me to apply a therapy called "reality." The reality is that 72 percent of Americans are Caucasian. Twelve percent are African Americans, about 5 percent are Asians, and every other race comprises the final 10 percent.

So, in your everyday interactions with people in this country, the odds are overwhelming that most of them are going to be Caucasian. Outside of large, cosmopolitan cities, the odds that you will have the opportunity to strike up a friendship with someone of another race are quite low.

This isn't something to feel guilty about. It isn't something to feel anything about. Most Nigerians don't have white people over to their houses on a regular basis. Most Inuit people will never have a Hispanic family over to their house. That's not because Nigerians or Inuit are racist. It's because there just aren't many white or Hispanic people around where they live.

This may seem like common sense, but it's not as common as you think. Peddling white guilt is part of the liberal agenda, but a lot of liberals actually buy into it. They truly feel guilty themselves, just for being who they are.

Movies and television help create this irrational guilt by portraying American society in a completely fictional manner. Every television show whose cast includes a group of children portrays the group as not only multiracial and multicultural, but equally represented by every race and culture on the planet.

No matter where the show takes place, you can expect every group of childhood friends to include a Caucasian child, a black child, a Hispanic child, an Asian child, and an Indian child. Despite the hard numbers that seven in every ten children are

Caucasian, one would have to conclude from watching children's television shows that no group of childhood friends in this country includes three or more Caucasian children.

I'm not saying there is anything wrong with showing children of different races playing together. What I do object to is portraying a false picture of American society, which contributes to the irrational guilt I was just talking about. If you are accepting of other people regardless of their skin color, you have nothing to feel guilty about, even if you don't have occasion to develop relationships with people of other races.

These contrived plots in which there are virtually no all-white groups of children plant the seed in children that there is something wrong if they don't have friends of other races. Instead, children should learn that race doesn't matter—character does.

What Are Western Values Post-Obama?

Western Civilization reached its apex in the United States of America, the freest, most prosperous, and most powerful nation in the history of the world. That civilization was built upon principles derived from English common law and tradition, Judeo-Christian morality, and the uniquely American principles of individualism and self-reliance.

What are Western values today? Shooting junk at night and taking a coffee enema in the morning? Sleeping with fifteen people at night and doing an herbal bath cleansing routine the next day? Are those our values now? Is this why everyone is into detoxing, because they know their souls are polluted?

Here we are, fifty years after the 1960s, when we were told

to eliminate all repression, to let it all hang out. If it feels good, do it. Why don't we do it in the road? Can anyone really say that has worked out well? We hear a lot about how repressed American society was before the 1960s, but not much about how much more well ordered and civilized it might have been.

John Adams famously said, "Our Constitution was made only for a moral and religious people." He was right. There has always been a protection against any federal-government-mandated religion in this country, as there should be. But religion or some equivalent moral set of principles is a responsibility that goes along with freedom. We can see the consequences of abandoning that responsibility all around us.

Americans barely notice as a rogue president runs roughshod over the Constitution, takes over the health-care system, floods the country with illegal aliens, and alienates our allies overseas. As long as the beer is flowing, football is available three nights a week, and porn is available 24/7, they'll stay fat, dumb, and happy.

One would be hard-pressed to answer whether the United States is still a land of opportunity or a land of dependency. One in eight Americans are receiving food stamp assistance.[17] Over one-third of Americans have government-subsidized health insurance.[18]

We have two opposing forces fighting in the world right now. We have the extremely religious Muslim fanatics who interpret their religion from a ninth-century point of view and are willing to kill for it. They'll kill boys for watching soccer, believing that watching a soccer game is the first step on a slippery slope to becoming transgendered. That is how insane these fanatics are.

The West is exactly the opposite. It has no values left. The left destroyed the church. They've destroyed all semblance of religion and morality. They've destroyed the American principles of private property, free enterprise, self-reliance, and personal responsibility. They've replaced them with atheism, hedonism, dependency, and political correctness. Man in the West today has no soul.

The Islamofascists are using this to their advantage. While they're conquering Afghanistan and Iraq militarily, they're conquering America with propaganda. They are spreading disinformation through academia and the media, including Hollywood. They're smearing as racist anyone who stands up to radical Islam.

They're using the same tactics against those who recognize the danger of Islamofascism as liberals used against McCarthy and others who recognized the dangers of communism sixty years ago. Even self-described feminist Dr. Phyllis Chesler, emerita professor of psychology and Women's Studies at the City University of New York, agrees with me on this.[19]

They'll even attack their own. When Bill Maher had a moment of clarity and hosted Sam Harris to talk about the real problems within Islam itself,[20] the progressive jackals descended on both of them, calling them racists and Islamophobes. Ben Affleck, a guest on the same episode, nearly burst a blood vessel, calling Harris's arguments "gross" and "racist." One blogger at the *Huffington Post* went so far as to level the ultimate slander at Maher, at least to the progressive mind. He called him "conservative."[21]

What do we stand for and what will we fight with? Our strength was built upon our values. When we were a moral and religious people, dedicated to individual liberty, personal responsibility, private property, and limited government, we were invincible. Those principles were the reason we had the mightiest economy and the most powerful military on earth.

Now those values are gone. They're all but extinct. The Islamofascists may be wrong, but they are dedicated to their creed and willing to die for it. We've abandoned our creed. What exactly are our soldiers supposed to die for today?

I certainly wouldn't want to put my life on the line for a lot of what I see around me. I don't even know what to say to a soldier who comes home from Afghanistan after defending a society which curses his service and protests movies celebrating his heroism.

Soldiers used to return from war to a society of high culture, innovation, and free enterprise, where institutions like private property, churches, and traditional marriage ensured a level of civility and prosperity that made their service worth the sacrifice and risk.

Today, they return to an increasingly unrecognizable caricature of that bastion of freedom they thought they were defending.

This is partly the result of Government Zero. When you have Zero Leadership, you can expect people to be led astray. But don't forget cause and effect. The government is largely a reflection of the people. The people elected it. The people decide what they want to ask it to do. Ultimately, it is the people who must take responsibility. The government can force them to buy health insurance, but not to abandon their values.

Any reform of the government must be preceded by a rebirth of American culture. Only a moral and religious people, who once again dedicate themselves to American values, can find the strength to defeat America's enemies, both without and within.

CHAPTER 7

Zero Immigration

What Country Is This?

Obama has flooded America with Africans, Middle Easterners, and Chinese over the past three years. Europeans need not apply for citizenship. You can see now what he meant when he promised to "transform America."

While Mexicans remain the largest immigrant population in the United States, the Progressive-Islamist administration has managed to increase immigration from the Middle East, Asia, and the Caribbean the most. Overall, the number of immigrants living in the United States, legally and illegally, is at an all-time high of 41.3 million.[1]

It wasn't too long ago that America was still a First World nation that led the world in commerce and military might. Despite decades of progressive assault, private property, free enterprise, Judeo-Christian values, and respect for law and order still dominated American culture.

English was the first and only language, and immigrants enthusiastically learned to read, write, and speak it in an attempt to become *Americans*. Upon these pillars was built the freest, richest, most powerful nation in human history.

Today, the entire foundation of American society is under assault by a Progressive-Islamist alliance that hasn't neglected reshaping our entire immigration policy. We're no longer a land of opportunity for ambitious, talented immigrants looking to escape social democracies with large welfare states. We're now a land of government handouts for waves of immigrants, both legal and illegal, who come here for the generous welfare benefits our progressive government keeps increasing.

We're also a target for Islamofascists who are actively infiltrating our free and open society for the express purpose of destroying American civilization. Turkey's former prime minister and now president, Recep Tayyip Erdoğan, once said, "We will ride the train of democracy to our ultimate goal," meaning a new caliphate based upon sharia law. He was talking about Turkey.

The Islamofascists want to ride our American democratic train to the same goal here. What they don't blow up they could eventually rule by voting.

Look at what the immigration policies of just a few decades have done. According to the U.S. Census Bureau, Hispanics made up 8.9 percent of the electorate as of November 2012.[2] We have to assume that number is even higher now. Immigrants in general, including these, largely vote Democrat.

Unlike previous waves of immigrants, this current wave coming from south of our border doesn't consider learning English or assimilating into American culture a responsibility that goes along with immigrating. They have demanded and received accommodations in their own language. Today,

Americans have to "press 1 for English" if they want service in the language in which their Constitution is written.

Some of them even consider their immigration here a Reconquista, meaning they are reclaiming the land which once belonged to their Spanish-speaking ancestors. Regardless of what you might think of their claims, they are open and honest about one thing: They aren't looking to assimilate into American culture. They are looking to assimilate the territory they settle into Mexican or Spanish culture.

Language is only the tip of the iceberg. Along with language, we're importing people with different political ideas. They come from largely socialist countries and are unlike previous waves of immigrants in that they don't necessarily come to get away from socialism. On the contrary, their voting patterns suggest they are attracted to the more generous welfare benefits than are available at home.

Instead of escaping socialist countries and oppressive governments to take advantage of free enterprise and individual liberty here, they are coming here to transform America into the image of the countries they left and plunder the accumulated wealth of America's freer past. How else could one explain their uniform support for the Democratic Party?

The other half of the Progressive-Islamic takeover is occurring through the federal government's Refugee Resettlement Program. Admitting largely Muslim refugees from war-torn and terrorism-plagued countries in the Middle East, the progressives are creating self-contained Muslim communities in virtually every state. These groups of refugees are riddled with terrorists that even the FBI says they cannot screen out. Those who aren't violent nevertheless represent a completely foreign culture that in no way shares our values.

This is all the result of legal immigration, assuming there is still any distinction between legal and illegal. Illegal immigrants are having an even worse effect. At best, they are illiterate in their own language and have grim prospects for employment. At worst, they are hardened criminals or terrorists themselves who are a grave threat to public safety.

Those of us who remember the America of not so long ago wake up every day and ask, "What country is this?" Those of you who don't will nevertheless ask the same question just a few years from now, unless the Progressive-Islamist takeover is stopped.

Sleeper Cells Among Us

While illegal immigrants continue to pour over our southern borders carrying potentially deadly diseases, socialist values, and no discernible benefit to American society, the progressives in control of the White House are also importing one hundred thousand Muslims per year as refugees.[3] Under the pretense of humanitarianism, these useless academics are creating the very sleeper cells FBI counterterrorism chief Michael Steinbach says now exist in forty-nine states.

The White House sorority and the useful idiots who parrot them constantly downplay the threat of radical Islam by saying there is no way for Islamofascist armies like ISIS to breach our borders. "It's not like we're going to wake up one day and find ISIS in New York," they sneer. They refer to the farcical prospect of ISIS invading the United States in a conventional military operation.

They're right about one thing. ISIS won't have to wait for

the progressives to weaken our military to that extent. ISIS is already here. But they didn't land Normandy-style in amphibious landing craft. They were brought in by our government as refugees and secretly resettled all over America.

Earlier this year, Rep. Trey Gowdy (R-SC) sent John Kerry a letter. He wanted more information about the dozens of foreign refugees from Syria, North Africa, and elsewhere coming into South Carolina.[4] It was the first time I know of that a congressman actually called the federal government to account for its unilateral decisions while bringing in seventy thousand refugees a year on average over the past few years.[5]

Congressman Gowdy asked all the questions one would expect from a conscientious representative of his constituents. Who in Congress or the state and local governments were consulted before the decision was made to resettle these people in Spartanburg, South Carolina? What services will taxpayers be obliged to provide these refugees? How many have criminal records? How many more are coming?

As glad as I was to see somebody in Congress actually pushing back, there are a few questions I'd like to ask Mr. Kerry myself.

First, why is the administration granting asylum mostly to Muslims from Syria, Somalia, Afghanistan, and Iraq, when a full-fledged holocaust is being perpetrated against Christians? Second, how do we know that ISIS agents posing as refugees are not among those the administration has admitted and put on a fast track to citizenship, just as the FBI has warned?

I know the answer to my first question, although I wouldn't expect the Islamophillic administration to answer it. Bringing in Muslims, even legitimate refugees, is consistent with the Progressive-Islamist takeover of America. These ready-made communities are just more pockets of anti-American, unassimilated foreigners who will eventually become citizens and vote Democrat. They further dilute Christianity as the dominant religion in America, English as the dominant language, and American values as the dominant culture.

As far as my second question, the FBI has already told us they aren't screening refugees for links to terrorism. As *World Net Daily* reported, "The U.S. simply does not have the resources to stop Islamic radicals in Syria from slipping into the country through the State Department's refugee-resettlement program, said Michael Steinbach, deputy assistant director of the FBI's counter terrorism unit."[6]

Leaving Christians to the Wolves

While we know the progressives want to do anything but bring more Christians into America, it is unconscionable that they would allow their political agenda to deter them from taking immediate, emergent action to address the genocide of Christians in the Middle East. While the Muslim in chief refuses to say the word *Islamic* when referring to the Islamic State, that very group is systematically exterminating the most ancient population of Christians in the world.

You wouldn't know this from listening to the president. Just like the Jews murdered by Islamic terrorists in a kosher Jewish deli in Paris became merely some "folks" randomly murdered by "zealots," the 147 Christians murdered by Islamic terrorists were nondescript "innocent men and women" murdered by "terrorists."[7]

There isn't any doubt that these were Muslims targeting

Christians. They were members of the Somali-based al-Shabab terror group, and they specifically asked the victims if they were Christian or Muslim before murdering them. Christians attempting to impersonate Muslims to save their lives were asked to recite a Muslim prayer. If they could not, they were killed.[8]

Similarly, Obama referred to the twenty-one Coptic Christians beheaded by Islamofascists in Libya merely as "Egyptian citizens." Yet, when ISIS kills Muslims they believe aren't practicing the faith properly in their insane opinion, Obama openly recognizes the religious identity of the victims, as he did "Ismailis and Alawites" in Syria.[9]

The president is always quick to remind us that ISIS has killed more Muslims than members of any other religion. He truly has a keen eye for the obvious. Most people in the region are Muslims, so it isn't surprising ISIS has killed more Muslims overall than Christians.

The difference is that Muslims are not targeted because they are Muslim. On the contrary, demonstration of one's dedication to orthodox Islam can save one's life and property in territories under ISIS control. Christians, on the other hand, are without exception dispossessed and exiled, if they're lucky, or summarily executed if they're not.

The president knows all of this, but he and the sorority have made up their minds to pretend the extermination of Christians isn't happening. That makes it a certainty Christians can expect little help from U.S. Immigration as long as the progressives control the White House.

Believe it or not, this is exactly what the so-called bleeding-heart liberals did during the original Holocaust. Their patron saint, that great "man of the people" Franklin Delano Roosevelt, and the Democratic Congress were in a similar position to help

Jews during the 1930s. But despite repeated pleas to increase the quota for German immigrants, the Democrats failed to do so.

As Kristallnacht and Auschwitz loomed, FDR's government kept the limit on German immigration at just over 27,000 immigrants per year. They failed to significantly raise the limit even after Jews were declared noncitizens in 1935. From late 1938 through June 1939, over 300,000 German refugees applied for visas, but most were unsuccessful.[10]

Even after the Holocaust was under way, the progressive FDR administration refused to believe the truth about it, although admittedly less deliberately than Obama appears to be denying the new holocaust.

Worst of all, the FDR administration didn't even admit all of the Jews the quotas would have allowed. Between 1933 and 1937, only 30,000 refugees entered the United States. The quotas would have allowed almost 130,000.[11] That means FDR could have admitted 100,000 more Jews without even fighting the political battle to have quotas raised, but he didn't.

You'll never believe the reason given for not admitting more Jews fleeing the Holocaust. They were afraid the refugees would be a burden on the welfare system. Can you believe that, coming from the Democrats? The same people who want to bring in tens of millions who can't read or write in their own language were suddenly afraid that Jews fleeing the Holocaust would be a burden on taxpayers. It would be funny if it weren't so tragic.

So much for the great defenders of the oppressed. If you're African, Muslim, or socialist, progressives will spare no expense to defend you against the slightest infringement of your rights. But if you're Jewish, Christian, or capitalist, they will look the other way even in the face of mass murder. They protested every war the United States fought against communism, but actively supported Clinton's intervention into Kosovo. Why? Because Clinton took the side of the Muslims against the Christian Serbians. Suddenly, the peaceniks were war hawks.

Now they are silent while Christians are slaughtered, just as they were during the Nazi Holocaust. The women's-rights activists who invent "rape culture" on college campuses and in the military have nothing to say about ISIS kidnapping ten-year-old girls and forcing them to get married. They say nothing about Yazidi girls abducted and turned into sex slaves for ISIS soldiers. Where is their outrage?

One has to wonder what could be in the minds of this administration, other than direct harm to the American people. Forget the lack of compassion for Christian refugees of this new holocaust. What possible benefit could the American people derive from bringing in 100,000 Muslims every year? Given a finite total number of refugees who can be accommodated, what possible reasoning would lead any sane person to choose Muslims over Christians?

He is bringing Shia/Sunni internecine warfare into America. It's like bringing viruses and bacteria into a healthy population.

The Sleepers Awaken

As I've said many times about this administration, it doesn't matter whether they are playing for the other side or just clueless academics in over their heads. Either way, the results for the American people are the same. These progressives are a clear and present danger to the American people every day they remain in office.

We can't necessarily just wait out Obama's term, either. Hillary Clinton certainly isn't talking about doing anything different. Picking up right where Obama will have left off, she's talking about LGBT activism, income inequality, and global warming. As I've discussed in other chapters, she's been friendly with the Muslim world for decades.

We don't have time to wait for the right people to get elected. Without a serious opposition party, it may not matter who wins the next election. Besides, the sleeper cells have already started to wake from their slumber.

In April, Abdirahman Sheik Mohamud was arrested for plotting to attack police or military personnel after returning from ISIS training in Syria. The initial reports sounded like something Obama's sorority had scripted for his latest press conference. Mohamud was initially described as "an Ohio man" and "a U.S. citizen."[12] You might have thought this was just an average local boy who fell in with the wrong crowd and was led astray.

In reality, Mohamud was a Somalian immigrant who was already plotting to commit terrorism within the United States when he became a U.S. citizen in 2014.[13] His communications with his brother indicate that becoming a citizen was all part of the plot to become an ISIS agent within our borders.

How did this man become a U.S. citizen? Where was DHS, TSA, and the rest of the security apparatus our billions fund? How does an immigrant from Somalia get through the process to become a citizen and receive a U.S. passport while NSA is intercepting the phone and e-mail metadata on every man, woman, and child in this country? Could it be they aren't looking for Somalian terrorists? Are they spending too much time targeting conservatives for tax audits?

Whatever the explanation, ISIS is laughing at us. Just think about this: If Mohamud hadn't been caught after returning from Syria, he would have been able to vote in the next election. How many more like him are out there?

Mohamud wasn't the first Somali immigrant to attempt this. Just a few days after his arrest, six men from the Somali immigrant community in Minnesota were arrested for attempting to travel to Syria to join ISIS.[14] And these six weren't the first from this community. Late last year, two other men attempted to travel to Syria to join ISIS from the same Somali community. One of them was successful.[15]

Over the past eight years, at least twenty-two people from "Little Mogadishu," as this Somali community in Minnesota is called, have left the United States to join the Islamofascists overseas.[16] Some have gone back to Somalia to join al-Shabab. Some have joined the rebels the White House sorority is funding in Syria against the Assad regime. Wherever they end up, they join the war against civilization being waged by Islamists on a global scale.

This isn't an isolated incident. Little Mogadishu has just had more time to develop into a full-blown terror cell. The government has an ongoing Refugee Resettlement Program that has resettled Somali refugees in Columbus, Ohio; San Diego, California; and Lewiston, Maine.

By the way, these cities were picked at least partly because of their generous welfare programs. I'm sure you're happy to hear you're funding this terrorist recruiting program.

I do not mean to imply the program is limited to these few states. The network of federal, state, and private agencies is able to resettle refugees in all fifty states.[17] Once you understand what is going on, the threat of terror cells in every state doesn't sound at all crazy. On the contrary, it's crazy to ignore what's happening before our very eyes.

From listening to our Soviet-style media, one could only assume our biggest challenge was to ensure Muslim Americans weren't discriminated against. I'm not saying some innocent Muslims aren't unfairly assumed to be violent in some cases. What I am saying is we have far more serious problems to worry about. We have an administration which is, intentionally or not, rolling out the red carpet for people who have not only sworn to kill all of us, but to enslave the entire world.

They can only succeed with a compliant government that puts its own needs above those of its people.

Importing Crime

Not every crime committed by an immigrant or illegal alien is an act of terrorism. Some are just ordinary crimes, committed by garden-variety criminals, who likewise should not have been admitted into the United States.

The Department of Homeland Security (DHS) is charged with making the removal of illegal immigrants who have criminal records a priority. On its website, DHS reported it "conducted a total of 577,295 removals and returns, including 414,481 removals and 162,814 returns" during fiscal year 2014.

That sounds like an impressive number, until you dig a little deeper. That's when you start hearing about the results of Obama's "prosecutorial discretion" in dealing with his so-called dreamers. In a report DHS provided to Senate Judiciary Committee Chairman Chuck Grassley, illegal aliens with criminal records released by DHS committed one thousand crimes in 2013.[18] These crimes included child sex abuse, carjacking, aggravated assault, and a host of others.

Those are just numbers for 2013. A separate report based upon Judicial Watch's analysis of 76 DHS documents concluded that almost 166,000 illegal aliens with criminal records were released back into American society as of April 2014.

America learned how tragically this can end when thirty-one-year-old Kate Steinle was shot to death by an illegal immigrant who had previously been deported five times.[19] Not only had Juan Francisco Lopez-Sanchez been deported five times before the shooting, he had seven prior felony convictions.

Sanchez was on an American street because San Francisco is a "Sanctuary City," meaning its government does not cooperate fully with federal immigration authorities.[20] Sanchez had been turned over to San Francisco deputies pursuant to a drug warrant by the U.S. Immigration and Customs Enforcement (ICE) with a request that they be notified if Sanchez were released. This routine request is called an immigration detainer and would have been honored by law enforcement elsewhere. It was not honored by San Francisco law enforcement because of the Sanctuary City policy.

This was by no means the first time the policy has resulted in tragedy. In 2008, Edwin Ramos, an illegal immigrant suspected of previous murders, shot and killed a forty-eight-year-old man and his two sons.[21] Ramos thought one of the sons was a rival gang member. Ramos had been twice protected by the city's Sanctuary City policy after committing crimes as a minor.

There couldn't be a better example of Government Zero than this. After letting the federal government run roughshod over the powers reserved to the states or the people, the one instance in which local governments push back is on an issue on which they actually should cooperate fully with the federal authorities. Had they done so this past July, Kate Steinle might still be alive today.

It is not just intentional violence one has to worry about. Illegal aliens are convicted of drunk driving and driving without a license or insurance. So if you're involved in a traffic accident with an illegal immigrant, you have zero chance of getting medical expenses or damages to your vehicle reimbursed, even if the accident was 100 percent the other driver's fault.

Juan Perez-Juarez managed to hit the trifecta. He managed a violent crime, indecent exposure, and a traffic accident involving injuries to another driver all on the same day.[22] It almost sounds like a joke, but it's not. The details are chilling.

It all started when the illegal immigrant from Guatemala saw a little girl playing in front of her house in Bensalem, Pennsylvania. Perez-Juarez first attempted to entice the little girl into his car. When she refused to get in, he got out of his car, exposed himself, and then urinated in the street.

Fortunately, the child's father came out to chase Perez-Juarez away. While making his escape, Perez-Juarez crashed his car into a pole. He was later involved in a second accident involving injuries to the other driver and was finally arrested.

All of this mayhem was caused by one criminal illegal alien released by the Obama administration. Just imagine Perez-Juarez's Saturday afternoon multiplied by 166,000. This is the kind of chaos the progressives are creating in a society where violent crime rates had previously been cut in half over the past twenty years. Just as they are destroying the world order with their Progressive-Islamist foreign policy, they're destroying civil society from within with their insane immigration policies.

Jonny Alberto Enamorado-Vasquez was apprehended

immediately after entering the country illegally in October 2012. He spent several weeks being passed around by several federal agencies, including ICE and the Department of Health and Human Services. He was released later that month due to "lack of space," according to the government.[23]

Two years later, Enamorado was charged with the January 2015 murder of Michael Phalen, a Houston smoke shop owner. Enamorado and two accomplices allegedly broke into the shop and killed Phalen in a gunfight.

It goes without saying that crimes like this are perpetrated by natural-born American citizens every day. I am not claiming people who were born here don't have the same dark side of their natures as people everywhere.

I am saying that American culture has traditionally been freer, more peaceful, and more law-abiding than many of the countries illegal immigrants are coming from. Even within those countries, the law-abiding people who want to emigrate obey the law and apply through the proper channels. Those who sneak in illegally have already demonstrated a lack of respect for the law. We shouldn't be surprised when they break other laws once here.

The government is never going to keep every criminal out of American society, but it should at least be trying to the best of its ability. Had Jonny Alberto Enamorado-Vasquez not been carelessly released in 2012, Michael Phalen would still be alive today.

Importing Disease

I've been warning about the danger of deadly diseases carried by illegal immigrants for over thirty years. I wrote a book on the subject called *Immigrants and Epidemics* in 1981, but I could not get it published, even though all of my previous books had sold. Why? I was told by every publisher that a book on that subject was off-limits, regardless of how well documented or factually accurate. They were all afraid to publish it for political reasons.

Now, the socialist dictator Obama has decided that elections don't matter and has used his phone and pen to rewrite immigration law himself. Besides being unconstitutional, he's risking an epidemic in America due to the diseases many of the illegals are bringing in.

As far as I'm concerned, he committed a crime against humanity in dumping many ill people on us, primarily mothers and children, in the summer of 2014. Many of them brought in measles, tuberculosis, and other illnesses. These kids came in from countries where those diseases are endemic.

This is one of the chief reasons we have immigration laws in the first place. At Ellis Island, when America was run by men who wanted to protect the population rather than infect it, people who looked sick or were not vaccinated were sent back to their country of origin. Sometimes, they were vaccinated and kept in quarantine before being allowed to enter the general population.

This was not a denial of their right to immigrate. It was an enforcement of their responsibility not to start an epidemic when exercising that right. It was protecting the right of the existing population not to be infected by diseased immigrants. That's one of the main reasons we have immigration laws.

Obama and his stooges at the CDC have covered up what has already been a crisis in new or previously eradicated diseases brought in by illegal immigrants. Tuberculosis, hand-foot-and-mouth disease, and Chagas disease, previously eradicated from Southern California, are all on the rise and testing positive in border patrol agents. The vice president of the Border Patrol Union, Chris Cabrera, confirmed this to Fox News in July 2014.

"Our agents don't like to see these kids in these conditions, especially coming off the long journey they have been subjected to, and then the diseases that some of our agents are contracting—we had one get bacterial pneumonia a couple days ago," Cabrera said. "A lot of our guys are coming down with scabies or lice."

He added: "The border patrol is trying to play catch up and we're having a lot of diseases coming in and some we haven't seen in decades and we are worried they'll spread throughout the United States especially if they [the immigrants] are being released and have the disease."[24]

Not only has the Obama sorority allowed thousands of sick immigrants to enter the country, it has then transported them all over the United States, over the objections of immigration professionals who are trying to do their jobs and contain any threat of contagious disease. Even ABC News reported on this. They also interviewed Cabrera:

> *"We are sending people everywhere. The average person doesn't know what's going on down here," said Border Patrol agent and Rio Grande Valley Union representative Chris Cabrera.*
>
> *Cabrera says agents are seeing illegal immigrants come over with contagious infections.*[25]

Whoever has permitted this, whether it was the stooge at the CDC, the stooge at the NIH, or Obama himself, is at least guilty of criminal negligence. Where are all the shyster lawyers who sue doctors for negligence when they make an honest mistake? They send their kids to college with money they made suing doctors, but they're nowhere to be found when the government is negligent and endangers us all.

One of the reasons health departments are overwhelmed is a huge spike in tuberculosis cases over the past two years. It isn't an isolated incident. Forget what the Department of Health and Human Socialism tells you. Tuberculosis has broken out at camps for illegal immigrant children at Lackland Air Force Base in Texas and Fort Sill in Oklahoma. As Fox News reported last July:

> *However, at least a half dozen anonymous sources, including nurses and health care providers who worked at Lackland, allege that the government is covering up what they believe to be a very serious health threat.*
>
> *Several of my sources tell me that tuberculosis has become a dangerous issue at both the border and the camps.*
>
> *"The amount of tuberculosis is astonishing," one health care provider told me. "The nurses are telling us the kids are really sick. The tuberculosis is definitely there."[26]*

I'll bet your local paper neglected to report that, too. Why would they? It might make Dear Leader Obama look bad. It might make it look like keeping his oath and doing his constitutional duty was probably a good idea after all. Don't expect to hear anything that contradicts the dictator from *Pravda* or *Izvestia*.

Outbreaks of the rare Enterovirus 68 (EV-D68) are also suddenly occurring all over the country, in areas as remote from the southern border as Missouri, Illinois,[27] and Buffalo,

New York.[28] Why is this suddenly happening all over the country? It couldn't be because Obama is putting sick illegal immigrants on buses and airplanes and transporting them all over the country, could it? No, Savage, that's crazy talk. Nothing Dear Leader does could possibly be so harmful.

It isn't just measles or the flu. Children have actually been crippled. The Centers for Disease Control and Prevention (CDC) itself was investigating whether the virus was causing symptoms similar to polio in at least nine infected children in September 2014.[29]

One would think that with all of this, the federal department whose sole reason to exist is to control and prevent disease outbreaks would be highly concerned. One might expect the CDC to issue the strongest recommendations to the president to take emergency steps to protect the public, his first duty as president.

Instead, the CDC claims it has no idea about the origin of these diseases. In a February 2015 update to its investigation on EV-D68 causing poliolike symptoms in children, the CDC reported it was now referring to the condition as "acute flaccid myelitis" and had verified cases of 112 children in thirty-four states who had developed the condition.[30]

The section titled "What CDC Is Doing" listed several bullet points on actions taken by the agency, including further testing, working with health-care professionals and state and local departments of health, and so on. What the update makes no mention of is any effort to determine the reason these outbreaks suddenly occurred all over the United States, immediately following Obama's new immigration initiatives.

The agency had said in its initial report in September it had "particular interest in characterizing the epidemiology and etiology of such cases." Apparently, it lost interest in the epidemiological aspect of the investigation. I wonder why. Is there some reason they suddenly don't want to know the origin of these diseases?

It has previously denied any link between illegal immigrant children and the virus, despite a peer-reviewed report linking EV-D68 to Latin American children.[31] Now it isn't investigating the origin of the disease at all, even though it has previously published a study on its own website calling EV-D68 "one of the most rarely reported serotypes, with only 26 reports throughout the 36-year study period."

Almost five times that many cases have been reported in a five-month period in 2014–2015, but the CDC isn't even curious why that might be. Perhaps that's because finding the answer could hurt the president politically.

They're doing the same fake science with tuberculosis. The Lynn, Massachusetts, scare was by no means an isolated incident, but it is interesting that there have been no statements by the CDC about the origin of the disease there. Remember how fast they were to announce the source of the "Disneyland outbreak" of measles in February 2015? Within days, the CDC had done genetic tests indicating the virus was "similar to strains seen in Indonesia, Qatar, Azerbaijan, and Dubai."

"We don't know exactly how this outbreak started but we do think it was likely a person infected with measles overseas," the CDC's Dr. Anne Schuchat told reporters.[32]

Why were they so quick to determine the origin of the measles strain, but not the origin of the much more dangerous tuberculosis outbreak?

I can think of one possible answer. The measles was likely carried into the United States by a tourist here legally and thus not politically damaging to the president, but the tuberculosis in Lynn was probably brought in by an infected illegal immigrant child carrying the disease into its overloaded Community Health Center. Announcing that would have been very harmful to the president politically. We're supposed to believe that's a coincidence. Do you?

Tuberculosis cases in the United States have been steadily declining in the United States for sixty years, from over fifty cases per hundred thousand in 1953 to just three per hundred thousand in 2013. Numbers for 2014 were not available at the time of this writing, but I assume that trend will continue, in spite of cases the administration may have brought in with its immigration policies. What if it doesn't? If there is an uptick in the number of cases for the first time in sixty years, will the CDC investigate then?

So far, the CDC's answer to sudden outbreaks of disease has been the same as Obama's answer to everything else: blame Americans. They blame the small percentage of parents who don't vaccinate their children. Never mind that this has been the case for decades and the outbreaks started only after Obama started inviting sick children into the country and then shipping them all over the States. Who cares about scientific concepts like controlling for other causes? Not the Lysenkoites at the CDC.

I've only given you a few examples of the dozens of deadly diseases that could potentially enter the United States as a result of the president's irresponsible, politically motivated immigration policy. Faith in federal agencies to control the spread of these diseases is obviously misplaced. Politics have corrupted their science, just as it has the IPCC's. How can we possibly trust the same people who have ignored ongoing outbreaks of tuberculosis, EV-D68, and other diseases to suddenly start doing real science when a more serious outbreak occurs?

Importing Socialism: Amnesty for Illegals

While the White House sorority is importing terrorism through its refugee program and deadly diseases through its immigration policies, it is simultaneously importing socialism.

The progressives have accomplished quite a bit in the century they've controlled public schools. But teaching progressivism takes time. It's taken generations to overcome the common sense inherent in the American people. Sometimes, critical thinking still rears its troublesome head, as it did with those schoolchildren at Pine Bush High School who refused to sit still for the Pledge of Allegiance being read in Arabic.

Fortunately for progressives, they have another source of low-information voters. Those they can't teach progressive socialism they simply import. That's the real reason they are so adamant about amnesty for illegals. It's not about compassion or fairness or freedom. It's about power.

Before talking about the present, let me enlighten you a little about the past. I'm going to let you in on a little progressive brainwashing that you didn't even know you were swallowing hook, line, and sinker.

How many times have you heard liberals argue that America lags behind Europe in quality of life because it doesn't have government-run health care or a larger welfare state in general? Have you heard that one? I hear people mindlessly repeating it all of the time. It's a mind trick, and a pretty good one at that.

What does this have to do with immigration? Think about it for a moment. What was America like when the huge waves of legal immigrants entered through Ellis Island during the late nineteenth and early twentieth centuries? Did it have government health care? Did it have a large welfare state in general? No.

In fact, that's precisely why those immigrants came to America, to escape governments with less freedom and large welfare states. That's why they called America "the land of opportunity." It was our free markets, limited government and culture of self-reliance, individual liberty and responsibility, and opportunity to become whatever you wanted if you worked hard enough. They came here because we had less government than they had at home, not more.

I'll bet you never thought of that, did you? It never occurred to you that the kind of government these liberals want to construct, the socialist paradises in Sweden or France, are precisely the kind of governments millions of immigrants came here to get away from. These were the immigrants who helped make America the greatest nation in human history.

German immigrants came here specifically to get away from the large welfare state in Bismarck's Germany. They waited in line at Ellis Island, learned to speak English, and studied to become citizens, not for a handout, but just for the opportunity to keep the fruits of their labor instead of having it stolen by the government.

It goes without saying that immigrants who came to America during this period knew they'd have to be productive members of society in order to survive. They would have to assimilate into American culture and find their place in the American economy. They weren't going to get a handout. They were just going to get a fair chance. That was all people like my parents or any other immigrants were asking for back then.

Even today, *legal* immigrants are far more likely to come to America for the same reasons. They come to attend American universities, earning degrees in medicine and engineering. They come to do highly technical jobs in fields where there is a shortage of their skills. They are more likely to start businesses and employ other people.

Part of the reason for this is the immigration process has been discriminatory in the past. I know, that's a bad word to progressives. Liberals have convinced people that any discrimination is bad. That's ridiculous. Discrimination is necessary for survival. If you can't discriminate between edible plants and poisonous ones, you'll die. Every day you must discriminate in a thousand ways to avoid death, financial problems, and other misfortunes.

The immigration system is supposed to discriminate between different types of immigrants. That doesn't mean it discriminates based on their race, religion, or national origin. It shouldn't. It discriminates based on each individual's risk for American taxpayers versus his or her potential value to American society. Will this individual add to American society or become a burden upon it?

No system is perfect, least of all when the government is running it, but it at least attempts to represent the interests of the American people in terms of who is approved to immigrate and who is not. It can at least screen people for diseases, find out what skills they have and what their plans are. That gives some indication of whether they will be a plus or a minus for American society.

None of this happens when people immigrate illegally. As we've already seen, they are bringing diseases into the country that have been previously eradicated or have never been present here before. They tend to be low skilled and much more likely to require government assistance than those who go through the proper channels.

Many of them can't even read or write in their own language.

After California passed a law allowing illegal immigrants to apply for driver's licenses, most were unable to pass the written test, even though it was offered in Spanish. Nevada had a similar experience after allowing illegals to apply for driver's licenses. Seventy-one percent failed the test in their own language.[33]

Nevertheless, Nancy Pelosi actually told reporters that immigrants who "flocked to our shores" provided "invigoration that made America the greatest country that has ever existed in the history of the world and will continue to."

What is she saying? Does bringing in two-year-old babies from El Salvador whose mothers don't even read or write in Spanish "invigorate" America? What jobs are they going to take? Are the two-year-olds going to work?

Of course, that's not why Pelosi wants them here. She wants them here to ensure the progressives have voters for the socialist welfare state. First, they get them in by any means possible. Then, they find a "path to citizenship" for people who literally invaded the United States without even needing an army.

They are the army. It's a progressive-socialist army that is going to change what's left of the United States after imported Islamists try to blow it all up. This is the new immigration policy under the Progressive-Islamist takeover. If you're illiterate and from a socialist country or Muslim and from a country rife with terrorism, you're admitted immediately and subsidized.

If you're educated, Christian, Jewish, or self-sufficient, you can get in line. The progressives may eventually let you in, but they are going to let in a hundred of the former group for every one of the latter.

This isn't an accident. Common sense will tell you that the people who have valuable skills are more likely to cooperate with a process that is going to base its decision to let them in at least partly on those skills. Those who have little or no skills will tend to avoid it. The former group will further enrich American culture, the economy, and the nation. The latter are more likely to become a burden.

But the illegals have one "skill" that liberals are extremely anxious to bring into this country. They are low-information voters who will vote Democrat if they get a path to citizenship. They come from largely socialist countries south of the U.S. border and are already indoctrinated into that worldview. All the Democrats have to do is get them in and make them citizens, and they can change this country forever.

Forget what the president might say about being compassionate or fair-minded. Obama and his party want to maximize immigration because even legal immigrants tend to vote Democrat. According to the Center for Immigration Studies, "the enormous flow of legal immigrants in to the country—29.5 million [from] 1980 to 2012—has remade and continues to remake the nation's electorate in favor of the Democratic Party."[34]

Nevertheless, most Republicans support reform of our immigration laws to make it easier for people to immigrate legally, even though it is politically disadvantageous for the party. That is precisely the opposite of the Democrats' strategy, which is to maximize the number of immigrants entering the United States, whether legally or not, regardless of the risks of violent crime or disease they pose.

They want to get them in at any cost, including the cost of deadly epidemics, and streamline their path to citizenship, at which time most will become Democratic voters. That's the real reason Obama announced he would violate his oath and cease doing his constitutionally required duty to "take care that the laws shall be faithfully executed."

Not only is he not enforcing immigration laws, he's encouraging illegal immigration with welfare benefits and tax breaks. At a time when ISIS is rampaging across the Middle East, committing terrorist attacks in Europe, and threatening the same within the United States, he and his party have held the Department of Homeland Security budget hostage to further his amnesty for illegals agenda.

It's the Cloward-Piven strategy in action, which calls for radicals to overwhelm public and private systems, so there would be a reason for the government to step in. This isn't a secret. Several Republican congressmen saw through Obama's tactic immediately. According to *World Net Daily*:

> *In the 1960s, Professors Andrew Cloward and Francis Fox Piven of Columbia University, Obama's alma mater, devised a plan to provoke chaos by deliberately overwhelming governmental systems and the U.S. economy to the point of collapse, paving the way for state intervention that would ultimately replace America's free-enterprise republic with a collectivist system.*
>
> *"I do feel this attempt to flood the border with illegals is a playing out of the Cloward-Piven theory," said Rep. Steve King, R-Iowa.*
>
> *"If you don't see them bring reinforcements down there to seal the border, that means that, yes, it's a Cloward-Piven maneuver to flood the country until we get to the point where we are an open-borders country that welcomes everybody, legal and illegal," he told WND.*[35]

In addition to overwhelming public and private systems, flooding the country with illegals who eventually get amnesty and vote also creates a whole new Democratic voting bloc.

Rep. Steve Stockman, R-Texas, agreed that Obama—who studied the chaos strategy at Columbia, according to a classmate—"is trying to do a Cloward-Piven thing with the border."... He said it's "an open secret Obama is trying to flood Texas with illegals to make it into a blue state," with a Democrat majority.

"If we lose Texas, and it becomes like California, then the Republicans lose the chance of ever getting a Republican elected president," the Texas lawmaker warned.[36]

Whether overwhelming public systems is intentional or not, it's happening. The mayor of Lynn, Massachusetts, says the influx of illegal immigrants over the past two years is stressing almost every service from trash collection to health care.

"We have been aware of the unaccompanied children issue for quite a while, and we were able to absorb a lot of these children early on," said Lynn mayor Judith Flanagan Kennedy. "But now it's gotten to the point where the school system is overwhelmed, our health department is overwhelmed, the city's budget is being sustainably altered in order of [*sic*] accommodate all of these admissions in the school department."[37]

Illegal Immigration for Profit

In addition to promoting the anti-American, Progressive-Islamist agenda, illegal immigration also makes billions for special interests. I followed the money. You may remember the reporting last year about the luxury hotels being rehabbed for the illegal alien "children,"[38] offering saunas, tennis courts, luxury pools, and more. The Obama administration actually bought a luxury hotel to convert into a facility for juvenile illegal aliens.

If you're a poor American, do you have a beauty parlor at your disposal for free? Do you have flat-screen TV? Do you have free lawyers, doctors, dentists? Do you have a workout gym? Do you have a swimming pool? Do you have a soccer field in your housing complex? They do. They will. Somebody's making a fortune off of this. Where is the money coming from? Who are the contractors who are going to make billions off the illegal alien amnesty surge?

I found the RFP[39] put out in January 2015 for housing and clothing and feeding these "children." The government was plotting to bring them in all along. But someone was making a fortune on it, I figured. But I didn't know who.

A $50 million federal government contract to house illegal aliens at another facility that was blocked and yet they're moving them in here? Many of the rooms are suites: private toilets and showers, flat-screen and cable TV, soccer fields. You get the picture, right?

Well, guess what: Some people are getting rich off the billion-dollar immigration surge, and they're not all Democrats. Only a handful of U.S. corporations have the honor of long-term contracts with federal agencies that deal with the "immigration problem." It's a closed shop. And for these companies, the latest surge from Guatemala and El Salvador has meant big business and big profits. That's why Obama is pushing for emergency funding for so-called "family detention centers" like the one in Texas.

They are more like resorts. Soccer fields with artificial turf, lighting, flat-screen TVs, and pools are amenities you might get on a vacation once a year, if you can afford to take a vacation at all.

So why are you and I spending so much money on those who break our laws? The answer is profiteers. Every television, every desk lamp, every blade of fake soccer grass has a huge markup to it. You heard about the $32 aspirin in hospitals, right? That's nothing compared to what these companies are making on these detention facilities. It's connected to the companies that run prisons for profit. Do you get the picture?

Do you know about prisons for profit? I dug into the particulars of one such company making a profit off the immigrant surge, the GEO Group. Who are they? In the past six years, GEO was awarded nearly $880 million in ICE contracts alone.[40]

Who is the parent company of GEO Corporation? Wackenhut Corporation, which owns a lot of private prisons and funded the American Legislative Exchange Council, or ALEC. ALEC is a lobbying group. They tell your elected officials what to vote on. They tell the elected officials where to eat, what to breathe, and how to operate. They run the country.

Are you ready for this? What I'm about to tell you will change your view of politics for the rest of your life. Who's running this company who helps fund ALEC and is behind all of these resorts for illegal aliens? Well, I have the names because you wanted to know the answers. The top shareholders include people you never heard of. It's an international organization. They own facilities in the UK, Australia, South Africa, and the United States. The management team includes George Zoley, John Bulfin, Norman Carlson, and Thomas Wierdsma.[41]

I don't know who they are. But maybe some of these hedge funds are familiar to you. They include BlackRock Fund Advisors; Credit Suisse; River Road Asset Management, LLC;

Eagle Asset Management, Inc.; Scopia Capital Management, LLC; Carlson Capital, LP; BlackRock Institutional Trust Company; Hotchkis and Wiley Capital Management; and Vanguard Group, Inc. If you have money in any of them, it may be helping fund GEO Group's holding facilities for the illegal alien children.

All of this is perfectly legal. Don't assume I'm saying there's anything illegal in what they're doing. I'm just telling you to follow the money.

Maybe you have mutual funds and you like the percentage you're making every year. Just know these companies are profiting from the illegal alien surge. You may say you're a conservative and against illegal immigration. Well, here are the mutual funds that hold GEO stock: Vanguard Specialized REIT Index Fund; Fidelity Small Cap Discovery Fund; iShares S&P Small-Cap ETF; Prudential Jennison Equity Income Fund; Eagle Series Trust Small-Cap Growth Fund; iShares Russell 2000 ETF; Vanguard Small-Cap Index Fund; Vanguard Total Stock Market Index Fund. Do you get the picture?

I'm just getting started. Who is on the GEO Group board of directors that is making billions off the illegal aliens living in luxury resorts? (And this may explain why the Republicans along with the Democrats have been lobbying for amnesty in one form or another.) Well, they're not household names, but they have names. In addition to CEO George Zoley, who is chairman of the board, the board of directors includes Richard Glanton, chairman and CEO of ElectedFace, Inc.; and Norman Carlson, former director of the Federal Bureau of Prisons.[42]

Let me pause right there. The former director of the U.S.

Federal Bureau of Prisons is on GEO's board. Think about that for a moment.

It gets even better. Also on the board is Anne Newman Foreman, former undersecretary of the U.S. Air Force. You were told women in the military would be much kinder and gentler. Well, there she is. She left the Air Force and she's on the board of directors of GEO Group.

As I said, it's all perfectly legal. It's business as usual. Look how well they're all doing. They came to do good and they did very well indeed. Clarence E. Anthony, president and CEO of Anthony Government Solutions, Inc.; Christopher Wheeler; and Julie M. Wood are also all board members.

Again, these are not household names, but wait until you hear the punchline, because you haven't heard it yet.

The Koch brothers, David and Charles, who are two of the richest people in the world, are key funders of the American Legislative Exchange Council (ALEC).[43]

There you have it. You thought it was all liberals who wanted amnesty. But conservatives are also guiding forces behind the illegal immigration surge because they own facilities with thousands of unused beds. And they want you to fill them and pay for them. It is big business, big government, and big religion, all in one bundle and getting paid off your back.

Can We Get America Back?

As our dear Marxist leader would say, "Let me be perfectly clear." I'm not against immigration. I'm the child of immigrant parents myself. Everyone living in this country is descended from immigrants, including the inappropriately named

Native Americans. They aren't indigenous to America, either. They came here from Asia. They just came before the Europeans. That's something else you probably didn't learn in school.

Immigrants helped build this country into the greatest nation on earth. I believe that every human being has a natural right to leave the country he or she is born in and seek a better life in another. But that right has the same natural limit that all rights have: "the limits drawn around us by the equal rights of others," as Jefferson so eloquently put it.

Among other things, that means you do not have a right to immigrate to another country carrying a potentially deadly disease that could harm the people living there. You don't have a right to enter that country illegally and subvert its constitution. Most obviously, you don't have a right to immigrate into a country for the express purpose of killing its citizens or overthrowing its government.

This is precisely the kind of immigration our government is actively facilitating. It's all about the type of people you attract with strictly enforced immigration policies based upon adding to American society versus those you attract with no immigration policies whatsoever. The latter is the most charitable description for what the White House sorority is doing.

The flood of illegals over our southern borders has been going on a long time. The Republican administration before Obama certainly didn't do anything to stop it. George W. Bush's brother Jeb wouldn't be any different. He thinks we need more immigrants.

Importing low-information voters from socialist countries is killing us slowly through the erosion of our legal traditions, language, and culture of free enterprise and personal responsibility. Importing terrorists could kill some of us tomorrow, as we've already seen with terrorist attacks by Islamofascists like the Tsarnaev brothers or the female would-be terrorists who plotted to attack New York City.

It all goes back to Government Zero. When you have a government acting in its own interests rather than those of the people, you have immigration policies like this. The Progressive-Islamist takeover benefits a government that wants to expand its power rather than secure the blessings of liberty.

You've heard about the Roman policy to "divide and rule." That's just what the government is doing. While it divides indigenous Americans over race, sex, and economic class with its economic and social engineering policies, it creates whole new groups of "Americans" who don't speak our language and don't share our values with its immigration policy. Some of them even want to kill us.

Then it champions their rights not to be discriminated against while trampling our rights to life, liberty, and the pursuit of happiness. While we're fighting each other and these government-sanctioned invaders, the government grows stronger and we get weaker.

I've been warning about the dangers posed by injudicious immigration policies for decades. Now those dangers are accelerating exponentially with the Progressive-Islamist takeover. If we ever want to see our country again, we need to stop it now. In another decade, it might be too late.

CHAPTER 8

Zero Religion
Lenin's Pope

Hitler's Pope

As part of their ongoing war on religion, leftists regularly attack the pope. One of their favorite smears is to call him a Nazi, a tactic they used most recently against Pope Benedict XVI. Pope Benedict had been in the Hitler Youth, but only because it was legally mandated for all fourteen-year-old boys in Germany at the time. It was the same as being drafted into the army. Had he not joined, they would have come to his house and made him join.

Those are facts, but facts are immaterial to the left. They have an agenda, and Pope Benedict being a Nazi fit that agenda at the time, regardless of all evidence to the contrary.

It wasn't the first time they ran the "pope is a Nazi" campaign. You may remember the 1999 book *Hitler's Pope* by John Cornwell. In it, Cornwell elaborates on a charge made previously against Pope Pius XII in Rolf Hochhuth's 1963 play *The Deputy*. Both claim Pope Pius XII helped the Nazis because, as cardinal secretary of state of the Church, he signed the Reichskonkordat.

The Reichskonkordat was an agreement with the German government stipulating that clergy would refrain from certain political activity in exchange for guarantees of the Catholic Church's rights. This, they argue, helped legitimize the Nazi regime and stifle criticism against it.

Never mind that the agreement was not signed by Hitler and doesn't even mention the Nazi party. Forget that Pope Pius actually saved many Jews from the Holocaust, was called "the mouthpiece of Jewish war criminals" by the Nazis themselves, and was mourned as a hero by Jews all over the world upon his death in 1958.[1] Even Cornwell himself has largely backed away from the allegations against Pope Pius in his own book.[2]

Again, leftists aren't interested in facts. They are interested in their agenda, and "the pope is a Nazi" fits their agenda. The pope and his influence over billions of Catholics stands in the way of their plans for a godless, socialist world order. So, in addition to attacking religion in every public space, they attack the pope when doing so meets their needs.

Politicizing the Papacy

That has certainly not been the case with Pope Francis. Pope Francis is different, because he is not a spiritual leader. He is a political operative, with all the earmarks of having been hand-picked for his office the way French president François Hollande and our own Dear Leader Obama were picked for theirs.

It wouldn't be the first time the Vatican has been occupied by a political rather than a spiritual leader. The papacy is two thousand years old. It has had good periods and bad periods, as has any long-standing institution run by imperfect human beings. There were popes who were honest, wise, and deeply spiritual, and others who were morons, scoundrels, or worse. There were times when the papacy was the spiritual center of the Catholic faith and times when it was little more than a political office, complete with rule over large areas of land and armies commanded by the pope to enforce that rule.

Pope John XII was definitely an example of the latter. He was simultaneously the secular prince of Rome and the pope, but he acted more like the pagan Roman emperor Caligula. He was accused of turning the sacred palace into a whorehouse, fornicating with several women there, including his own niece, and then blinding his confessor.[3] He put deviant liberals in Hollywood to shame.

Pope John was eventually deposed as both ruler of Rome and pope, but subsequently regained both offices, brutally mutilating prisoners captured in his victory. He is said to have died in the act of committing adultery.[4]

Pope Benedict IX was also accused of rape, murder, and other atrocities, while Pope Boniface VIII demolished several towns while feuding with a powerful family. The ironically named Pope Innocent IV tortured heretics, including Galileo, for the "heresy" of claiming the Earth revolved around the sun.

Were the Church not nourished by the Holy Spirit, it might never have survived some of its darker times. But it did survive, and in modern times the Church and the papacy have concerned themselves much more with saving souls than politics.

That's not to say the pope should have no political opinions at all. Pope Pius XI, who was actually the sitting pope when the Reichskonkordat was signed, said,

When Politics come near the Altar, then Religion, the Church, the Pontiff have not only the right but the duty to give directions and indications to be followed by Catholics.[5]

"When politics come near the altar" means when governments infringe upon or attempt to influence the Church on spiritual matters. That's precisely the opposite of the pope using his position as spiritual leader to influence politics, but that's what Pope Francis has been doing. Not only has he abused the trust placed in him for political purposes, he's sold out to the socialists who'd love to abolish all religion if they could get away with it.

Pius XII was wrongly called "Hitler's Pope." The charge didn't fit the facts, as the author who wrote the book eventually admitted himself. But Pope Francis can very appropriately be called "Lenin's pope." Let's consider the facts supporting *that* charge.

Channeling Lenin

Just eight months after taking office, Pope Francis published *Evangelii Gaudium*, an apostolic exhortation in which he makes the same spurious criticisms of capitalism Lenin used to lead the Bolshevik revolution. As just one example, he says,

We can no longer trust in the unseen forces and the invisible hand of the market. Growth in justice requires more than economic growth, while presupposing such growth: it requires decisions, programmes, mechanisms and processes specifically geared to a better distribution of income, the creation of

sources of employment and an integral promotion of the poor
which goes beyond a simple welfare mentality.[6]

The left always talks about the free market as if it were being run by someone and income was being distributed. That's counterintuitive. By definition, a free market does not run according to a plan, and no one decides how income is distributed. Each individual decides whether to buy or sell, at what price, and at what quantity. They aren't told what to do by anyone. That's why they call it free.

The pope doesn't believe freedom works. He wants "decisions, programmes, mechanisms and processes" to be imposed on people. He wants income *redistributed*, meaning forcibly taken from some people and arbitrarily handed out to others.

This is just what Lenin did after the 1917 revolution in Russia. He implemented decisions, programmes, mechanisms and processes based on Karl Marx's maxim, "From each according to his ability; to each according to his need."

Guess how that worked out? Things got so bad in Russia that Lenin was in danger of being deposed by 1921. The Soviet Union survived only because Lenin's "New Economic Policy" restored some semblance of a market economy.[7]

The Soviets, the Vietnamese, and the Chinese all learned the hard way that communism doesn't work. They all abandoned it on their own after suffering miserably trying to make it work.

We often refer to China as "Communist China" because the Communist Party still asserts autocratic rule over the political process. But China might be less communist economically today than the United States. In some ways, China is the most capitalist society on earth.

The United States doesn't have a completely capitalist system. The free market has been continually altered since the progressive assault on it began over a hundred years ago. We have a mixed economy like Europe, although the United States has more capitalism than socialism in the mix, at least for now. But politicians still interfere with the peaceful exchanges of property that would occur without interference in a free market. Too often, voters choose politicians based on how much of other people's money they are going to get or what industries are going to get subsidies or favors.

China's system is very similar. They just don't bother with the fraud of elections. Americans went to the polls in 2014. They voted against the leftist policies of the imposter in the White House. They said *nyet* to the Communist Democrat Party of America.

What was the result? The next day, the arrogant, lame-duck president laughed at us and said our votes don't count because only a small number of people voted, meaning white people and working people. He said, "Wait until 2016 when I flood America with 20 million illegal aliens and fill the streets with Occupy Movement radicals. I'll get them all registered and they'll all vote. Then, you'll see who really runs this country." I'm paraphrasing, but that's what he really meant.

China practices the same sort of state-directed capitalism as the United States, without the political need to appeal to voters. There are no elections. Instead, everything is done through bribery. If you want to start a business in China, make sure you bribe the right government officials.

In America, you may not have to bribe politicians directly in order to start a business, but you do have to pay for permits. If you want to build a house, there are permits for that, too.

If you want your kids to go to an elite college, you might have to make a "donation" to fund a new building or an academic department. It's bribery in all but name.

The Chinese are more honest about it. They just hand over $5,000 gift cards directly and dispense with the whitewashing. Say what you want about them. Their economy is booming while ours continues to contract, regardless of phony government statistics indicating it's recovered.

In any case, China is not a communist state. They learned the hard way how lethal communism is. They paid an even bigger price in human life than Russia, where full communism was abandoned earlier. But every country that has tried communism has had the same results.

Even Vladimir Putin admits it was a mistake. He reminded President Obama about the horrors of communism at Davos back in 2009, in an attempt to dissuade Obama from pursuing his $800 billion disaster of a mortgage bailout.

> In the 20th century, the Soviet Union made the state's role absolute. In the long run, this made the Soviet economy totally uncompetitive. This lesson cost us dearly. I am sure nobody wants to see it repeated.[8]

Apparently, Pope Francis does want to see it repeated. Not only is he advocating thoroughly discredited socialist theories, he's completely misinformed on the economic conditions he says he wants to improve. He mentions inequality eleven times in his apostolic exhortation, calling it "the root of all social ills" and saying it is "increasingly evident." He says the "need to resolve the structural causes of poverty cannot be delayed."

He reiterated this in a letter to the president of Panama earlier this year:

> *Inequality, the unfair distribution of riches and resources, is source for conflicts and violence among peoples, because it involves the progress of some to be built on the necessary sacrifice of others and, to live with dignity, they have to fight against the rest.*[9]

There is only one problem. By every objective measure, inequality is not increasing. It's decreasing at rates orders of magnitude greater than at any time in human history. According to the *Economist*, the poverty rate worldwide has been cut in half in the past twenty years.[10] Not only has poverty decreased spectacularly, but it has done so precisely because so many countries have shifted away from the kind of socialist policies Pope Francis advocates and toward the free market system he condemns.

I am not saying the pope is evil. He probably believes the things he says just as millions of leftist voters do. Why wouldn't he? Pope Francis was born and raised in socialist South America. He was immersed in anticapitalist thinking his entire life. He probably believes in socialism as much as American businessmen believe in free enterprise. As the *Economist* said of an interview the pope gave in 2014:

> *By positing a link between capitalism and war, he seems to be taking an ultra-radical line: one that consciously or unconsciously follows Vladimir Lenin in his diagnosis of capitalism and imperialism as the main reason why world war broke out a century ago.*[11]

As you can see, I am not alone in recognizing the influence of Lenin on the Holy See. Whether it is conscious or unconscious, it's still socialism and terribly destructive. For a man whom billions trust to hold these views is terribly dangerous for a world in need of more freedom, not less.

This is why borders and culture are important. It is no accident that the first non-European pope in twelve hundred years would have these radical views. We believe the things we are raised to believe. If you elect a pope from a socialist country, as Argentina was for most of Pope Francis's life there, you should expect him to have socialist views on the economy. When you allow millions of people from a socialist country to cross your border and eventually become citizens who vote, you should expect socialist representatives and eventually socialist laws.

This is all the more dangerous because the people destroying your freedom believe they're right. It's very hard to accept that the things you have been taught since you were a child are wrong. People living in socialist countries have been taught all their lives that free enterprise is something to be feared, rather than embraced. They have been taught that business owners exploit workers, rather than give them an opportunity to be far more productive than they could be on their own.

The Power of Religious Authority

People subscribing to bad ideas is not something to be feared in and of itself. That's one of the rights the First Amendment is designed to protect: to believe and say very stupid things, as long as we do not do harm to others. But when you combine stupid ideas with power, it can be very dangerous. Power wielded based on stupid ideas *can* do harm to others. It can destroy society, the economy, even an entire nation. Just ask Vladimir Putin, when he's in the mood to be honest, as he was at Davos in 2009.

Power can come in many forms. Certainly, our crypto-Marxist president is an example of stupid ideas combined with great power. He wields that power directly, as commander in chief of our military and executor of our laws.

Large voting blocs also wield great power, although they wield it indirectly by deciding who holds office. When you deliberately invite tens of millions of people with very bad ideas into your nation and give them a path to citizenship, you are investing them with the power to elect the people who will eventually harm you.

The pope wields a third kind of power: the power to influence ideas. Millions of honest Catholics look to the pope for guidance on how to live a good, Christian life. When he's guiding people on how to emulate Jesus in their personal lives, he is a tremendous force for good in the world. But when he's acting as a political operative, he's just the opposite.

Besides, with all due respect, he doesn't know what he's talking about.

It's a little like medicine. The United States has the greatest doctors in the world when it comes to diagnosing and treating acute illnesses. That's what they're trained to do, and no system trained them better than America's former free market health-care industry. If you get a serious illness and the most effective treatment is medicine or surgery, there is nowhere on Earth you're in better hands than with an American medical doctor. At least for now.

However, medical doctors are not experts in nutrition, in

wellness, or in preventing you from getting sick and need-ing their help. This is something I know a little about. I earned a Ph.D. from the University of California, Berkeley, in nutritional ethnomedicine.

Medical doctors can tell you exactly what is going on with your body and can suggest medical solutions. But as far as liv-ing a healthier life when you're not sick, they are little more than very intelligent laypeople. When they are giving you the same nutritional or fitness advice as Michelle Obama, you may want to do some research on your own.

The same goes for the pope. He doesn't hold a degree in economics. He's never even run a business. On economics, he's *less qualified* than most Catholics, who at least work in the private sector and understand the realities of the business world. The pope has a few years' experience as a chemical engineer, a janitor, and a bouncer in a bar. These are all honest professions, but they hardly qualify him to opine on complex economic subjects.

Unfortunately, millions of Catholics believe they have to agree with him on economics, even though he knows less about it than they do. The Church dogma of papal infallibility helps bolster this misconception. Many well-meaning Catho-lics believe they have to agree with the pope on everything because they're taught he's infallible.

Catholics, I have news for you. You don't have to agree with the pope on economics to be a good Catholic. The Church doesn't teach that and, in all fairness, even Pope Francis has said this:

> *I am only infallible if I speak ex cathedra but I shall never do that, so I am not infallible.*[12]

The Church defines papal infallibility very narrowly. They only consider him infallible when "in the exercise of his office as shepherd and teacher of all Christians, in virtue of his supreme apostolic authority, he defines a doctrine concerning faith or morals to be held by the whole Church."[13]

On other subjects, his opinion is just that—an opinion. When he tells Catholics to care about the poor and work toward a world with less poverty and suffering, he's advancing the message of Jesus. When he opines on the best economic system to make that happen, he's out of his depth.

He was similarly out of his depth when he supported Dear Leader Obama's overtures toward Cuba. First, he hosted meetings between Raul Castro and President Obama at the Vatican. Then his secretary of state issued a letter applauding "the historic decision taken by the Governments of the United States of America and Cuba to establish diplomatic relations, with the aim of overcoming, in the interest of the citizens of both countries, the difficulties which have marked their recent history."[14]

Now, there have been arguments made by conservative, free market proponents to establish diplomatic relations and trade with Cuba as a way of showing Cuba's people the benefits of capitalism and eventually inspiring them to overthrow Castro and the Marxists. But that was not what Lenin's pope had in mind. He doesn't see the Castro regime as evil and in need of being overthrown. He considers it at least equal to the American government. He probably believed the regime would treat its people better after he stuck his nose into international relations.

Exactly the opposite happened. Immediately after Obama announced sweeping changes to U.S. policy on Cuba, the communist regime banned a free speech protest in Havana. Not only did the government arrest three dissidents before the event even started, it cut off calls to the organizer's cell phone.[15] Instead of the prison island becoming more liberated or more liberal, it has become more draconian.

Anyone who understands the inherent connection between socialism and authoritarianism would have seen this coming a mile away. But leftists don't see the connection. They believe socialism provides more freedom, regardless of an entire century's evidence to the contrary. Democratic politicians regularly praise communist leaders as wise and caring, even as those same leaders murder millions, stifle all dissent to their rule, and otherwise oppress their people.

Speaking in support of Obama's Affordable Care Act at a town hall meeting in 2009, Rep. Diane Watson said, "And I want you to know, now, you can think whatever you want to about Fidel Castro, but he was one of the brightest leaders I have ever met."[16]

That same year, Obama's communications director, Anita Dunn, had this to say at a high school graduation:

> "The third lesson and tip actually comes from two of my favorite political philosophers: Mao Zedong and Mother Teresa — not often coupled with each other, but the two people I turn to most to basically deliver a simple point which is: you're going to make choices; you're going to challenge; you're going to say why not; you're going to figure out how to do things that have never been done before."[17]

Yes, she praised the same Mao Zedong who intentionally killed tens of millions of his own citizens in political purges and unintentionally killed at least fifteen million more trying to implement his disastrous, Marxist economic policies.

Liberal politicians and media do this all the time. They correctly criticize Hitler for killing six million people, but turn a blind eye toward the killing of tens of millions by socialist dictators.

This is certainly the way Obama looks at communists like Fidel and Raul Castro and is likely the way Pope Francis sees them, too. He may not condone the oppression of the Castro regime, but he can rationalize it away as long as the regime remains committed to the "social justice" of communism.

As I've always said, liberalism is a mental disorder. A liberal can completely ignore crimes against humanity by a socialist dictator just because he is a socialist. And liberals will rationalize away horrific crimes committed by someone if that person shares a race or religion with others who are victims of prejudice. If a white man commits a violent crime, they want him prosecuted. If a black man commits the same crime, they want to blame white people for what the criminal did.

That's actually true racism. It is judging people not by their actions or character but by their race or religion. I believe everyone should be subject to the same rules, regardless of race or religion. Everyone should enjoy the same rights and privileges and should be held equally accountable for his actions, regardless of race, religion, or sex.

The Pope Attacks Free Speech

That's why I wish Lenin's pope would spend more time condemning the jihadists torturing and beheading Christians instead of attacking free markets and free speech. He couldn't even bring himself to condemn the horrific murders of the

Charlie Hebdo employees without making excuses for the murderers:

> *"There is a limit," he said, speaking in Italian. "Every religion has its dignity. I cannot mock a religion that respects human life and the human person...If [a close friend] says a swear word against my mother, he's going to get a punch in the nose...One cannot provoke, one cannot insult other people's faith, one cannot make fun of faith."[18]*

You read that correctly. The pope actually made excuses for the Islamofascist murderers, just as progressive-socialists like him do at every opportunity. It would have floored me if I didn't see through this fakir from the beginning. He's the perfect complement to our Progressive-Islamist president.

Pope Francis says free speech should be limited and one can expect to be answered with violence for saying something insulting. That's completely ridiculous. The definition of free speech is the right to say controversial, even insulting things without fearing violence, either by the government or individuals.

People don't have to like what you say or agree with you. They can say insulting things back. The appropriate response is to answer them with reason or ignore them, not break into their offices and gun them down.

Thomas Jefferson actually refuted the pope directly. "The legitimate powers of government extend to such acts only as are injurious to others. But it does me no injury for my neighbour to say there are twenty gods, or no god. It neither picks my pocket nor breaks my leg."[19]

Jefferson is saying something we all learned in kindergarten:

Sticks and stones can break my bones but names can never hurt me. He's talking about government power, rather than violence committed by individuals, but the principle is the same. The reason governments aren't allowed to infringe upon free speech is because enforcing the law is a violent act. When the police show up to enforce the law, they don't hand you an invitation. They take you away and use violence if you resist.

The principle behind the First Amendment is that speech itself, regardless of how offensive, cannot justifiably be answered with violence. I didn't like much of the liberal nonsense *Charlie Hebdo* put out, but I'm free to disagree with them or not listen at all. That's how freedom works.

Again, this is cultural. I'm not surprised at all by Pope Francis's view on how speech should be limited. He's the product of a socialist culture where stifling free speech goes hand in hand with stifling economic freedom. You can't have free speech in a socialist society. Too many people would start asking each other why they're working so hard and still getting poorer and poorer.

I know. Your whole life you were told, "Oh, watch out for those right-wingers. Those right-wingers will take away your freedom of speech. Those right-wingers will tell you what art you can produce." Yes, all those fears were valid, but you were afraid of the wrong people. When you have a damaged optic chiasma, you see everything upside down and backward. It's not the people who want the government to leave you alone that are the problem. It's the ones who want it to help you that you should be afraid of.

I know this firsthand. I'm the only member of the American media who is not permitted to enter Britain based on statements I never even made. As I said, facts don't matter. It wasn't right-wingers who banned me but Britain's wonderful, caring, liberal Labor Party government who did it. These are the great defenders of free speech.

In fairness, Cameron and his phony conservatives haven't overturned the ban. They're about as conservative as Hollow Man Boehner.

Don't forget that the First Amendment doesn't just protect free speech. It's also about the separation of church and state. When did the Catholic Church become so brazen as to suddenly step over that important firewall?

I'll tell you. When the Catholic Church was given billions of dollars by the federal government to help usher in millions and millions of illegal aliens because they need the pews filled with illiterates from Central America. That's when it happened.

Once the Catholic Church and Baptist Family Services and certain Jewish and Protestant organizations were corrupted by Obama with billions of dollars in taxpayer-funded resettlement programs, the churches, the synagogues, and others became useless as institutions of religion and instead became arms of the community organizer Barack Obama.

So it's about much more than free speech. It's about destroying all semblance of civilized society. Stalin, Mao, and Pol Pot weren't the only communists who committed atrocities. All of them did. Look up the 1944 Battle of Meligalas in Greece. Calling it a battle is disingenuous. It wasn't a battle; it was a massacre.

What Is the Pope Defending?

Communist guerillas rounded up fifty nationalist soldiers and more than a thousand villagers and butchered them to the last man, woman, and child. That is what the communists did in Greece. That is what communists always do. They have that in common with the maniacs calling themselves the Islamic State.

Contrary to what the communists in America, who like to call themselves progressives, might tell you, socialism is a brutal, violent ideology. Free enterprise is stifled by force. Property is redistributed by force. You cannot complain because speech is repressed by force. The so-called progressives are the most vicious subpopulation in this country. That's why they don't speak out against the massacres occurring daily against Christians and other minorities, including homosexuals, by their friends, the Islamists. They are used to all of their heroes doing the exact same thing.

Ironically, most of them would be the first ones lined up against a wall for a firing squad or sent to the gulag in a traditional socialist country or tortured and beheaded in an Islamic one. If they had any sense they'd side with the forces of civilization against both. Lenin's pope was raised in a socialist, oppressive society like this and those influences are showing.

The Pope Promotes Junk Science

If you think he was wrong about economics and foreign relations, wait until you hear what he has planned next. He has already said, "Climate change, the loss of bio-diversity, deforestation are already showing their devastating effects in the great cataclysms we witness."[20] Now he's writing an encyclical letter on the subject and plans to support Obama on climate change initiatives in the United Nations.

Remember when I said the Church limits papal infallibility to a very narrow range of subjects? Well, encyclicals have traditionally been issued by popes on only the most important religious issues. That naturally limits them to subjects the author knows something about.

The pope knows less about climate science than he does about economics. I actually worked to save rain forests as an environmental activist, before that moniker became synonymous with *socialist*. Pope Francis has never done environmental work. His only scientific experience is as a chemical technician, which has nothing to do with climate or the environment. The only thing the pope knows about climate is when it rains, his aides open up an umbrella for him.

In an attempt to represent him as a scientist, the progressive left has propagated the myth that Pope Francis has a master's degree in chemistry. He doesn't. According to the *National Catholic Reporter*, he doesn't have a college degree in any subject, neither a master's nor a bachelor's degree.[21]

That doesn't stop him from rendering his utterly valueless opinion. In the absence of any actual scientific understanding of climate or the environment, he just repeats liberal talking points, putting a religious spin on them:

"I don't know if it (human activity) is the only cause, but mostly, in great part, it is man who has slapped nature in the face," he said. "We have in a sense taken over nature."

"I think we have exploited nature too much," Francis said, citing deforestation and monoculture. "Thanks be to God that today there are voices, so many people who are speaking out about it."[22]

Yes, shame on those who have "slapped nature in the face," but nothing but excuses for jihadist lunatics who cut people's heads off merely because of their religion. No wonder the most anti-Christian president in American history is wrapping himself in the robes of the Holy Father. They think alike on so many things.

So, here is the pope again using his office to promote a political movement. I say "political" rather than "scientific," because that's what the entire environmental movement has become. It's not about saving the planet anymore, if it ever was. It's about money and control. Like every other crisis the left dreams up, the proposed solution to climate change is politicians getting more of your money and controlling more of your life.

What never ceases to amaze me is that anyone believes the climate change narrative. When you take a step back and think about what we're asked to believe, it really is quite ridiculous. It requires us to forget the basic science we all learned in grade school.

Most of us learned about the recurring ice ages that have occurred throughout Earth's history somewhere around the fifth grade. They were all ended by global warming, which was obviously occurring long before the industrial revolution.

In fact, the first ice age occurred over two billion years ago, during the Proterozoic Eon. As you may have surmised, the warming period that ended it wasn't caused by human activity. It wasn't dinosaurs engaging in heavy industry, either. They wouldn't exist for over a billion years themselves.

The truth is that the earth has cooled and warmed in cycles during its entire existence. Technically, we are still in the last of five major ice ages in Earth's history. What most people refer to as the end of the last ice age around ten thousand years ago was really just the end of the last glacial period. The current ice age as defined by real scientists won't end until there is no glacial ice anywhere, including in Antarctica.

Even within the current interglacial period there have been significant fluctuations in temperature. Right after your fifth-grade science class, you may have learned in history class about the Norse settling Greenland. They were able to do so around 1000 AD because of the Medieval Warm Period,[23] which made Greenland much more hospitable. At the time of their arrival, Greenland's climate was "relatively mild (i.e., as "mild" as it is today)" according to Jared Diamond.[24] Its rivers were more navigable, trees and herbaceous plants were more abundant, and crops could be grown farther north.

The Norse settlements ended abruptly during the 1400s with the onset of what is now known as the Little Ice Age, a period of dramatic cooling.[25] The details of their demise are uncertain, but all theories include the effects of cooler temperatures on farming and navigation. There was less land to farm and less wild vegetation, and the North Atlantic Ocean was harder to navigate due to more abundant ice. All of these pressures combined with new competition from the Thule, ancestors of the Inuit, and mistakes the Norse made themselves in managing resources.

What is important to take away from their story is that much more violent climate changes than anything experienced since the industrial revolution have always occurred on this planet. The Medieval Warm Period and Little Ice Age are not controversial theories. They are accepted scientific facts, although the Intergovernmental Panel on Climate Change

(IPCC) has tried to mitigate *their* "inconvenient truths" by characterizing them as regional climate patterns.

Perhaps the biggest whopper the climate change cult wants us to swallow is that carbon dioxide causes global warming. They've actually called carbon dioxide a pollutant. Yes, I'm talking about the same carbon dioxide that is necessary for photosynthesis and without which all plant life would die. This is something you probably learned in fourth grade, but the enviro-socialists want you to forget that, too.

The data they rely on does show a correlation between warming periods and carbon dioxide. But the increases in carbon dioxide always occur *after* the temperature increases.[26] So, increases in carbon dioxide don't cause global warming. Global warming causes increases in carbon dioxide.

Obviously, a point-by-point scientific rebuttal to the climate change theory would require its own book. I do deal with it at greater length in the next chapter. I've come to my own conclusions as a scientist, knowing the historical background behind this movement. Common sense will serve you just as well.

I invite you to do your own research. You'll find every major assertion of the climate change hoax completely refuted by qualified scientists. As with everything else, the leftist media ignores the evidence and goes on repeating the lies.

Even the scientists the IPCC relies on don't tell anywhere near the same story about climate change the politicians do. They still debate quite a bit about what causes it, how dramatic it has been or will be, or even if it is ultimately harmful or helpful to human life.

That's right, the IPCC's own scientists aren't even sure global warming won't be a good thing.

Before getting back to the pope's role in all of this, I invite you to ask yourself a few questions you don't have to be a climate scientist to answer:

If the climate change question is so settled, why does the IPCC need to kick scientists out for dissenting? Have you ever heard of any other multidisciplinary research team behaving this way?

Why did everyone stop calling the phenomenon "global warming" and start calling it "climate change"? Absolutely no one pushing this theory calls it global warming anymore. Could the reason be that there has been no warming since at least 1998? Look it up. It's true.

The overwhelming majority of scientists not kicked out of the IPCC are dependent upon the politicians running the organization for funding for their research. Under any other circumstances you can imagine, wouldn't this be considered a conflict of interest?

The Real Agenda Behind the Climate Change Scam

Last, but not least, let's consider who is leading the charge to have this theory accepted and government policy based upon it. They are exclusively the hard left, the same people who were so wrong about everything in the twentieth century.

Most people forget that at the beginning of the twentieth century, the left actually argued that socialism was a better system than capitalism. They didn't say it was necessary to save the planet from global warming or pollution. They said it was a better system on its own merits.

The next one hundred years was like a laboratory experiment

to test that theory. It wasn't a completely controlled experiment, because even the United States was partially poisoned with socialist policies. But Russia, China, and many other countries tried full-out communism. It was a disaster.

Even discounting the hundreds of millions who died in wars or purges under communism, it still failed. Eight thousand years after the discovery of agriculture, tens of millions just plain starved to death, all directly as a result of the economic system imposed upon them. It was the single most tragic failure of an idea in human history. That's why Putin said nobody wants to see it repeated.

Now, the very same people who pushed this tragic failure of an idea are pushing the climate change narrative. Being familiar with his writing on economics, it is not surprising to see the pope lining up with them. Cardinal Wuerl confirmed this when he made the familiar Marxist "sustainable development" argument at an international forum on economics and the environment in May.[27]

We're supposed to believe that it's no coincidence that the only possible way for us to save the planet is for us to accept the same failed sociopolitical system that killed hundreds of millions in the twentieth century.

Pope Francis may be a lot of things, but he's not stupid. No one rises to the highest office in an organization as large as the Catholic Church without being creative, smart, and educated. That doesn't mean he is intentionally promoting something he knows to be wrong. Again, he was raised in an anticapitalist culture within which socialist fallacies are constantly reinforced. Even intelligent people can form emotional attachments to ideas that overcome their reason if those attachments are formed early enough.

The same may not be true for the people he's siding with. When Al Gore left office as vice president of the United States in 2001, his net worth was less than $2 million. By 2013, it was estimated at over $300 million.[28] He's made it all on climate change and other left-wing scams, including selling Current TV to Al Jazeera, who used its assets to launch Al Jazeera America. He's also made a nice bundle trading on companies that received government subsidies for green technology. Do you think he's shrinking his "carbon footprint"? Not a chance. Gore spends over $30,000 a year on electric and gas bills.[29] That's over twenty times the national average.

When you follow the money, you find a rogues' gallery of people making money off this scam, including friends and relatives of congressmen and wealthy executives of "green energy companies." The latter benefit when their companies' stock prices soar because of government funding or loan guarantees, only to fall like a stone when it turns out their product doesn't work or is too cost-prohibitive. They don't care. They sell out when the stock is high and live happily ever after, leaving taxpayers with the losses.

Everybody involved in this scam gets what they want. Politicians get to tax, spend, and regulate more. Crony capitalists get to make fortunes, returning a portion to their politician friends in the form of campaign contributions. Bought-and-sold scientists get funding to continue their research, which they then intentionally misinterpret and misrepresent.

All of this comes at a cost, and guess who gets the bill? You do. It's not just the $22 billion directly stolen from taxpayers and wasted by the government on this nonexistent problem. It's also the higher prices you pay for energy, which will go even higher if Obama and Lenin's pope are successful. It's the higher prices of other products due to energy costs driving up the price of bringing them to market. It's the costs passed onto consumers of complying with all of the insane regulations imposed to avert the phony crisis.

There is also the opportunity cost of stifling creativity, distorting market prices, and overriding consumer choices inherent in the socialist system they're building based on this sham. Who knows? In a truly free market, someone may have already discovered a better energy source than fossil fuels. We'll never know. The capital that might have funded that discovery was wasted on Solyndra and other tax-subsidized green-energy disasters.

I have no problem with people making money, even lots and lots of it. That's what a free country is all about. Freedom is the opportunity to work hard and change your economic circumstances by providing great benefits to others. That's how true capitalists become wealthy. They provide society with billions in products and get billions of dollars in return. Everybody wins.

That's not how socialism works. In a socialist system, the ruling class extracts everything everyone else produces and offers nothing in return. It's what I call trickle-up poverty. The ruling class keeps living large off the people, the middle class shrinks, and the lowest class expands.

Many people mistakenly believe there was no income disparity in the communist Soviet Union. That's not true. If you think Joseph Stalin lived in a one-room apartment like his "comrades," you're sadly naïve.

Stalin actually lived like a king in his dacha at Sochi, a luxurious palace in the resort town that recently hosted the Winter Olympics.[30] The difference between Stalin's wealth and Steve Jobs's was the latter earned it and the former stole it. Jobs made billions by producing products for which people voluntarily exchanged their money. Stalin pointed a gun and said, "Give it to me or I'll shoot." Actually, some dissenters were lucky enough to go to the gulag.

One can't help noticing the similarity to our vacationer in chief or the First Lady with her seventy-five ladies-in-waiting. Serving in the federal government was a financial hardship for many of our founding fathers. During his second term as vice president, John Adams had to rent a room from Secretary of the Senate Samuel Otis and his wife.[31] For the Obamas, it has been a huge step up in lifestyle, just as it was for Stalin.

This is the truth about socialism. It isn't about equality. That's just the sales pitch. It's about rulers and the ruled. It's about a few people at the top living like royalty while everyone else struggles to get by, all the while being told that thoughts of keeping their own money are selfish and unpatriotic. It's a scam.

It also always ends in disaster, as it did in Russia, China, and every other country that tried it. It will end in disaster in Europe, too. It's just happening more slowly there because they have a mixed economy. They've attempted to mix capitalism and socialism to get the benefits of both. It hasn't worked, because it can't work. The European social democracies will all eventually collapse, just as Greece has. The taller trees just take longer to fall.

Let's hope it's not too late to keep the United States from proving no tree is too tall.

That brings us back to what Lenin's pope and Obama are *really* teaming up to do. The pope will release his encyclical on climate change and lend his full support to the lame-duck

Marxist signing the Kyoto Protocol or something worse at the United Nations. Then the people who failed to convince American voters that socialism was a good idea will have an excuse to impose it on them anyway as the only solution to climate change.

The Marxist Encyclical: On Care for Our Communist Home

Remember when I said the Church limits papal infallibility to a very narrow range of subjects? Well, encyclicals have traditionally been issued by popes on only the most important religious issues. That naturally limits them to subjects the author knows something about.

Pope Francis has thrown that principle out the window for purely political reasons. His *Laudato Si: On Care for Our Common Home*[32] is a thinly veiled political manifesto, combining pronouncements on both economics and climate science the pope has no expertise in whatsoever. In it, he takes all of the scientific and economic fallacies I've already talked about and stamps them with the official seal of the Church.

The encyclical opens with some quotes from Saint Francis of Assisi that appear cherry-picked to sound like the leftist, New Age "Gaia" narrative. That's no accident. The pope's scientific advisor for this letter is the radical Gaia-worshipper and climate hoax scientist Hans Joachim Schellnhuber. Consider this passage:

> *In the words of this beautiful canticle, Saint Francis of Assisi reminds us that our common home is like a sister with whom*

we share our life and a beautiful mother who opens her arms to embrace us. "Praise be to you, my Lord, through our Sister, Mother Earth, who sustains and governs us, and who produces various fruit with coloured flowers and herbs."[33]

Saint Francis's poetic language here may sound like paganism, but not when taken within the whole context of his writing. He was certainly very concerned about the environment and all of God's creatures, but he didn't worship the Earth itself as a goddess, as the pagans did. Neither did he consider it a living organism, as the modern, secular Gaia cult does. But look where the Pope takes that imagery in the next paragraph:

This sister now cries out to us because of the harm we have inflicted on her by our irresponsible use and abuse of the goods with which God has endowed her.[34]

That didn't come from Saint Francis; it came from the pope. Or, I should say it came from Schellnhuber, as this is straight Gaia cult nonsense, wherein the Earth is alive and human beings are inflicting violence upon her.

Schellnhuber's beliefs include a whole range of radical ideas that would horrify most Catholics.[35] Not only does he embrace the idea that the Earth is a living, conscious organism, but he sees human beings as a threat that must be diminished. He has said the "carrying capacity" of the Earth is below one billion people, although he's backed away from that statement when confronted.[36] Schellnhuber belongs to a whole subgroup of radical liberal environmentalists who believe the human population must be vastly decreased to save their Earth goddess.

In fairness to the Pope, he somewhat disclaims this portion of Schellnhuber's insane worldview, although I wish he was a bit more emphatic:

> *At one extreme, we find those who doggedly uphold the myth of progress and tell us that ecological problems will solve themselves simply with the application of new technology and without any need for ethical considerations or deep change. At the other extreme are those who view men and women and all their interventions as no more than a threat, jeopardizing the global ecosystem, and consequently the presence of human beings on the planet should be reduced and all forms of intervention prohibited. Viable future scenarios will have to be generated between these extremes, since there is no one path to a solution.[37]*

The solutions will have to be "generated between these extremes"? What does that mean? Do we just need to eliminate a few billion people, not six billion as Schellnhuber implies with his "carrying capacity" statements? How can there be any compromise at all with these insane theories?

With Schellnhuber advising him and his own Marxist biases, Pope Francis has produced a gargantuan piece of leftist propaganda that includes just about every hard-left fallacy ever foisted upon the gullible, including the Gaia cult narrative, the climate change hoax, Marx's thoroughly discredited economic theories, and the standard class warfare our demagogic president promotes every chance he gets.

He even manages to work in a deferential reference to Islam, quoting an Islamic poet in a footnote to a passage on the "mystical meaning to be found in a leaf, in a mountain trail, in a dewdrop, in a poor person's face."[38]

There ought to be an impeachment process for popes when they use the power of their office to mislead the faithful so egregiously.

Throughout his treatise, the pope cites excessive consumption as one of the root causes of both environmental damage and global poverty. If you and I would just lower our standard of living, everything would be fine. Of course, the pope doesn't seem to realize there is something quite hypocritical about a man who flies around the world on a private jet lecturing the rest of us about our standard of living. Like all socialists, he believes he is an exception to his own rules about what wealth everyone else is entitled to.

He certainly has some rules in mind for *your* money. He confirms the real agenda behind the global warming hoax here:

> *To blame population growth instead of extreme and selective consumerism on the part of some, is one way of refusing to face the issues. It is an attempt to legitimize the present model of distribution, where a minority believes that it has the right to consume in a way which can never be universalized, since the planet could not even contain the waste products of such consumption.*[39]

Isn't that convenient? We need a different "model of distribution," meaning government redistribution of wealth, because if everyone consumed as much as the "minority" there would be too much waste. This is so illogical it's hard to know where to start.

First, the Pope conveniently forgets that rich people

consume more because they've produced more *for other people.*
A billionaire acquires his billions by providing billions of dollars in products to his customers. Who consumes the products
the billionaire sells to get his money? It isn't the billionaire. It
is his customers, the mass market.

Second, the pope nonchalantly implies this "minority"
doesn't have a *right* to spend money they've earned by providing products of equal value to other people. How can that be?
When a businessman exchanges $1 million in products for $1
million in money, why do his customers have a right to consume $1 million in products if he has no right to consume the
money he received in exchange for them?

These are garden-variety socialist fallacies, but the pope
doesn't end there. He actually trots out one of Marx's theories
that is so discredited even modern-day Marxists have backed
away from it:

> *Production is not always rational, and is usually tied to eco-
> nomic variables which assign to products a value that does
> not necessarily correspond to their real worth. This frequently
> leads to an overproduction of some commodities, with unnec-
> essary impact on the environment and with negative results
> on regional economies.*[40]

Marx's theory of overproduction was a foundational plank
in *Das Kapital,* or *Capital* in English. Marx argued that a capitalist system results in firms producing so much that they
force down the prices of their own goods, thereby diminishing profits and ultimately necessitating layoffs. Workers find
themselves poor "in the midst of plenty," unable to afford the

goods they previously produced. This is the root cause of what Marx described as the inevitable "crisis" of capitalism.

This is what the pope refers to when he says irrational production results in "negative results in regional economies." He very appropriately links alarmism about destruction of the environment to this communist claptrap. After all, promoting Marxism is what the environmental movement is really about.

Academia still hangs on to Marx's lunatic ravings, even after history has proven him wrong again and again. Over the course of the nineteenth century, consumer prices did fall dramatically as productive capacity and efficiency increased. But it didn't make workers poorer. It made them richer, especially since wages went up even as prices went down. These facts are not in dispute.

Marx's theory doesn't even make logical sense in a classroom. Even if wages had remained the same, what economists call their real wages would have risen, since purchasing power increases as prices fall. This isn't rocket science. If the cost of apples falls from two dollars per apple to one dollar per apple, you can buy twice as many apples with the same ten-dollar bill.

This century hasn't been any kinder to Marx. As I mentioned before, worldwide poverty has been cut in half precisely because so many previously socialist countries have dramatically reformed their economies to be more capitalist. Just as workers in nineteenth-century America realized a spectacular rise in living standards as the American economy became more productive, so, too, are Third World nations today seeing millions escape from poverty by essentially doing exactly the opposite of what the pope says they should do.

Regardless, the pope is still pushing the same program as our Marxist president. He wants the most productive people in America and other First World nations to lower their living standards to accommodate wealth redistribution to Third World nations, even as he and the golfer in chief continue to live like kings, just as Stalin did in his communist paradise. Somehow, this will also save the world from global warming:

> *That is why the time has come to accept decreased growth in some parts of the world, in order to provide resources for other places to experience healthy growth. Benedict XVI has said that "technologically advanced societies must be prepared to encourage more sober lifestyles, while reducing their energy consumption and improving its efficiency."*[41]

This is the same reasoning that produced the War on Poverty in America, which has given us record numbers of people on food stamps and other forms of government welfare. Obama, the pope, and the rest of the Marxist progressives want to employ the same model on a worldwide scale.

Heaven help us if they succeed.

CHAPTER 9

Zero Science

Earlier this year, a study by Germany's Max Planck Institute for Meteorology[1] dealt what American climate scientists Pat Michaels and Chip Knappenberger called a "death blow" to global warming hysteria.[2] The study proves what any real scientist already knew: the Intergovernmental Panel on Climate Change (IPCC) models that predict significant warming with increases in atmospheric carbon dioxide are wrong.

Nevertheless, the president continues to pursue his Climate Change Action Plan[3] with strong support from progressives, including the pope, who use this imaginary crisis to pursue their all-out attack on private property and free enterprise. This isn't just my opinion. Maurice Newman, the chief business advisor to Australian prime minister Tony Abbott, said precisely that in an op-ed earlier this year.

"This is not about facts or logic. It's about a new world order under the control of the UN," he wrote in the *Australian*. "It is opposed to capitalism and freedom and has made environmental catastrophism a household topic to achieve its objective."[4]

Scientific evidence refuting the progressive climate change

scam continues to mount up, yet progressive politicians, media, educators, and politically captured scientists continue to advance the theory as if it were scientifically proven fact. This is what happens when the government hijacks science for political purposes. It's happened before and it's happening right now in America.

Lysenkoism: Then and Now

Science was hijacked by the government in the Soviet Union under Obama's role model, Joseph Stalin. For more than three decades, the Soviet scientific community entered a dark age now known as Lysenkoism. It was a period when all scientific discovery and advancement halted and regressed, thanks to the political dominance over Soviet science by a man named Trofim Lysenko.

I remember studying genetics in the late 1950s, when genetics was a huge subject. We were all fascinated by learning the structure of DNA. James Watson and Francis Crick put out *The Double Helix* ten years later. It was one of the most exciting periods for science in my lifetime. But there was one place in the world where Watson and Crick's great accomplishment wasn't being celebrated.

In the Soviet Union under Stalin, people were forbidden to believe that genes exist, just like people in Obama's America are forbidden to believe that man-made climate change *doesn't* exist. Marxists have to stamp out the truth or no one would tolerate their rule. That's why Stalin needed a fake scientist to push Lysenkoism in the USSR and why Obama needs fake scientists to push global warming in the USSA.

Lysenko rose to prominence during the 1930s. The Soviet

agricultural system was dying and people were starving because of communism. Russia had once been an exporter of wheat, but after Stalin collectivized the farms, production plummeted.

So the perversion of science in the Soviet Union was a direct result of the economic failures of communism. The pattern might sound familiar. First, Stalin attacked the middle-class farmers. Calling them kulaks, he said they were exploiters. He accused them of robbing from the people by charging too much for the produce of the land.

Does this sound familiar? Does it sound like the fairness doctrine—the litany you hear from Al Sharpton and the brigades of spineless sea creatures on the left about "fairness"?

Once Stalin had successfully demonized the middle-class farmers, he stole their land and turned it into government-owned-and-operated farms. But the government can't manage anything. It couldn't do it in Russia and it can't do it here.

How's the postal service working? It's so great that Federal Express and other private services are used by most businesses. Are you looking forward to Obamacare, which is Stalin-care in drag? You think government will give you better doctors, shorter wait times, or lower costs? The Russians did. That's why thirty million Russians starved to death as a direct result of collective farming and other idiotic socialist ideas.

So, along comes this crackpot Lysenko, who says he has found a new way to increase agricultural production in Russia. It was based on a Lamarckian view of heredity, meaning it was based on the work of Jean-Baptiste Lamarck. Lamarck preceded Darwin by several decades and is an important figure in the history of science. However, the basis for many of his theories, that *acquired* traits can be passed on to offspring, was acknowledged as mistaken even in Lysenko's day.

The idea that acquired traits can become hereditary is almost as ludicrous as the theory that man is causing global warming with industrial activity. One of Lamarck's examples of an acquired trait was the long necks of giraffes. Lamarck theorized that giraffes living in areas where they needed to reach the leaves on high trees stretched their necks in attempting to reach them and somehow this stretching was passed on to their offspring.

He didn't say Darwinian natural selection occurred, where over many generations the giraffes with longer necks survived at a higher rate than those with shorter necks and eventually only the long neck trait survived. No, Lamarck believed that when a giraffe stretched its neck, *that giraffe itself* passed on the newly acquired trait to its own offspring.

It's like believing a person with an average physique who changes his body style with intensive weight training can pass on the body builder's physique he acquired to his children. Today, it sounds so ridiculous that one wouldn't even require scientific proof to dismiss it. But it was the only acceptable theory in the Soviet Union for decades. This is what happens when science becomes the stepchild of politics.

Lysenko rejected the theories of evolution based on Gregor Mendel's work, which is the basis for all modern genetic theory. As I said, Lysenko actually believed genes didn't exist, a view shared by Stalin. Stalin denounced genetic theory as "idealist," a pejorative he used often for anything that didn't please him. It was one of his favorite "snarl words" for anything that didn't fit into his confused worldview.[5]

Stalin also believed the combination of Mendel's ideas with Charles Darwin's theory of natural selection sounded too much like the competition inherent in capitalism. How biological processes can possibly have any relevance to economics is hard to imagine, but Stalin wasn't the only one who held this view in the Soviet Union back then.

However, there was a more pressing, practical reason for Stalin to support Lysenko's crackpot theories: the faster results he promised to deliver in increasing agricultural production. Since Lysenko claimed plants could pass acquired traits to offspring, he could achieve new species of plants, including wheat that would grow in colder temperatures, a lot faster than the real scientists studying genetics. Stalin needed quick results to combat the famine he caused with his disastrous socialist policies.

Do you see the connection between socialism and pseudoscience? The people were against farm collectivization, just like Americans today are against carbon taxes or open borders. This resistance, along with the inherent problems of socialism itself, combined to destroy agricultural productivity. Stalin needed a miracle from his scientists not only to make agriculture more productive, but to convince the people not to completely revolt against socialism.

The problem was that real science didn't promise miracles, any more than it does today. Any improvement to Soviet crops through genetics would take many generations, which was time Stalin didn't have. He needed immediate gratification. So, just as people suffering from the mental disorder called liberalism ignore economic reality, Stalin threw his support behind a man who ignored scientific reality. What real scientists said would take years or decades, the crackpot Lysenko promised to do in months. As David Joravsky tells us, they even started to believe their own nonsense.

But Stalinist bosses saw themselves as popular leaders in the creation of an abundant new society; after a few disappointments with agricultural science, they angrily switched their support to pseudoscience. They needed to believe the line they were handing out, that collectivization was creating the most advanced farming system in the world.[6]

There was only one problem. It wasn't true. Regardless of how much Stalin or Lysenko wanted to deny the existence of genes or affirm the theory of acquired traits, any experiments based on those idiotic beliefs were bound to fail, just like everything the academic socialists in Washington do fails.

They did fail, but Lysenko was either too incompetent or too obstinate to recognize it. Not being a real scientist, Lysenko was able to break all the rules of the scientific method I described to you and not realize, or at least not admit to himself, that anything was wrong.

It is just like when the unemployment number falls because they stop counting people who have given up looking for work, not because they found jobs. Our Marxist in chief actually believes he's done something good. That's part of the mental disorder. Liberals aren't just stupid. They're delusional.

Regardless of the absurdity of his theories, Lysenko rose to become the most powerful scientist in the Soviet Union, all because his crackpot theories fulfilled a political purpose. Science ceased being a search for truth and became a search to validate Stalin's policies, just as climate science is no longer a search for truth, but a search to validate cap-and-trade and more regulation on businesses.

While Lysenko never had any support among real scientists, he was passionately supported by government journalists, just like the climate change con artists are supported by the media today. They only wanted to report what the government wanted them to report, that communism was working fine. Doesn't that sound familiar?

Purging Scientists Who Dissent

With Stalin and the press behind Lysenko, anyone in the Soviet Union who stood up to him was publicly denounced, the way Obama denounces people today. They lost Communist Party membership, the way you are thrown out of clubs today if you express conservative views. They lost their jobs, the way you can lose your job if you talk about affirmative action being a disaster for America or about the lie of global warming.

You didn't know you could lose your job if you didn't go along with the global warming con artists? Didn't your local newspaper carry that, either? Well, it happens all the time in the new Soviet America. It didn't start with Obama. Mr. Scam Artist himself, Al Gore, was doing it over twenty years ago.

In 1993, Gore fired physicist William Happer from his job as director of energy research for the U.S. Department of Energy. Happer had testified to Congress that the scientific data didn't support the alarmist fears being propagated at the time about ozone depletion and global warming. "I was told that science was not going to intrude on public policy," said Happer. "I did not need the job that badly."[7]

It can get even worse. Just as he purged anyone who resisted his political and economic agenda, Stalin purged scientists who rejected Lysenko's crackpot hereditary theories. He certainly wasn't going to let science intrude on public policy, either.

We don't have purges yet here in the United States, but only because the radicals promoting climate change know they can't get away with it. But listen to their rhetoric. They call Tea Partiers "terrorists" and openly call for "climate change deniers" to be jailed. Wrote Adam Weinstein in Gawker:

> *Man-made climate change happens. Man-made climate change kills a lot of people. It's going to kill a lot more. We have laws on the books to punish anyone whose lies contribute to people's deaths. It's time to punish the climate-change liars.*[8]

Don't be so quick to dismiss people like this as the lunatic fringe. The Nazis and Bolsheviks were fringe right up until the day they took over. This is just how it started with Lysenko. The press just loved him because his dumb theories validated Stalin. The Soviet press played a major role in bolstering Stalin's persecution of scientists who disagreed with him.

The same forces that were at work in the Soviet Union under Stalin are attacking scientific truth in America today. This is what Obama has done to science, to medicine, and to reality itself. We are living in a new Soviet era in America.

How Real Science Works

Let me speak to you as a scientist for a moment. That's right: I am a scientist, who has actually done scientific research *scientifically*. I earned a bachelor's degree in biology, two master's degrees in ethnobotany and anthropology, respectively, and a Ph.D. in nutritional ethnomedicine from the University of California, Berkeley. In order to earn these degrees, I had to not only collect and analyze data, but draw scientifically valid conclusions that other scientists concurred with.

When I say I did scientific research scientifically, I mean that I followed the standards commonly referred to as the scientific method. The scientific method has certain rules you have to follow or you're not doing science. You have to ensure the integrity of your data. You have to make sure your data is representative. You have to control for other possible causes of your results.

Once you've completed your study and published your results, they are subject to what scientists call peer review. That means that other scientists examine your work. They try to confirm you haven't made any errors in the way you've collected data or errors of logic in your conclusions.

I had to follow all of these principles to earn my Ph.D. It doesn't take an advanced degree to understand them. They're common sense. But when the government takes over science, common sense goes out the window.

Lysenko didn't follow any of these principles, because he wasn't a real scientist. He was a political appointee whose crackpot theories were accepted only by politicians and journalists for political reasons, just like the climate change scam is accepted only by politicians and scientists who want more government, more taxes, and more regulations.

That political action group posing as a scientific community, the Intergovernmental Panel on Climate Change (IPCC), says the debate is over about man-made global warming. That's how you know they're not real scientists.

Real scientists never say "the debate is over" about anything. All scientific knowledge is open to challenge at all times. That's how all great advances have been made. Imagine if the debate had been over when Isaac Newton had published his theories, meaning Albert Einstein never published his. Imagine if the debate had been over when scientists concluded that man could not fly.

The IPCC is a collection of politicians and bought-off scientists who are producing junk science for political reasons. It's Lysenkoism all over again. They've broken every rule of the scientific method, just as Lysenko did.

First, their samples aren't representative. One of the reasons NASA's Goddard Institute for Space Studies (GISS) was able to report 2014 as "the hottest year on record" is because of huge increases in part of South America, encompassing parts of Brazil, Paraguay, and Argentina. Guess what? There are almost no weather stations in the region.[9] What few stations there are certainly can't be representative of such a massive region.

They also use temperature readings from thermometers located in places that are obviously hotter than the larger surrounding area, like parking lots, concrete buildings, or inside metal beams. Do you think maybe that skews temperature readings a little warmer than they otherwise would be? Meteorologist Anthony Watts saw right through it. He studied the positioning of the so-called weather stations and called out the con artists.

The question remains as to why they continue to use a polluted mix of well-sited and poorly-sited stations.[10]

Just like Lysenko, the bought-and-sold climate scientists consistently fail to control for other causes of temperature changes. In attempting to answer Watts's questions about the location of weather stations, the fake scientists say satellite data confirms the findings on the ground. Watts called them on that scam, too. It's a classic case of failure to control for other possible causes.

> *I don't dispute the satellite measurements, but they are measuring temperature of the atmosphere above the Earth, and that includes all cities and populated areas as well as rural open space... My premise is this: if you want to see the effect of CO_2 on warming, you need to look in areas that have not been affected by urbanization to find the true signal.*[11]

No one disputes that temperatures are warmer in and around cities. It's not because of greenhouse gases. Cities just generate more heat. If man was causing global warming, the temperature should be higher in the country, too. As I said, you don't have to be a scientist. It's just common sense.

A larger percentage of the Earth has been urbanized over the past several decades, so satellite measurements read higher temperatures. Watts was quick to recognize this, as any real scientist would be. It didn't occur to the climate change pseudoscientists because they aren't interested in finding the truth. They are interested in promoting their political agenda.

Global Warming and Cooling Are Natural

Increased urbanization isn't even the most significant reason there might be warmer temperatures. The real reason the planet is warmer today is that it's *normal* for the Earth to go through warming and cooling periods. It's been doing so for millions of years, long before man inhabited this planet, much less started building factories.

Neither temperatures nor CO_2 levels are anywhere near their peak over Earth's history. During the Cretaceous period, approximately 145 to 66 million years ago, mean atmospheric CO_2 content was about 1700 ppm. That's six times what it was just before the industrial revolution. In October 2014 it was 395.93 ppm, still orders of magnitude lower than during the Cretaceous period.

Mean surface temperature during the Cretaceous period was 18°C, 4°C higher than it is now!

During this period of significantly higher atmospheric CO_2 and temperature levels, life was flourishing. Dinosaurs continued to dominate the land, but new groups of mammals, birds, and flowering plants appeared.[12] That's not a big surprise. Contrary to what fake scientists tell you, higher CO_2 levels are good for plants and warmer temperatures are good for life in general.

As I've said before, you don't have to go back millions of years to find much warmer temperatures than anything we've seen during the industrial age. Temperatures were warmer and ice sheets smaller during the Medieval Warm Period, just one thousand years ago. Dr. Reid A. Bryson, universally recognized as the father of modern climatology, confirms that even today the ice in Greenland covers old Viking farms.[13]

No one disputes Bryson is a real scientist, not even the climate change hucksters. Do you know what he says about hysterical cries that glaciers in the Alps are receding? He says it's all happened before.

What do they find when the ice sheets retreat, in the Alps?...A silver mine! The guys had stacked up their tools because they were going to be back the next spring to mine more silver, only the snow never went.... There used to be less ice than now. It's just getting back to normal.[14]

Bryson's a real climate scientist, the father of the whole discipline, and he doesn't believe the climate change scam at all. He's not alone among real scientists. There are actually thirty-one thousand who have signed the following petition to formally register their dissent to this politically motivated hoax:

We urge the United States government to reject the global warming agreement that was written in Kyoto, Japan in December, 1997, and any other similar proposals. The proposed limits on greenhouse gases would harm the environment, hinder the advance of science and technology, and damage the health and welfare of mankind.

There is no convincing scientific evidence that human release of carbon dioxide, methane, or other greenhouse gases is causing or will, in the foreseeable future, cause catastrophic heating of the Earth's atmosphere and disruption of the Earth's climate. Moreover, there is substantial scientific evidence that increases in atmospheric carbon dioxide produce many beneficial effects upon the natural plant and animal environments of the Earth.[15]

Obviously for these tens of thousands of scientists, the debate is not over. For real scientists, it never is. That means the IPCC's scientists' work hasn't passed peer review at all. The IPCC simply smears or ignores any scientist who doesn't concur.

As I've said, one of the things peer review helps scientists avoid is basic errors in logic. Well, the fake scientists in the

IPCC have made an error so long recognized it actually has a Latin name: *cum hoc ergo propter hoc*. Literally, it means "with this, therefore because of this." Sometimes we restate it as "correlation does not necessarily imply causation."

They haven't just made this classic error, they've built their entire house upon it. Here's what happened. They looked at data that indicates warming periods have been accompanied by increased levels of carbon dioxide in the atmosphere over time. That could mean carbon dioxide causes warming. It could mean warming causes increased levels of carbon dioxide. Or, it could mean neither. Maybe something else caused both temperatures and carbon dioxide levels to rise.

That's how a real scientist would think. That's how I had to think to complete my Ph.D. dissertation. But since the IPCC scientists' agenda from the beginning was political instead of scientific, they immediately assumed the higher carbon dioxide levels were *causing* the warming. They never considered the alternatives, because the alternatives wouldn't support the socialist politicians.

Inconvenient Research—The Vostok Ice Core Samples

They got away with it until some very inconvenient research occurred. Many of you have never heard of the Vostok ice core samples. But have you heard about Al Gore's big lie sample? Well, look up the Vostok ice core sample.

This research is very important. It's real data. It's not created by Al Gore. It's not created for the pope. It was obtained by drilling down into the ice above Lake Vostok in Antarctica to a depth of ten thousand feet. French and Russian scientists obtained deep core samples allowing them to look at, among other things, the history of temperature and carbon dioxide over the past 420,000 years.

Guess what? The samples did show that increases in carbon dioxide always accompanied increases in temperature, but the increases in temperature always came first.[16] The increases in CO_2 *consistently lagged behind temperature increases* by about eight hundred years.

That proves increased levels of carbon dioxide in the atmosphere *didn't cause warming*. How could it have, if it didn't happen until after the warming? This knocks over the whole house of cards.

That's not all the Vostok ice core samples tell us. As Joe Martino reports, 325,000 years ago, global temps and CO_2 levels were higher than they are today.[17] I guess Barack Obama didn't get any of this when he was at Columbia learning how to become a community agitator.

In fact, we are right now near the end of another warm interglacial. And those of us who are educated in science know we're actually heading into another glacial cooling period where global temperatures will drop and ice will again form heavily at the poles. It's already happening. The Antarctic has just had the greatest growth of ice in a very long period of time.[18] Don't take my word for it. Research it yourself.

So what can we say about this group of political radicals and their fake climate change research? In short, they don't do scientific research scientifically. Their data is not representative of the Earth's climate as a whole. They don't control for other causes of temperature change. Their methodology and results are not approved by their peers, other than those bought off by the politicians. But that's not the most damning evidence against this scam.

Where's the Warming?

If I were a news reporter, my editor might say I've buried the lead. Until now, I've given the climate con artists the benefit of the doubt that they are at least working with real data. They're not.

Remember when I told you the very first thing a scientist has to do is protect the integrity of his data? To ensure that it was really being gathered accurately and properly? Well, it goes without saying that there is no integrity in your data if you're intentionally altering the results yourself. It turns out that's just what these climate change scientists have been doing.

At the time of this writing, what Chris Booker of the *Telegraph* called "the biggest science scandal ever" was just coming to light. Booker says that future generations will be shocked at "the extent to which the official temperature records—on which the entire panic ultimately rested—were systematically 'adjusted' to show the Earth as having warmed much more than the actual data justified."[19]

Booker has been following the work of several researchers who have proved conclusively that even the temperature data the IPCC cites as evidence of its theory is completely bogus. Not only have measurements been altered to show warming trends where there is no trend at all, they have actually had the audacity to turn cooling trends into warming trends. Traust Jonsson, who formerly headed climate research at the Iceland office, expressed surprise that current reporting "completely 'disappears' Iceland's 'sea ice years' around 1970, when a period of extreme cooling almost devastated his country's economy."[20]

They did the same thing with data at three different sites in Paraguay. For all three sites, high temperatures in the 1960s were adjusted downward and lower temperatures thereafter were adjusted upward to turn a fifty-year cooling trend into a warming trend.[21]

It's not just Iceland and Paraguay. They've changed temperature records all over the world to show warming where it doesn't exist, including Australia, Canada, New Zealand, England, New York, Costa Rica, and Alaska. The whole list is too long to reproduce here, but Joseph D'Aleo and Anthony Watts have put together a comprehensive report called "Surface Temperature Records: Policy Drive Deception?"[22] I suggest you read it. Then you'll start to see what is really going on.

You can't say the climate change con artists aren't creative. They are even willing to combine unrepresentative data with data manipulation to get the results they want. Here's an excerpt from this report:

> The Ria Novosti agency reported that the Moscow-based Institute of Economic Analysis (IEA) issued a report claiming that the Hadley Center for Climate Change had probably tampered with Russian climate data:
>
> "The IEA believes that Russian meteorological station data did not substantiate the anthropogenic global-warming theory. Analysts say Russian meteorological stations cover most of the country's territory and that the Hadley Center had used data submitted by only 25% of such stations in its reports. The Russian station count dropped from 476 to 121

so over 40% of Russian territory was not included in global temperature calculations for some other reasons rather than the lack of meteorological stations and observations."

The data of stations located in areas not listed in the Hadley Climate Research Unit Temperature UK (HadCRUT) survey often show no substantial warming in the late 20th century and the early 21st century.[23]

Engineering physicist and heat transfer specialist Mike Brakey found similar tampering with climate history records in the State of Maine. In his own words:

Over the last months I have discovered that between 2013 and 2015 some government bureaucrats have rewritten Maine climate history... (and New England's and of the U.S.). This statement is not based on my opinion, but on facts drawn from NOAA 2013 climate data vs. NOAA 2015 climate data after they re-wrote it.

We need only compare the data. They cooked their own books.[24]

Brakey goes on to present chart data proving his allegations conclusively.

Does that seem shocking to you? It isn't to me. It's what happens when a crypto-Marxist president and his allies in Congress get control of the scientific community. It's Lysenkoism. Just like Stalin, Obama needs fake science to convince the public to accept an economic system they've already rejected at the polls, just as the kulaks rejected collective farming. Instead of Lamarckian hereditary theory, it's man-made global warming. But it's still fake.

One might ask why the polar ice caps are melting, if there really is no warming occurring. The answer might be simpler than you think. They aren't. In fact, Antarctic sea ice is increasing so rapidly that the operations manager of the Australian Antarctic Division says he may have to move some of this division's research locations.[25]

Of course, that's completely opposite of what's happening in the Arctic Circle, where sea ice is diminishing rapidly, right? Wrong. A May 2015 NASA data update shows polar ice caps at five percent above the post-1979 average in extent.[26]

Nineteen seventy-nine was an important year, because it marked the end of a thirty-year cooling trend, when ice caps were abnormally extensive. Lest we forget, the same group of socialists who want the government to take over everything because of global warming were telling us an ice age was coming during the 1970s.

When the cooling trend ended, they managed to have 1979 declared as the baseline for polar ice cap extent, even though it was atypical in terms of ice caps being much more extensive than they had been in almost sixty years.[27]

Even with this obfuscation, the data is still against the warmists. That's how crackpot this whole theory is. Even when they cheat, its supporters can't make the story stick.

How could Al Gore win the Nobel Peace Prize for his lies? How can the IPCC continue to push global warming when the data denies everything they allege? How could the pope come out and say he wants to give a speech on global warming at the UN?

It's all about politics. It's all about politics and ripping you off just as Obama rips you off to pay for the slackers, scoundrels, and grifters in our society. I'm setting the record straight by talking about the pope lining up with Obama on this global warming scam. The science does not support the big lie. It's all about stealing money from productive citizens to redistribute it to dependent voters and political cronies.

Junk Journalism for Junk Science

Just as Lysenko had an army of state journalists to smear and discredit anyone who opposed his crank theories, man-made climate change proponents and the Obama administration receive the same kind of support from the mainstream media. Anyone who suggests that politics may be compromising the science done by members of the IPCC is labeled a climate change denier. Anyone questioning the scientific validity of the CDC's statements about illegal immigrants and disease is labeled a xenophobe or a racist.

This is why we have a free press, regardless of which party is in power. The media is supposed to be skeptical of the government at all times. Even when reporters believe what politicians are telling them, they're supposed to play devil's advocate and ask the toughest questions they can think of. That's the only way to keep the government honest. It's one of the ways the people are represented, besides their political representation in Congress.

Like all dictators, President Obama abhors freedom of the press. He said so himself:

> *But a lot of it has to do with the fact that a) the balkanization of the media means that we just don't have a common place where we get common facts and a common worldview*

the way we did 20, 30 years ago. And that just keeps on accelerating, you know. And I'm not the first to observe this, but you've got the Fox News / Rush Limbaugh folks and then you've got the MSNBC folks and the—I don't know where Vox falls into that, but you guys are, I guess, for the brainiac-nerd types. But the point is that technology which brings the world to us also allows us to narrow our point of view. That's contributed to it.[28]

Obama prefers "a common place where we get common facts and a common worldview." That's what *Pravda* was in the Soviet Union. During Lysenko's reign over science, one of the common facts the media provided was that genes didn't exist. Another was the government was going to feed the people. How did those common facts work out?

The president would prefer that all dissent to his policies and the junk science used to support them were eliminated. Then, he makes the bizarre statement that technology increasing our source of news beyond the state-controlled media *narrows* our point of view! Orwell couldn't have written it any better. But Obama is probably delusional enough to believe it himself.

Lysenkoism eventually came to an end in the Soviet Union, as it inevitably had to. Scientific reality can be denied for only so long. Eventually, the people themselves just stopped believing the lies, regardless of the state media, and forced the Khrushchev regime to turn its back on Lysenko.

Lysenko was stripped of all of his power, and real scientists who had always rejected his crackpot theories stopped being persecuted. All of this happened when the people themselves refused to go along with the government nonsense that led to one crisis after another.

We have the same challenge in America today that those peasant farmers faced in Russia. We have a government that is perverting science and medicine to advance its political agenda. Pseudoscience as absurd as Lysenko's is officially recognized by the state, while real scientists are silenced or ostracized.

Just as in the Soviet Union fifty years ago, we have so-called journalists on the far left who continue to support these obtuse theories that have no validity whatsoever, and they smear anyone who dissents.

Like the Russians, we have to free ourselves from this. We have to continue to fight for the integrity of science, medicine, and the truth. Unchecked, the government will destroy the truth itself.

It won't happen this year or next year. But we will rid ourselves of these Stalinist liars in America. It will happen in our lifetimes. The truth shall set us free. It must. It's the only thing that can save us from Obama's Soviet era.

CHAPTER 10

Zero Business Sense

The Grand Illusionist's Bubble Economy

Back in March, Federal Reserve System chairwoman Janet Yellen made an unexpected announcement. She told Wall Street that a long-expected interest rate increase was unlikely. Based on that statement, the stock markets exploded out of negative territory to post huge gains.[1] That just means the bubble economy blew up a little bigger.

I've been telling my listeners for years that higher education is a bubble, caused by all the same government interventions that caused the housing bubble: cheap money and government-guaranteed loans to people who can't pay them back. It's misallocated and wasted trillions in capital, and it will end very badly.

I have news for you. It's not just the education sector that's a bubble. It's the entire U.S. economy. The grand illusionist in the White House has everyone believing that, somehow, his disastrous policies have resulted in an economic recovery. They haven't.

We haven't experienced a recovery. We've simply allowed the government and its central bank, the Federal Reserve, to blow up another bubble. Just like housing, this one is going to end badly, but it's going to be much wider in scope. Just imagine what happened in housing back in 2008 happening again, only over many sectors of the economy instead of just one. That's what is coming unless we change course now.

The key to the grand illusion is your apathy. There are few subjects more boring than monetary policy, interest rates, inflation data, and job market participation. That's what the Fed and the government count on. These numbers are reported in the media and then forgotten by 99 percent of the population. But they tell a very ominous story.

All the public is aware of is the stock market, which is at historic highs, at least nominally. It's astounding that any journalist can report on the market making new highs without emphasizing that the Federal Reserve has held interest rates at zero for over six years.

Actually, no real journalist can avoid pointing that out. We just don't have journalists in the media. We have propagandists who conveniently ignore details like unprecedented Fed intervention so they can tell us fairy tales about Obama's "recovery."

That's why Grandma Yellen's March announcement was so important. The market was deep in negative territory, because Wall Street was expecting her to say the Fed would finally start raising interest rates. That would have meant the party was over and would have resulted in a correction in the markets. It also would have meant a recession, which would hurt in the short term but is necessary to the long-term health of the economy.

That's a Savage Truth the media won't tell you. But it's true. The only way for us to get out of a bubble is for the inflated stock market prices to correct and the millions of people in jobs that wouldn't exist without the bubble to leave them and find new jobs that are sustainable without inflation. That's what happens when a bubble pops.

You have to understand how the Federal Reserve keeps interest rates down. It's a lot simpler than people think it is. The Fed creates money out of thin air and buys securities with it. That *increases* the supply of money, resulting in a *decrease* in the price of money. That's all interest rates are: the price of money. When supply goes up, all other things being equal, price goes down.

So, the Fed floods the market with new money whenever its friends on Wall Street are in danger of realizing losses. The fat cats love it, because stock prices go up. But there is a cost to everyone else. Capital gets directed to unsustainable businesses like green-energy companies, who employ people to make products that don't sell. It also makes the price of everything else go up.

I wasn't surprised when Yellen blinked at the last minute. What's good for the American people and the long-term health of the American economy doesn't matter to these crooks. All they care about is pushing the stock market higher so their fat-cat friends can rake in more billions. Then, they get out of the market or short sell it when the inevitable collapse occurs and make even more, while millions of Americans struggle to survive.

The longer the Federal Reserve keeps the stock market inflated and unsustainable businesses capitalized, the more people will be unemployed when it's over. Not only will people be unemployed, but prices will be higher because of the Fed's inflation. When the price of money goes down, the price of everything else goes up.

The media isn't telling you any of this. They're telling you there is no inflation and unemployment is low. These are all lies based on skewed government statistics. This didn't start under Obama. They've been manipulating these numbers for a long time, under Democratic and Republican presidents. Presidents of both parties are completely complicit in all of it.

Look into something called the president's Working Group on Financial Markets.[2] That's where the White House and the Fed get together to conspire on how to make the markets go up, no matter what the cost to the rest of us. It's also referred to as the Plunge Protection Team. Note that it was created by Ronald Reagan, a Republican.

The White House and the Fed have other accomplices in misleading the public. The Bureau of Labor Statistics says unemployment is down to 5.6 percent. Everyone knows that's not true. That's because they don't count unemployment the same way they used to. When an unemployed person gives up looking for work, they stop counting him or her as unemployed. That doesn't mean they have a job. They're just not counted.

Occasionally, someone from the establishment is courageous enough to call out these deceptions. Jim Clifton, the CEO and chairman of Gallup, did just that when he penned an article called "The Big Lie: 5.6% Unemployment." In it, he wrote:

> *Right now, as many as 30 million Americans are either out of work or severely underemployed. Trust me, the vast majority of them aren't throwing parties to toast "falling" unemployment.*
>
> *There's another reason why the official rate is misleading. Say you're an out-of-work engineer or healthcare worker or construction worker or retail manager: If you perform a minimum of one hour of work in a week and are paid at least*

$20—maybe someone pays you to mow their lawn—you're not officially counted as unemployed in the much-reported 5.6%. Few Americans know this.[3]

In reality, if we measured unemployment the way it was measured during the Great Depression, the numbers would look very similar to those of the Great Depression. When counting long-term discouraged workers, which were always counted before 1994, the rate goes from 5.6 percent to 23 percent![4] That's why nobody's real-world experience seems to agree with the media narrative on Obama's recovery.

So, we have a twofold problem with employment. We have millions of people unemployed that the government won't even admit to. Plus, we have millions more employed in the wrong jobs—jobs that wouldn't exist if it weren't for the bubble. That doesn't mean they would be unemployed, too. If the Federal Reserve weren't misdirecting capital with its inflationary policies, capital would flow to where it's needed to create *real* jobs.

Unemployment isn't the only number being manipulated. We're told inflation has been lower than 2 percent for years. That doesn't jibe with the experience of most Americans trying to pay their bills. That's because the government plays all kinds of tricks with the Consumer Price Index, too.[5] One of them is to simply remove items whose prices go up from the basket of goods it measures.

It's the same trick they do with unemployment. When something contradicts the narrative, they just don't count it. That doesn't change the truth. The truth is prices are rising rapidly. I don't think I have to tell you that. But by manipulating the official statistics, they accomplish two goals. They avoid paying higher cost-of-living adjustments to Social Security beneficiaries, and they lend apparent legitimacy to the government's economic recovery narrative.

The key to the grand illusion is your willingness to accept the lies. As I said, interest rates, inflation statistics, and unemployment rate adjustments are *boring*. Nobody wants to be bothered with these details. Frankly, nobody should have to worry about them. The government isn't supposed to be engaged full-time in deceiving us.

Unfortunately, it is deceiving us full-time and has been for many decades, under both Democratic and Republican administrations. But this one has really taken deception to a new level and the media has been more complicit than at any time in history. Let me give you a few examples.

First, we constantly hear that Obama inherited a mess in terms of the economy. That's true; he did. But no one seems to remember the mess George W. Bush inherited at the beginning of his term. The NASDAQ crash occurred in April 2000, while Bill Clinton was still in office. Bush inherited a recession caused by that bubble popping, but the media still talk about Clinton as if he did something wonderful for the economy. All he did was ride a bubble, as both Bush and Obama did after him.

I'm no fan of George W. Bush, but fair is fair. If we're going to be constantly reminded Obama inherited a recession, we should also acknowledge Bush inherited one as well. That one didn't take seven years to end, either.

In reality, neither Clinton, Bush, nor Obama did anything to help the economy. They just happened to be in office while the Federal Reserve inflated the money supply and blew up bubbles during their terms. Clinton and Bush were just unlucky enough to still be in office when their respective bubbles popped.

Not surprisingly, the media don't seem to remember the recession that started on Clinton's watch. He also gets a complete pass on the housing bubble, even though he signed the Community Reinvestment Act and appointed Franklin Delano Raines as CEO of Fannie Mae. Both were instrumental in causing the housing bubble,[6] but all anyone seems to remember is that the bubble popped when Bush was president.

Bush certainly didn't do anything to help, but facts are facts. One of the few things the Bush administration did right was to warn Congress about the risks in letting Fannie Mae assume such huge amounts of mortgage debt, which it did repeatedly starting in 2002.[7]

Regardless, Bush publicly went right on cheerleading what he called the Ownership Society while it scored him political points, even though he knew it was built on a faulty economic foundation. So, I assign equal blame to Republicans and Democrats for that disaster. If either party had been representing the American *people*, instead of their buddies on Wall Street, it could have been avoided or at least mitigated.

This may seem like ancient history for a public with a twenty-four-hour attention span, but it's important. The media narrative about Clinton's wise economic stewardship, Bush's exclusive responsibility for the financial meltdown, and Obama's phony recovery all serve one purpose. They lend legitimacy to what Obama is doing to further destroy the economy now. So do the phony economic statistics on unemployment and inflation.

As long as most of the people believe most of the lies most of the time, Obama is free to continue his rampage over the economy. He's already signed the Dodd-Frank act, chasing investment away from America even faster than Bush's

Sarbanes-Oxley Act, while making the big banks even more "too big to fail" than they already were.[8] So he protected Wall Street while setting up Main Street for another disaster with one stroke of his famous pen.

He's still going to try to raise taxes and increase regulations based on the global warming scam, which I've discussed in other chapters. He continues to push for these damaging policies, regardless of the mounting scientific evidence that the man-made climate change theory is mistaken at best, a hoax at worst.

Yet the media continue to promote this myth and defend all of the misguided policies associated with it. Late last year, the *Washington Post* ran an article entitled "Remember Solyndra? Those Loans Are Making Money."[9] The article claimed that despite a few loans that went bad, like Solyndra and Fisker Automotive, the loan program for green-energy companies was a net positive overall for taxpayers.

It turns out this was just more shady government accounting. When the profits from the program were calculated, the interest that DOE pays the government to finance its lending wasn't included in the calculations. When those costs are added, the program will actually cost taxpayers over $2 billion.[10]

At least the government is consistent in its methods. When it wants to report low unemployment, it simply doesn't count everyone who is unemployed. When it wants to report low inflation, it doesn't include products whose prices went up. When it wants to report one of its boondoggles is making a profit, it simply leaves out some of the costs.

You and I would go to jail for accounting like this. But the Grand Illusionist gets praise from the media instead.

He wouldn't be able to get away with any of this if it weren't for the Federal Reserve's unprecedented inflation and the willingness of average Americans to believe a mountain of official lies, despite indisputable evidence right before their eyes. That's why I call Obama the Grand Illusionist, and he's not finished yet.

Destroying the Dollar

One of the consequences of unprecedented inflation is supposed to be a weaker currency. When the supply of currency units go up, their value in relation to other goods goes down. That's simple supply and demand. Yet the U.S. dollar has rebounded sharply during the past year. How can that be?

The most likely explanation for this is that as bad as the Federal Reserve has been, the central banks in other First World nations have been even worse. Some, like the European Union's ECG, have inflated to fight unemployment and bail out even more socialist members like Greece, even though its mandate is strictly price stability,[11] unlike the Fed's dual mandate.

Meanwhile, export nations like China continue to manipulate their currencies downward intentionally in order to maintain trade surpluses with the United States.[12] This has hurt U.S. economic growth, but it's just another foreign policy issue the sorority has either bungled or intentionally ignored.

Keep in mind, the dollar has remained relatively stable against gold for over two years now.[13] So it's not buying more gold and it's not buying more food, health care, or stocks. Those prices have all gone up. It's not buying more of very much at all for the average American, unless you believe the phony CPI numbers put out by the Bureau of Labor Statistics.

But it is increasing in value against a number of foreign

currencies, which means the buying power of Americans is increasing for foreign goods. That's good for the average American, but bad for multinational corporations looking to sell out American workers and consumers even further. As you might expect, the media have come out in a full court press lamenting the strengthening dollar.

We're told a strong dollar will increase trade deficits, deflate stock prices, and cause a recession. Those are half-truths. Yes, it will be cheaper for Americans to buy foreign goods, but it will also be cheaper for American manufacturers to import foreign materials to make goods here. Corporate profits from overseas sales may decline slightly, but investment in new production in the United States will increase.

Do you see the connection to everything else I've talked about? A strong dollar is good for Americans living on Main Street in America. It gives an incentive to multinational corporations to make investments in America. It sacrifices a few quick profits today for long-term job and general economic growth within the United States.

As Larry Kudlow notes:

Between 1982 and 2000, as the dollar increased 178 percent, King Dollar (with lower tax rates and lighter regulation) presided over a stock market gain of 1,099 percent, a jobs increase near 40 million, and 3.5 percent average annual real GDP.

During the recent dollar decline period, from 2001 to 2011, as the dollar fell 25 percent, jobs increased a paltry 2.3 million, real GDP growth averaged less than 2 percent, and the S&P gained a measly 15 percent. [Emphasis in original.][14]

I'm not surprised the media is conducting a propaganda war against a stronger dollar. It coincides perfectly with the internationalist, progressive agenda to turn America into a depressed, European-style social democracy. A weaker dollar means foreigners own more of America, the average American can buy less with his wages, and the fat cats on Wall Street can make quicker profits without reinvesting in America.

That Americans believe the lie that a strong dollar is bad for the economy just gives Grandma Yellen one more excuse to keep pushing back the interest rate hikes necessary to arrest the enormous bubble blowing up over the whole economy.

If you want to see high-paying jobs and domestic production return to the United States, you want the dollar to stay on its upward trend. That's one bright spot in an otherwise dark and cloudy American economic landscape.

Trade Treason

There is a trade deal this traitor in the White House has been trying to push and the Republicans have supported him. They're all traitors. This deal is such a sellout for America that even Harry Reid opposed it.[15] Of course, I'm talking about the Trans-Pacific Partnership (TPP), a twelve-nation free-trade agreement that our beloved dictator has decreed be kept completely secret.

It was kept so secret that even Nancy Pelosi opposed it. Those lawmakers permitted to look at the deal had to go into the basement of the building where the documents were hidden and were not allowed to take notes with them or discuss what they read afterward. I'm not making this up. As *Politico in Europe* reported:

"It's like being in kindergarten," said Rep. Rosa DeLauro (D-Conn.), who's become the leader of the opposition to President Barack Obama's trade agenda.[16]

I call it trade treason. No one really knows what this trade deal is, but I can tell you this: It's a sellout of the American worker by both Obama and the Republicans. They want to give Asia a trade deal that will destroy us economically.

The only thing the Republicans care about is their connected friends in big business. Anything that lowers costs for gargantuan corporations is good for America, according to this faux opposition party, even if it actually harms most Americans. Another hundred thousand jobs are migrating overseas? That's okay. My friends on Wall Street will make another couple billion. The stock market will go up. That's how too many of today's Republicans think.

As far as I'm concerned, Mitch McConnell is one of the worst Benedict Arnolds in America. He said the "bipartisan effort" would help grow opportunities for "our constituents."[17] He must have meant the lobbyists. The only opportunities that will result from this deal are those pushed by the Better Business Bureau and those few multinational corporations that will benefit.

As for the bill being bipartisan, that could only be true if we had two political parties. But we don't. We have one party, the Government Zero Party.

The only ones standing in the way of this sellout right now are the Democrats and a few authentic, conservative Republicans. The Democrats oppose this because if they didn't they'd have to go back to the workers in their districts and explain why they betrayed the working man once again.

The monster in the White House, the world's worst bully, tried everything he could to scare the heck out of his own party, but they wouldn't cave. They stuck to their guns and voted down an attempt to get the Trade Promotion Authority (TPA) bill giving Obama fast track authority on this trade deal through the House.[18] The progressives would not cave in to this bully, who is wholly owned by Google, Microsoft, General Electric, and the rest of the multinational corporations.

It was actually a Progressive-Conservative coalition that defeated this bill, at least for the moment. There are a few authentic, nationalist conservatives in the Republican Party who joined the progressives in blocking this. That coalition provided a glimpse of what a true nationalist coalition would look like.

Unfortunately, it didn't last long. The House had actually voted to approve TPA the first time around, but voted down the Trade Adjustment Assistance (TAA) bill that would appropriate aid to workers who lost their jobs due to the trade deal itself. Because TPA, or "fast track," was originally contingent upon passage of TAA, Democrats were able to vote for TPA and still make sure it failed by voting against TAA, which they would otherwise support.

If that sounds confusing, welcome to Washington politics. To make a long story short, the two bills were separated, and TPA was brought up for a vote just a week later and passed the House.[19] The Senate quickly passed the House version and sent it to Obama to be signed into law.[20] This means that Obama can bring the final deal to Congress for an up-or-down vote, with no amendments allowed and debate severely restricted.

Government Zero always wins in the end.

The deal is being sold as one that will open new markets to

U.S. exports, which sounds great. But that's not what's really going to happen. We know that because they told us the same thing when they rammed the North American Free Trade Agreement (NAFTA) down our throats. Instead of increasing exports of U.S. products, it increased exports of U.S. factories and jobs.

Back when I was on the radio in the mid-1990s, I opposed NAFTA. I said it would destroy jobs in America. I said it would destroy factories in America. I said it would bring illegal aliens and drugs into America.

Was I wrong or was I right?

NAFTA decimated American manufacturing. It destroyed America's entire industrial base.

Remember what I told you about the World Trade Organization (WTO)? Has that worked out for America? No. It's also weakened American manufacturing.

Fast-forward to 2015. The United States ran $50 billion in trade deficits in March alone,[21] and Obama wants to make it even worse.

The president has repeatedly claimed the deal will result in more auto sales to Japan. "If you drive around Washington, there are a whole bunch of Japanese cars. You go to Tokyo and count how many Chryslers and GM and Ford cars there are. So the current situation is not working for us," Obama said in April.[22]

Like everything else that comes out of this man's mouth, this is a lie. This deal won't result in more American cars being sold in Japan. Japan doesn't even have a tariff on American cars. They don't sell in Japan because the Japanese want smaller, more fuel-efficient cars.

The U.S. does place a tariff on Japanese cars, however,

which this deal will eliminate. So, the TPP will actually do exactly the opposite of what Obama says it will. It will increase the sale of Japanese cars in the United States, meaning increasing competition for domestic sales, and it will do nothing to increase sales of U.S. cars in Japan.

Believe it or not, I'm with the liberals and the labor unions on this one. They're not always wrong about everything. The majority of Republicans are wrong about this, because they're not representing the American people. They're representing their pals on Wall Street and in the board rooms of big corporations.

I'm sorry if I'm shocking you, but I don't have to go party line. I'm not in the Rush Cartel. I call them as I see them. It's that simple.

Real conservatives should be against this bill for constitutional reasons. In addition to selling out our workers and manufacturers, it also has serious implications for our national sovereignty. The deal creates an international tribunal that would have the power to override our own state and federal laws and levy fines against U.S. taxpayers.[23]

Just before the House voted on whether to grant Obama fast-track authority on this sellout, yet another bombshell broke: This supposed trade treaty would massively expand the traitor in chief's authority on immigration.[24] According to Rosemary Jenks, the director of government relations at Numbers USA, Obama has not told Congress or the American people the truth about his secret deal.

"He has told members of Congress very specifically the U.S. is not negotiating immigration—or at least is not negotiating any immigration provisions that would require us to change our laws. So, unless major changes are made to the Trade and Services Agreement—that is not true," said Jenks.[25]

Frankly, I'd be surprised if we found out this pathological liar *was* telling the truth about anything. But a few naïve conservatives out there may still be surprised the Republicans who knew about this would back it. I'm not.

Today's Republicans are so bought and sold by big business that they don't even care about their own long-term survival. As long as Larry Ellison, Mark Zuckerberg, and the rest can print as many H-1B visas as they want to replace American science, technology, engineering, and mathematics (STEM) workers with foreigners, the Republicans don't care if they rip up the Constitution and make Obama a king over immigration.

These businessmen running multinational corporations feel no allegiance to America whatsoever. They are going to do whatever increases their bottom line, regardless of the long-term damage it does to this country. You would think at some point they would have enough money. How many yachts can they own? How many castles can they own? How many islands?

Greed is like nymphomania for these people. There isn't enough gold or money in the world for them. Their insatiable appetite for wealth is decimating American workers, like those at Disney who lost their jobs to foreigners so Bob Iger can make more than $46 million next year. This is greed on a scale unlike anything we've seen since the Aztecs were decimated by the Spaniards.

After the Spaniards had virtually destroyed the Aztec culture, one of the survivors said their greed was a disease for which there was no cure. I say the same about Ellison, Gates,

Zuckerberg, and the rest of these plutocrats. They're like the conquistadors. They'll lay waste to this entire country trying to satisfy their lust for wealth and it still won't be enough.

And they own the Republican Party. That's Government Zero personified.

Obama ceding national sovereignty is no big surprise, either. He's an internationalist who hates America and has shown little regard for any constitutional limits on what he does. But again, one would think the Republicans would at least defend the Constitution, if not American workers.

They aren't even doing that. Senate Republicans have agreed to give the president fast-track power,[26] meaning Congress would have to approve it as is, without any ability to propose amendments, just to appease their big donors and connected friends.

That just shows you their other positions on constitutional and national sovereignty issues are a sham. The minute their pals in big business can make a few extra billion, they'll give the rest of the world the keys to America and let it empty the vault.

Any free-trade deal with poorer countries in Asia is going to be a one-sided arrangement under which middle-class jobs move out of America and even more cheap, foreign-made goods flood our markets. It will be great for big business and Wall Street, lethal for small business and Main Street, and will expand our already overflowing welfare rolls.

It's another double-win for our Marxist in chief. With one stroke of his unconstitutional pen, he'll direct billions more to his crony capitalist friends and further overwhelm the system, Cloward-Piven style, in his quest to turn America into a socialist welfare state.

Selling Out STEM Workers with H-1B Visas

While working on a deal to export the last manufacturing jobs out of America, the administration continues the practice of outsourcing high-tech jobs to visiting foreigners through the H-1B visa program. Earlier this year, Southern California Edison laid off four hundred employees and replaced them with foreign workers visiting the United States on H-1B visas.[27]

This program's stated mission was to admit temporary workers from foreign countries to do jobs there are no U.S. citizens to fill. Southern California Edison claimed that was what it was doing, but California congressman Darrel Issa wasn't buying it.

"This appears to be an example of precisely what the H-1B visa is not intended to be: a program to simply replace American workers en masse with cheap labor from overseas," he said in a statement.[28]

The progressives are torn between their ties to big labor and their unqualified support of the president in bringing in as many immigrants as possible, whether legally, illegally, or through programs like this. The far left within his own party oppose the program. Bernie Sanders managed to get a restriction on H-1B visas for the banking sector into the American Recovery and Reinvestment Act, cosponsored by Republican senator Chuck Grassley.[29]

Establishment Republicans like Jeb Bush line up with the internationalists in supporting the program. Bush said it would be foolish not to extend the H-1B visa program.[30] Unlike the trade deal, however, Republicans are not so uniform in their support of the H-1B sellout.

The problem for defenders of the program is there is no shortage of STEM (science, technology, engineering, and mathematics) workers in this country. On the contrary, there is a shortage of jobs for them,[31] as several studies have indicated.

The real reason the program enjoys the political support it does is cost. Big business realizes huge cost savings by employing visiting workers on this program. Officially, workers hired on H-1B visas are supposed to be paid on the same scale as American workers filling that job would be. But there are all sorts of ways to get around that requirement, as Southern California Edison demonstrated. The company can simply lay off its STEM workers and coincidentally hire H-1B workers for "new positions."

Don't misunderstand me. I am all for companies being aggressive in cutting costs and getting the most talent for their money. I don't believe anyone is entitled to a higher salary. Everyone should compete in the market with other candidates for the jobs they seek. But "the market" shouldn't include foreign workers from much poorer countries that offer no similar opportunities in return to American workers.

The H-1B visa program is just another point of agreement between progressives and establishment Republicans to sell out the American people for big business and their international agenda. Support for this program alone should eliminate Jeb Bush as a viable candidate for anyone who opposes the progressive agenda.

As with illegal immigrants, our legal immigration policies should put the needs of Americans first. Instead, our Government Zero uses this program to reward multinational corporations and promote the progressive anti-Americanization agenda.

A Big Zero for the American Economy

Overall, every one of the administration's policies weaken the American economy for Americans and benefit America's economic rivals or enemies. The progressives are more worried about equal opportunity for Asians and Muslims than protecting American workers and small businesses. The nonexistent Republican opposition cares only about big business and Wall Street.

We don't need a progressive or even a conservative economic policy. I'm not sure if *conservative* means anything anymore, with Republicans like Mitch McConnell calling themselves by that name.

We need a nationalist economic policy. We need representation for the 315 million Americans who live in this country, not for multinational corporations or the rest of the world. It's not the government's job to help Third World countries be more competitive. It's the government's job to represent the interests of the people who elect and pay them.

CHAPTER 11

Zero Liberty

Zero Free Speech

In May, two homegrown Islamic terrorists claiming allegiance to the Islamic State opened fire on a free speech event in Garland, Texas.[1] The event, organized by activist Pamela Geller, included a "Draw Muhammad" cartoon contest. For this, American-born U.S. citizens under the influence of radical Islam decided they must die. But for the heroic actions of an off-duty traffic cop, they would have.

Instead, only the two terrorists were killed. That's the good news. The bad news is free speech may have been seriously wounded, thanks to the propagandists in the media.

Free speech is a topic I know an awful lot about. I'm in the free speech business. Without the First Amendment, I wouldn't be on the radio, which would please many on the left who don't believe in free speech at all. They believe in controlled speech. They believe in government speech. They believe in progressive speech.

In other words, they believe in *their* hate speech and no one else's. As with everything else, you can count on progressives to side with the Islamists on free speech issues and smear anyone who tries to stand up to them.

Deniers of the new holocaust constantly tell us ISIS is not a threat to the United States. They mock conservatives who talk about the danger of sharia law as "conspiracy theorists." As I tell listeners on my show, *The Savage Nation*, the conspiracy theorists of twenty years ago have become the news reporters of today.

We are fighting right now to preserve our most basic principles in the face of a Progressive-Islamist takeover that is attacking them on every front. Both liberals and supposed conservatives in the media are playing for the other side, whether they realize it or not.

I'm talking about how Bill O'Reilly and Greta Van Susteren bent over backward to blame the victims. They didn't attack the Islamic murderers. They didn't attack the religion itself for putting hatred in the minds of these throwbacks. No, they attacked the person who provoked them, Pamela Geller:

> *Insulting the entire Muslim world is stupid...It does not advance the cause of liberty or get us any closer to defeating the savage jihad...Now, the group that did the insulting says it's entitled to profane Mohammad, because in the Islamic religion, any kind of depiction of him is a sin. They say they can do that in America because of freedom of speech. Well, it's true. They have the right to do it here. But again, it's stupid. It accomplishes nothing."[2]*

O'Reilly couldn't have been more wrong. It accomplished an awful lot. It flushed out hateful terrorists and hateful liars in the media. It showed us there are Muslims ready to kill over a cartoon and it showed us who in the media is on the side of hate.

Two Muslim fanatics, as we know, did the shooting. Pamela Geller didn't do the shooting. Two Muslim fanatics, identifying themselves as ISIS, have now attacked in America, right in our homeland. O'Reilly, Van Susteren, and liberal journalists, who are really one and the same, deplored Geller's exercise of free speech and blamed the victims.[3]

O'Reilly said what Geller did was stupid. Insulting the First Amendment is even more stupid. Nor does that advance the cause of liberty.

The media said Geller provoked the radical Islamists into attacking the event. Of course she provoked them. She did it on purpose to show the world what they're capable of. Today, it's cartoons of Muhammad. What is it tomorrow?

You have to understand that large numbers of Muslims don't just want to ban pictures of Muhammad. They want to ban any speech critical of Islam. And I can guarantee you Hussein in the White House is already drawing up plans to ban the criticism of Islam.

Soon thereafter, ABC News described Geller's group as "notorious for its anti-Islamic views." Notice that they didn't say the Islamists were notorious for killing. They didn't condemn the fatwa issued by ISIS against Pamela Geller for drawing cartoons. They didn't condemn the maniacs setting people on fire while they are still alive. No, the cartoonists were the problem, not the killers.

Indeed, everything is upside down, just like in *Alice in Wonderland*. That evening, on Monday, all of the so-called networks were repeating the description of Geller's group as a hate group. They probably based that on the Southern Poverty

Law Center's (SPLC) website, which lists Geller's American Freedom Defense Initiative (AFDI) as an anti-Muslim hate group. The SPLC is the real hate group. It's a leftist, fanatic hate machine. The people who run this left-wing propaganda center are some of the sickest, most demented, Soros-funded people in America.

The SPLC itself encouraged violence against the conservative Family Research Council. After the SPLC labeled it a hate group, along with conveniently identifying its headquarters on a "hate group map," a left-wing shooter showed up at the council's offices and attacked.[4] So, in my opinion, the Southern Poverty Law Center is far more responsible for having encouraged violence than Pamela Geller or other opponents of radical Islam. Look into old Morris Deeds, Mr. Holier-Than-Thou, and his Al Sharpton–like SPLC. You'll find out who the real hate groups are.

Based on sources like the SPLC, the AFDI was smeared on MSNBC, CNN, and elsewhere. NBC terrorism analyst Evan Kohlmann even claimed the AFDI was not holding a free speech event. Can you believe that? He said, "These people are not standing by that principle, they're standing by the principle of hatred for other people."[5] So Kohlmann now wants to define what speech is. This is how obnoxious it's become.

I'll quote Winston Churchill again, who said that the object of the protections of free speech is to protect offensive speech. I've said it to you a thousand times. Polite speech does not need the protection of the First Amendment. It's obnoxious and offensive speech for which the First Amendment was written.

Kohlmann actually made my arguments unintentionally when he went on to say, "The police told them in order to hold this event they would have to have $10,000 worth of security on hand. They had a SWAT team outfitted like it was Baghdad. So obviously someone knew there was a likelihood that some stupid person would do this."[6]

He was trying to further blame the victims, but his comment actually begs the question: Is it even America anymore when one has to hire a SWAT team for protection just to draw cartoons? Why don't those who mock and insult Christianity have to hire SWAT teams? Why don't the media claim they are "provoking violence" when they put pictures of Jesus in bottles of urine? Do I have to remind you that the National Endowment for the Arts subsidized the maker of *Piss Christ* in the 1990s?

Obama was quick to denounce the "Innocence of Muslims" video his administration tried to blame for causing the Benghazi attacks, but he had no objection to this desecration of Christ when it was displayed in Manhattan in 2012.[7]

Do you remember what the Brooklyn Museum did when they showed a dung-covered art work of the Virgin Mary? The man running the Brooklyn Museum giggled, saying the exhibit was protected by the First Amendment. The National Portrait Gallery promoted a video of a crucifix with ants crawling over the body of Christ. Was that freedom of speech? We were told it was.

The answer is it was freedom of speech. We have room for that in America, but not in Muslim America. The throwbacks want to bring their backward world to your community. And with the Progressive-Islamist media's help, they just might succeed. Most of you don't know this war of Islam against the world has been a war of attrition, spanning a millennium. It didn't start on 9/11. It started a thousand years ago. But thanks to multiculturalism, no one knows the truth anymore.

Multiculturalism metastasized under Bill Clinton, who opened our borders in a way they were never intended to be opened. Since then, the nation has been flooded with people whose views are antithetical to the views of America. They're refusing to join the melting pot. They want you to melt into their retrograde world.

If you think these two shooters in Texas are alone, you have more naïveté than Bill O'Reilly and Greta Van Susteren combined.

Not long after the attacks, I came across a story on PJ Media, one of those rare media outlets not bought and sold by progressives. They reported:

> A Kansas City mosque that petitioned Barack Obama to ban free speech defaming Islam in 2012 will hold a funeral for one of the two jihadists killed in a shootout Sunday outside a Dallas-area convention center that was hosting a "Draw Muhammad" cartoon contest...Back in September of 2012, [this Islamic center] launched an online petition calling for Barack Obama to sponsor a bill limiting the free speech of American citizens by criminalizing insults to religion (namely, Islam) following international protest of the "Innocence of Muslims" video.[8]

Now this would be the equivalent of holding a public funeral for 1930s Nazis who tried to murder Americans and were killed in the process. Imagine if a German Lutheran Church had then wanted to have a funeral for them. That never happened, but you can imagine the outrage you'd hear from the liberal media even then.

We actually tolerated Nazis in America back in the 1930s more than we do patriots today. The Nazis once had events in America on stages where they had a Nazi flag on one side and an American flag on the other. I'll never forget learning that when I was a little boy in the 1950s. I was going through old magazines and I found out that the Nazis had been that prominent in America as far as the late 1930s, and brazen enough to hold rallies in Madison Square Garden and other venues here in the United States of America. We didn't stop them, because we believe in freedom of speech in this country. That's how committed to it we are. Do you remember the American Nazi Party marching in a Jewish neighborhood in Skokie, Illinois, forty years later? They were defended by the American Civil Liberties Union, made up mainly of Jewish lawyers, who said, "They have every right. We don't agree with the Nazis, but we'll defend their right to march." Where were all those good, Jewish liberals in May? Why weren't they defending Pamela Geller?

By the way, one of the board members of the Kansas City mosque supported the requested ban on free speech back in 2012. Mohammed Kohia, who helped start the petition, said, "Insulting somebody else or putting somebody down can insight [*sic*] violence and lead to people losing their lives. We're trying not to give these people a chance to misbehave."[9]

Surprisingly, the ACLU actually stepped in and disagreed. I was pleasantly shocked by what the ACLU attorney said:

> *Somebody's speech is no excuse for violence, that's right...but you can't punish the speaker for the violence practiced by others. While I understand why they're upset, their proposition is clearly unconstitutional.*[10]

I'd like to hear the ACLU's opinion today. By the way, this same mosque "had hosted internationally renowned Islamic hate speaker Khalid Yasin, whose controversial statements include calling for the death penalty for gays and describing the beliefs of Christians and Jews as 'filth.'"[11]

The Garland, Texas, shooting showed you what is under the surface in this country. Every sane member of the military in my audience knows what the battle really is. Ask any soldier who fought in Afghanistan or Iraq what they saw Muslims doing in the countries they were deployed in to liberate. Ask them and find out what terrorism really is. You don't even have to go that far. Just remember watching people being set on fire while they are alive. Ask about the Yazidi women being raped as young as eight years old by these "peace-loving Muslims" in the Middle East. Ask about the kidnapping and the murders. Ask about all of these things and you'll understand what the battle really is. You'll understand that the event in Texas was only a spark in America. It's a global war of attrition that has spanned a millennium.

Pamela Geller is not the problem. She's the solution. The real problem here is cowardice. The real problem is not understanding that this is about freedom of speech, not about freedom of speech according to some. Geller may be a pro-vocateur, but she did nothing wrong. She and those who participated in that event were peacefully exercising their right to free speech, in opposition to the murderous violence that occurred in France related to *Charlie Hebdo* and many others who have suffered or have been murdered because they dared to criticize Islam.

There is no excuse for violence simply because someone said something or drew something you find offensive. That's not the American way. What's next? Is it okay for the LGBT crowd to bomb churches because their pastors provoke them by speaking out against homosexuality? Is it okay for some to attack liberal churches because they promote abortion?

Of course not.

This is pure evil. Pure evil kills for a cartoon. The essence of free speech is being threatened by Muslims in the United States of America and the world trying to shut down any criticism of their Quran and Muhammad. I have read the Quran. It is quoted extensively in my novel *Countdown to Mecca*. In over one hundred places they called for killing the infidel. Why doesn't the *New York Times* talk about the holy book itself? Why doesn't the *New York Times*, which attacks the Catholic Church on a regular basis, look into the Quran and see the more than one hundred verses, or suras, that call Muslims to war with those they call nonbelievers? *Nonbelievers* means anyone who isn't Muslim. Why doesn't the *New York Times* look at Sura 5:51, which says that Muslims are not to take Jews and Christians for friends? Allah describes them as "unjust people."

The answers are quite clear. We are living in a twisted world. Islam is at war with the West. We have a president who won't say the word *Islamic* and a Soviet media who takes the side of Islamic murderers against Americans exercising their right to free speech. Liberty itself is under attack. These two would-be Islamic murderers were by no means alone. The FBI said they overlooked the Texas Muslim shooters' violent tweets because there are so many like them. Think about what that means. Officials said there are so many like them that you have to prioritize your investigations.

That wasn't entirely honest. Did you know they were tracking the shooter in Texas for eight to nine years? Why didn't they stop him when he bought his AK-47? Why didn't they stop him when he bought his bulletproof vest? Why did the FBI permit the jihadi to come to Texas and open fire with his automatic weapon?

Immediately after the thwarted attack, the Islamic State said they have at least seventy-one active Islamic State members in the United States trained to kill.[12] One has to wonder why the FBI isn't actively pursuing these people. They may be on the FBI watch list, but the FBI is too busy watching Christians, returning war veterans, antiabortion activists, and constitutional conservatives. That time and money would be better utilized looking at radicalized Muslims. Why are they bothering with patriotic Americans instead? In plain English, it's because Hussein is in the White House.

It should come as no surprise that the Muslim in chief didn't back the defenders of free speech, either. He didn't support or criticize Pamela Geller. He ignored the event entirely. This is the president who has never hesitated to weigh in on a shooting when it suits his demagogic agenda. When it allows him to further inflame racial division, he's at the podium immediately. When he can use a tragedy to attack the Second Amendment, he's as reliable as Old Faithful.

I remind you that none of the local school or police shootings are any of his business. They are not within the jurisdiction of the federal government. They are state issues. Obama's statements after each one of them have been as unnecessary as they have been harmful.

However, when the shooters claim they are acting on behalf of an international organization with whom the United States is actively at war, attacking American citizens on American soil— that is precisely when he *should* get involved. Instead, the president flew to New York the night of the shootings to appear on David Letterman. When pressed, his press secretary, Josh "the new Goebbels" Earnest, said, "In the mind of the president there is no form of expression that would justify an act of violence."[13]

That's great to hear. Why didn't we hear it from the president firsthand? Why wasn't he at his podium talking about taking executive action against Islamic sleeper cells, instead of disarming law-abiding Americans? Why wasn't he saying "American lives matter"? Why is he suddenly silent when the shooters are Muslims and the victims are white?

To be fair, at least Josh Earnest affirmed that it is still permitted to criticize Islam, at least for now. When asked, "Is it time for individuals or groups or even publications to stop depicting the Prophet Muhammad in cartoons or any other types of drawings?" he replied,

> *Well, that's obviously a judgment that we leave up to individual media organizations. The principle that I restated yesterday is one that applies, which is, that there is no expression, however offensive, that justifies an act of terrorism or even an act of violence. And that apparently is what these two individuals in Texas were trying to do.[14]*

By the way, whenever I hear the words "the Prophet Muhammad," I'm a little disturbed. Why doesn't anyone say "the Lord Jesus?" Why do they refer to Jesus merely by his first name, but to Muhammad as "the Prophet Muhammad?" Does that mean Muhammad is a prophet and Jesus isn't the Lord?

I'm just trying to show you how language is used. In the new Progressive-Islamist America, Islam is constantly legitimized and Christianity is constantly ridiculed and scorned.

Incidentally, ISIS called Jewess Pamela Geller *khanzeer*, which means "pig." I'm afraid to tell all of you good, liberal Jews who are wringing your hands that this is the essence of the whole problem. You have a pathologically willful blindness to what is going on in the world. You have no idea what U.S. Muslim attitudes are toward Jews and Christians. You like to think that because they appear at interdenominational events they're on your side. You ought to find out what they're saying about Jews and Christians behind your backs.

This is the beginning of the battle. Geller may be repugnant. Geller may be obnoxious. Geller may be a provocateur, but she did the world a favor. She exposed the hatred that exists within Islam itself. She showed everyday Americans why they need to wake up and realize their own lives and liberty are threatened by these fanatics right here in the United States.

As I've said numerous times, if you look back into the Jewish Bible, the Old Testament, it's filled with hate. It says to kill homosexuals, kill adulterers, and more. I've read Leviticus, including on the air. But modern Jews, even modern Orthodox Jews, don't kill homosexuals and they don't stone adulteresses. They know the difference between a five-thousand-year-old text and the real world, the civilized world built upon Judeo-Christian values, but which eschews those passages that obviously proceed from man's barbaric past and not from the mind of God.

Christianity also used to put people to the sword for blaspheming Jesus. That was in the fifteenth century. But Christianity went through a reformation. Islam has not gone through a reformation. It needs to. Don't take my word for it. We heard precisely this from one of the bravest women alive today, Ayaan Hirsi Ali. Ali is a Somali-born former Muslim herself, who once believed in fatwas and supported the Muslim Brotherhood. She had a revelation after the 9/11 attacks, when Osama bin Laden used the Quran to justify them. She renounced Islam and became an activist against its many outdated, barbaric tenets. Her life has been regularly threatened by the throwbacks ever since.

Earlier this year, she wrote an op-ed in the *Wall Street Journal* in advance of her new book, *Heretic*, in which she said a lot of the same things I've been saying for years. The problem isn't just with "radical Islamists." It is an inherent part of the religion itself, as understood even by peaceful Muslims today. In her own words, "the call to violence and the justification for it are explicitly stated in the sacred texts of Islam." She goes on to say,

> *It is not just al Qaeda and the Islamic State that show the violent face of Islamic faith and practice. It is Pakistan, where any statement critical of the Prophet or Islam is labeled as blasphemy and punishable by death. It is Saudi Arabia, where churches and synagogues are outlawed and where beheadings are a legitimate form of punishment. It is Iran, where stoning is an acceptable punishment and homosexuals are hanged for their "crime."*[15]

This is why the majority of armed conflicts around the world involve Muslims at war with their neighbors. As I said before, it's not just with Israel. Muslims are fighting non-Muslims or each other in dozens of countries. Ali quotes the late political scientist Samuel Huntington, who said in 1996, "Islam's borders are bloody and so are its innards."

How did the media react to Hirsi's brave statement, made under death threats from the maniacs beheading people all over the world? Did they commend her for her bravery and thank her for defending freedom and tolerance? Of course not. They made excuses for the maniacs and mercilessly attacked this heroic champion of freedom.

Time magazine called her proposals "a tone-deaf declaration rather than an opening of a conversation."[16] Its reviewer Carla

Power says Hirsi "doesn't get" Islam. Can you believe the nerve of this Ivy League white liberal? She has a degree in Middle Eastern studies from an American ivory tower, so she thinks she knows more about Islam than a woman who grew up a Somali Muslim and was the victim of female genital mutilation at age five.

Massachusetts-born Haroon Moghul was quick to jump on the bandwagon, saying Hirsi is "in over her head" when talking about Islam and calling *Heretic* "one of the worst books, period."[17] He said Islam has already had a reformation. Really? We ought to air-drop him into Iraq and let him experience the reformation himself. He's another ivory tower liberal with a degree from the same universities teaching global warming and rape culture.

Of course, the media assault on Hirsi wouldn't have been complete without court jester Jon Stewart wading in. He had Hirsi on his show for an interview,[18] which was really about discrediting her arguments almost from the moment she sat down. Of course, he took the opportunity to remind everyone how terrible Judaism and Christianity are and how violence was committed in the names of those religions seven hundred years ago.

That's the point, Jon. It was seven hundred years ago. Nobody disputes that. Show us the Christians burning people alive today. Show us the Jews beheading people for drawing cartoons.

Instead of attacking Ayaan Hirsi Ali and Pamela Geller for exposing the true nature of the "religion of peace," the media should be investigating what animates the morons at the lowest level of what some call a political movement disguised as a religion. But they're not interested in that. The leftist media is interested in tearing down the Judeo-Christian foundation of American society and replacing it with atheist progressivism. If they have to turn a blind eye to the atrocities committed in the name of Islam and smear defenders of free speech to do so, they're willing to do just that. It's an all-out propaganda attack on our basic freedoms, starting with the first, most important freedom: freedom of speech.

They are aiders and abettors to radical Islam, who are using a Trojan Horse approach to get into this country and try to tell us how to live. Today they object to cartoons, tomorrow it's pork on the menu. After pork on the menu, it's other graven images they don't like. After that, they'll take down the crosses off churches, because they find them offensive. They've already accomplished similar coups in places in Michigan. They've stopped church bells from ringing.

We found out just how biased the media really is when the Clinton Cash scandal broke earlier this year. Virtually every national media organization one could name has made sizable contributions to the Clinton Slush Fund, which poses as a charitable organization.[19] Many of these contributions were in the millions of dollars. Does anyone seriously believe media outlets forking over this kind of cash to the Clintons are reporting the news objectively?

Politico was kind enough to publish a list of the media outlets who contributed, broken down by the size of the contribution. I've included it here:

$1,000,000–$5,000,000

Carlos Slim, chairman & CEO of Telmex, largest *New York Times* shareholder

James Murdoch, chief operating officer of 21st Century Fox

Newsmax Media, Florida-based conservative media network

Thomson Reuters, owner of the Reuters news service

$500,000–$1,000,000
Google
News Corporation Foundation, philanthropic arm of
    former Fox News parent company

$250,000–$500,000
Houghton Mifflin Harcourt, publisher
Richard Mellon Scaife, owner of *Pittsburgh Tribune-Review*

$100,000–$250,000
Abigail Disney, documentary filmmaker
Bloomberg Philanthropies
Howard Stringer, former CBS, CBS News, and Sony
    executive
Intermountain West Communications, local television
    affiliate owner (formerly Sunbelt Communications)

$50,000–$100,000
Bloomberg L.P.
Discovery Communications
George Stephanopoulos, ABC News chief anchor and
    chief political correspondent
Mort Zuckerman, owner of New York *Daily News* and
    U.S. News and World Report
Time Warner, owner of CNN parent company Turner
    Broadcasting

$25,000–$50,000
AOL

HBO
Hollywood Foreign Press Association, presenters of the
    Golden Globe Awards
Viacom

$10,000–$25,000
Knight Foundation, nonprofit foundation dedicated to
    supporting journalism
Public Radio International
Turner Broadcasting, parent company of CNN
Twitter

$5,000–$10,000
Comcast, parent company of NBCUniversal
NBCUniversal, parent company of NBC News,
    MSNBC, and CNBC
Public Broadcasting Service

$1,000–$5,000
Robert Allbritton, owner of *Politico*

$250–$1,000
AOL Huffington Post Media Group
Hearst Corporation
Judy Woodruff, *PBS Newshour* coanchor and managing
    editor
The Washington Post Company

We don't even have to ask that question about George
Stephanopoulos, who gave at least $75,000 to the Clintons
without disclosing it, as any journalist with integrity would

have. But Stephanopoulos isn't a journalist and never has been. He's a paid male escort for the Clinton machine. His involvement with the Clintons since becoming a news anchor goes much deeper than the well-publicized $75,000 contribution.[20]

Stephanopoulos certainly isn't the only political operative posing as a journalist. Propagandists claiming to be news reporters are endemic in American media.

Zero Freedom of the Press

I wonder if the media would be so eager to support the Progressive-Islamist government if the Muslim in chief were ever to get his way. He's stated openly he's against a free press. He complained about a "balkanization of the media" and longs for "a common place where we get common facts and a common worldview."

That's what they had in the Soviet Union.

While he simply ignored the Garland shootings, he certainly made clear his contempt for freedom of the press shortly thereafter. Opining during a summit on poverty about how terrible conservatives are for criticizing the most opulent welfare state in human history, the president actually came right out and said freedom of the press should be abolished:

> And so, if we're going to change how Rep. John Boehner (R-OH) and Sen. Mitch McConnell (R-KY) think, we're going to have to change how our body politic thinks, which means we're going to have to change how the media reports on these issues, and how people's impressions of what it's like to struggle in this economy looks like.[21]

In case you have any doubt, *we* means "the government" to our socialist dictator. He came right out and said he wants to control how you think and how the media reports the news. He's openly called for recreating the Soviet Union right here in America. What does this man have to say or do to receive the impeachment he so richly deserves?

He didn't waste much time putting his plans into action. Three days after his comments about "changing the way the media reports," the administration "urged" the media to change the way it reports on ISIS. Emily Horne, spokeswoman for retired general John Allen, the State Department's special envoy leading the international coalition against ISIS, made the following statement:

> *We are urging broadcasters to avoid using the familiar B-roll that we've all seen before, file footage of ISIL convoys operating in broad daylight, moving in large formations with guns out, looking to wreak havoc.... It's inaccurate—that's no longer how ISIL moves.*[22]

The Obama administration continues to advance its narrative that ISIS is on the run after its defeat at Tikrit. But the terrorist organization invested little in defending that city, and in May it won a victory in the more important Ramadi in Anbar province. Critics say that ISIS is far from being defeated, even if their method of transport has changed.

Whose narrative is truer? There is no way to know. The administration won't allow journalists to embed in the most fiercely contested areas of Iraq and Syria, so we're just expected to take its word that victory over ISIS is near. It looks like Obama has succeeded in changing the way the media reports about this already. There is a saying many conservatives used to repeat. I think you've heard it. "Free speech is not free." We're about to learn it the hard way if we don't stand up for it now. The graves of our warriors across Europe and America are filled with people who fought for the right to criticize others without getting killed for it.

The battle has come home.

Zero Civilian Security

Standing up for free speech isn't the only thing that will bring the progressive media jackals down on your head. The propagandists have also been busy smearing anyone who questions the suspicious militarization of federal agencies.

While the administration wages an all-out war on local cops, it continues to arm to the teeth federal agencies, some of which have no business carrying weapons at all. We still haven't received any explanation for why the government purchased billions of rounds of ammunition for the Social Security Administration and Department of Homeland Security.

After initially refusing to answer at all, then secretary of homeland security Janet Napolitano eventually said about half the rounds purchased were allocated to U.S. Customs and Border Protection. That's fine, but what about the other half? What possible use could the Social Security Administration have for hollow-point bullets, which aren't even allowed on the battlefield according to the Geneva Conventions? This government believes these are questions they don't need to answer. We should just trust them implicitly, regardless of how many times they lie to us about keeping our health insurance if we like it or exactly what the NSA may be doing in terms of spying on *us* rather than our enemies.

It is this arrogance and dishonesty that led to a major controversy over the government's infamous Jade Helm 15 training exercise this past summer. This was a gargantuan, multistate military training exercise that involved war game operations on private land, in cities and towns, and in the countryside. Not only did American citizens see an unprecedented military presence in their midst, but covert agents were instructed to infiltrate civilian populations, identified only by armbands. According to the U.S. Army's own presentation, "Some participants will be wearing civilian attire and driving civilian vehicles."[23]

The government claimed this massive exercise was designed to get military personnel used to dealing with unfamiliar terrain and infiltrating civilian populations in other countries. Many speculated they were training for martial law during an emergency here.

Let me be clear from the start. I never believed some of the wilder conspiracy theories about this exercise. I did not believe the federal government was planning to invade Texas or establish martial law. But I do have a problem with this and the media reaction to anyone who questioned it.

First, I don't understand why such a massive military operation within our borders is necessary to train what is already the mightiest military force in human history. This is a military that hasn't lost a battle since early in World War II. If the administration is as committed as it says it is not to put boots on the ground in any new conflict, then why do we need boots on the ground in seven U.S. states?

Second, what precedent does this set? Not everyone who objects to this exercise believes it's a military coup d'état. But there are legitimate concerns that conducting operations like this desensitizes civilian populations to a military presence in their midst. One of the bedrock principles of our free society is a suspicion of "standing armies." It is especially disturbing that some of the trainees will be operating covertly. Regardless of what the pedantic academics running the current government might intend, it's fair to ask whether it would be easier for a future administration with more sinister intentions to oppress a population already accustomed to seeing military personnel and ordnance on American streets.

What I find most disturbing about this is the media reaction. Just as they did with Pamela Geller and Ayaan Hirsi Ali, the majority of the media reflexively pounced on those standing up for freedom. Anyone who questioned the exercise for any reason was immediately lumped in with the most paranoid fringe elements and smeared as a kook. Most egregiously, the media often misrepresented what critics of the program said. CBS News, the *Washington Post*, and others all seemed to link by association the questions Alex Jones's Infowars website raised about the program with a bizarre theory that closed Walmart stores were part of the conspiracy and would be used as prisons or death camps.[24] There was only one problem: Infowars had already publicly debunked that theory before the media implied Alex Jones endorsed it.[25]

It wasn't just the national media that smeared all dissenters to this overkill. The local alternative newspaper *Phoenix New Times* ran a story with the headline "'Jade Helm 15' Operation in Arizona by U.S. Army Worries Wackos." Can you believe that headline? I call attention to it only because it had the decency to publish updates from concerned citizens who disagreed with the writer. Here are some of the very sober, legitimate concerns of one local resident:

Really wish you didn't disparage legitimate concerns with the term "wacko". Set the knee-jerk conspiracy theorists aside for a moment. These operations are going to be held throughout towns and small businesses in the States specified. Go to the presentation made by the Jade Helm vendor to the Big Spring County Supervisors meeting in TX and hear for yourself (YouTube). The citizens are supposed to "notice" the arm bands worn by all of the participants (which will also include role-player volunteers) when they see armed kidnapper's, tanks, swat, etc. Think of the elderly, the children and the uninformed...All I'm asking is that you take a mature even handed look at what is being foisted on the citizenry and the raw panic that has and will ensue as folks watch it unfold and keel over from a heart attack aka War of the Worlds, remember? That was fake, too, Ray.[26]

Does this person sound to you like a wacko? I encourage you to read the whole letter. The woman who wrote it was originally a New Yorker who was educated and had "decades of top level Fortune 100 experience." Not everyone who questions the government is sitting in his mother's basement wearing a tinfoil hat. Real, everyday Americans are concerned about this exercise, and they have every right to be.

Keep Your Mouth Shut and Obey

Any one of these stories and the way they were reported are cause enough for concern. We should be vigilant in guarding our liberties against even the slightest infringement. That's a core American value. Remember, the Boston Tea Party was about what would today be considered a minuscule tax. It was the principle that was important to our founders.

Taken together, these stories and dozens of others like them constitute a pattern. It is Government Zero trampling liberties we once took for granted and replacing them with the new normal in American culture: *Keep your mouth shut and obey.*

We've had a president who recognizes no constitutional limit on his power, and it's now trickled down to the cities and towns of America. If you criticize Islam or the president's refusal to recognize the new holocaust, you're a bigot. If you criticize the welfare state, you're a racist. If you object to large-scale military training exercises on the streets of your town, you're a wacko.

Meanwhile, the president is openly and admittedly seeking to control the media, just like Joseph Stalin or Chairman Mao. To a large extent, it looks like he's succeeded. Media outlets are being told how to report the war against ISIS, and none of them is allowed to send reporters to verify the administration's claims. They, too, are to just shut up and obey.

Worst of all, the administration and like-minded gangs posing as "community groups" are waging an all-out war against local police that looks frighteningly similar to the war on local cops waged by Hitler. If you think you've seen police brutality, you haven't seen anything like what you might see when the entire nation is policed by an occupying army of federal police, ultimately answerable to one man or one woman.

Government Zero means zero liberty.

CHAPTER 12

Zero Police

Obama's Endgame: A Federal Police Force

After yet another city lay in flames thanks to his divisive rhetoric and relentless war on local police, the Grand Illusionist in the White House had this to say:

> But we know that some communities have the odds stacked against them, and have had the odds stacked against them for a very long time—in some cases, for decades... And in some communities, that sense of unfairness and powerlessness has contributed to dysfunction in those communities. Communities are like bodies, and if the immunity system is down, they can get sick.[1]

As usual, the president glosses over the violent crimes committed by rioters and looters, calling them "dysfunction" while making excuses for the inexcusable mayhem perpetrated by the thugs. But that's just more of what we've heard from the Marxist in chief since he took office. What he proposes to do about the crisis he helped create is even worse.

Obama is working around the clock in the remaining months of his reign of terror to make certain he destroys the soldiers of our immune system, the police.

I'm something of an expert on immunity. I wrote a book on it back in the 1980s, during the height of the AIDS crisis. It was called *Maximum Immunity* and was published in six languages. It was a study of the immune system that compared white blood cells and other immune bodies that protect us against invaders to our soldiers, marines, navy, coast guard, and police.

Obama knows very well that if you take down the immune system, a body can be destroyed. The invaders can take over and destroy the body politic. The president seems determined to destroy local police forces and replace them with federal police. I believe I was the first one to warn my listeners of this, but it doesn't matter who said it first. We can all see it now. He is unleashing community organizers on crime-ridden cities.

This is a new mission. He's found $163 million to be distributed to gangs. He calls them "community organizations," but in reality, they're gangs. What else can one call the Cincinnati Black United Front? How about the American Civil Liberties Union? The ACLU is a gang with law degrees. They're the cowardly side of the revolution.

Obama's new attorney general is giving these groups money to tell local police how to behave. They're not going to be telling the police, "We back you. Keep the gangs under control." No, they're going to be telling police, "Be careful how you treat the thugs or you'll find yourself out of a job."

I've told you many times that history repeats itself. It's repeating itself here in a very chilling way. Taking control of and nationalizing the local police was a hugely significant step for Hitler in consolidating his power. Let me be clear: I am not saying Obama is Hitler. I've never said that. But he has all the dangerous instincts of a dictator. Nevertheless, what the Obama administration is doing to local police before our very eyes is horrifyingly similar to what Hitler did to create the Gestapo. Now, we know why he appointed Loretta Lynch to replace the worst attorney general in U.S. history. Lynch is worse than the worst.

I told my listeners Loretta Lynch would be worse than Eric Holder the minute I saw Al Sharpton demand she be made America's top cop! I was right. Her very first announcement after confirmation by the Senate confirmed this. Did she announce she was going to disarm the gangs in our cities? Did she say she'd target the communist front groups responsible for all of the violence and terrorism in our streets?

No. Instead, Loretta Lynch announced she was going to hand out $163 million to thuggish groups like the ACLU, who will work with the actual street thugs who do the damage. Lynch is going to dictate new guidelines to teach local police how to deal with gangs. This is very similar to how the Gestapo was born.

Upon becoming chancellor, Adolf Hitler appointed Hermann Goering minister of the interior for Prussia. This gave Goering control of the police. His position was roughly parallel to our U.S. attorney general, although Loretta Lynch doesn't have control of our local police. That's because we have a federal Constitution and state governments, which are supposed to function separately to avoid a dictatorship. State and local governments are supposed to carry out the majority of the police work in the United States.

Unfortunately, we have a madman surrounded by demagogues in the White House. They want to take over every aspect of our lives, and checks on their power like the state governments and local police forces stand in their way. Hitler was actually a fierce opponent of what we would call states' rights, as are all dictators. As was reported at the time,

> *Under the impact of the Nazi revolution, Hitler was able to go much farther than the most sanguine had dared to dream. Politically speaking, Prussia, Bavaria, and other once proud kingdoms have ceased to lead an independent existence.*
>
> *One will—that of Hitler—now extends from Berlin to the farthest corners of the Reich.*[2]

"One will" is what it's really all about. That's what a dictator is: one who seeks to run an entire nation according to his will alone, rather than through powers delegated by the people to exercise the will of the people. You might say Hitler ruled Germany with his pen and his phone, although there were much more brutal consequences for anyone who resisted than there are in the United States today. At least so far.

Hitler also created the first national health insurance program in a noncommunist state. Just like Obamacare, this was more about consolidating power and attacking capitalism than providing better health care for the poor and lower middle class. Helping the poor was just the sales pitch. Let's not forget Hitler was a socialist. "Nazi" is just a shortened version of his party's name, the National *Socialist* Party.

Just like Americans today, Germans at the time were blissfully ignorant that Hitler's attacks on states' rights and free enterprise in health care had anything to do with their personal liberty until it was too late. That was when Hitler launched his war on local police. It was directly prosecuted by Hermann Goering. It started when Goering prohibited the official local police from interfering with Nazi Brownshirts. The Brownshirts were officially known as the Sturmabteilung (or SA), which means "Storm Detachment." They were Hitler's paramilitary group, which he had employed to intimidate opposition for over a decade by the time he came to power. Their modus operandi was to inflict violence in the streets against the Nazis' political opponents. This had the dual effect of eliminating official opposition directly and terrorizing the populace through the violence.

The gangs that burned down Baltimore and riot in cities across America with their protests are today's Brownshirts. They may not be acting under the government's direction, but they have the same effect on the populace, and they get a pass from the government after the fact.

They destroyed Ferguson, Missouri, and got away with it. They burned businesses and other property in Baltimore and got away with that, too. They had the president covering for them, just as Hitler and Goering backed the Brownshirts. They own the streets of Oakland, California.

Goering's support of the Brownshirts and neutering of the local police left German citizens defenseless, just as law-abiding citizens are defenseless in American cities today when the rioting starts. The Brownshirts also looted local businesses, just as the rioters in Ferguson, Oakland, and Baltimore looted.

Goering was more ruthless in his attack on police than our Dear Leader wants to appear. He simply purged fifty thousand local police who didn't tow the Nazi Party line and replaced them with deputized Brownshirts. Once these street thugs had the power to arrest people, jails overflowed and more space was needed to accommodate the huge increase in prisoners. Thus, the concentration camp system was born.

Fraulein Lynch might not get away with anything as overtly dictatorial as Goering's purge, but she very well could accomplish the same ends through different means. We've already seen a blueprint for purging local police with Obama's purge of the military after Benghazi.

Once community groups begin advising local police departments, watch for a parade of cops with productive records being dismissed or put on administrative leave for petty violations of the new, politically driven code of conduct. It will be the same game plan used by the grand deceiver to purge the military of top-ranked opponents.

The purges would likely enjoy public support, given the all-out propaganda campaign being waged against local police. This isn't just my opinion. Former NYPD commissioner Howard Safir sees it the same way:

> *"After 20 years of incredible crime reduction accomplished by thousands of dedicated police officers, the public has become complacent now that they are safer," said Safir, who led the nation's largest police department from 1996 [to] 2000. "They have let the anti-police pundits and talking heads convince everyone from the president to the attorney general that police are racist and brutal."[3]*

The American Council on Public Safety (ACPS) also recognizes what is going on. In a press release following a speech by the president in May, they said,

> *The President has chosen to politicize and endanger the safety of our nation's police officers. Instead of leading America towards reconciliation or strengthening community policing,*

the President has again opted to propose policies that place blame on police for unrest while weakening their ability to defend themselves and protect communities. As the blood of police officers runs in the streets, the President seems intent to embolden those who drive the false narrative that our nation's cops—not the criminals—are the problem.[4]

All of this has resulted in an increase in line-of-duty deaths for police officers. Just like Hitler's Brownshirts, Obama's Brownshirts have responded without specific instruction to assist the purge in brutal fashion. That may not be the president's intent, but it is a consequence of his deplorable responses to the riots. The number of cops killed in the line of duty nearly doubled to fifty-nine in 2014.[5] That's a number that had been dropping for decades until last year.[6]

The war on local police and eventual takeover of policing communities by the national government is how the Gestapo was born in Germany. It's also how Obama is giving birth to a new Gestapo in America. He's just doing it more subtly. His rioting gangs are called victims; the police are called thugs. He's reversed everything. He's legitimized mayhem like we've seen in city after city, blamed the cops, and now wants to take national control of them as the solution.

Obama's Brownshirts don't have the power to arrest cops themselves, but the federally funded spies sent to oversee them will accomplish the same result by reporting them for their treatment of the thugs burning down our cities. Once the precedent is set that local cops can be removed based on information the federally subsidized gangs like the ACLU provide about them, there could be a parade of cops thrown out of their jobs and replaced with useless political hacks who are properly sympathetic to the criminals setting businesses on fire.

Then, law-abiding citizens in America will be as defenseless as law-abiding Germans in 1930s Germany. Then, they'll be sufficiently terrorized to support a proposal for a national police force. That's the endgame.

We've already seen the mayhem start to shift from mainly destruction of property to assaults on innocent citizens. Protesters in Cleveland pepper-sprayed bystanders sitting at outdoor tables in restaurants.[7] Let's not forget how bad it can get. During the 1992 L.A. riots, innocent motorists were pulled from their cars and murdered. That was with a real president in the White House, which wasn't tacitly condoning the violence.

Barack Obama is the greatest illusionist in the history of the presidency. Make no mistake: He's a grand illusionist. Instead of screaming in German, he speaks softly in English, but threatens everyone in the United States of America with his reign of terror on a daily basis.

Meanwhile, ISIS is taking over one city after another in Iraq, and Obama's sorority tell us they're not losing any sleep over it. The world is burning and they're attacking American police.

Let's get back to history for a moment. After taking complete control of the local police, Goering created the Geheime Staats Polizei, shortened to Gestapo for convenience. The Prussian police had done Goering an unintentional favor by creating a huge cache of secret files on the Nazis. Goering took that idea and ran with it. He not only used the existing Prussian files against any internal Nazi opponents, but had his Gestapo continue the practice against everyone.

Do you remember those FBI files the Clinton administration requested and received back in the 1990s? Maybe those are the secret files that are keeping Republicans silent today while the progressives tear down this nation. It's possible, although the Obama administration wouldn't need twenty-year-old paper files to blackmail Republicans or anyone else today. It has the NSA collecting metadata on every phone call and e-mail sent by anyone in this country, despite a federal court ruling the practice illegal earlier this year.[8]

Or, maybe the Republicans are just greedy cowards who aren't interested in going out of their way to oppose the president on his terrifying mission. We know the establishment Republicans are willing to sell out our freedom. We saw that when Mitch McConnell tried to ram through renewal of the Patriot Act and defended the NSA's bulk collection of metadata without warrants or probable cause.[9]

Either way, we're on a very dangerous road that America wouldn't be the first to travel. With free speech and freedom of the press under attack, the military scaring the daylights out of civilians with massive training exercises in our cities and towns, and a president giving tacit support to nascent Brownshirts in our midst, the local police are our last line of defense. They are our antibodies against the disease of chaos and destruction invading our body politic.

That's why the progressives are trying to destroy them.

CHAPTER 13

Saving a Nation with Nationalism

Abandoning Conservatism

I know you've sought out this book for answers. I am going to give you answers, but perhaps not the ones you expect. Extraordinary problems require extraordinary solutions. A nation that has been radically changed for the worse may need to be radically changed back to its best form.

It's time to abandon conservatism as the defining principle of our movement. It has become meaningless. *Conservative* has come to mean anything anyone who joins the Republican Party says it means. It means "small government" to one person and "big government" to another. It means "military intervention-ism" to one and "isolationism" to another. It is "nationalism" to one and "internationalism" to another.

Any movement that could include Jeb Bush, Ted Cruz, Lindsey Graham, Marco Rubio, and Ben Carson isn't a movement at all. It has no defining principles. It is merely a buoy in the ocean to cling to while gainsaying the other side. We've tried that approach in election after election. It hasn't worked. The progressive juggernaut continues to swamp us while radical Islam attempts to finish us off.

Don't get me wrong. I remain as much a conservative as I've ever been, in the true sense of the word. I seek to "conserve" those long-standing social and legal traditions that have protected our individual liberty and national greatness for hundreds of years. That's what *conservatism* really means in the classic sense. But when Jeb Bush can promote Common Core in our schools, open borders, and Spanish as a second American language and call it conservatism, the word has lost its meaning, just as *liberal* has.

At one time, *liberal* meant laissez-faire capitalism, limited government, and personal liberty. While I believe in each of those principles, they are missing one important component that makes the rest of them possible: duty. Liberty and prosperity are not possible without commitment to preserve and defend the nation without which their existence is impossible.

I'm not talking about being enslaved to the government. I'm talking about responsibility to the nation. *The nation and the government are not the same thing.* That's what the progressives don't understand. Our forefathers pledged their lives, their fortunes, and their sacred honor to *each other*, not to any government.

The government is just a tool. It can be a means toward preserving the nation or destroying it. I don't think I have to tell you how it's been used for as long as you or I can remember. Decade after decade, the progressives have chipped away at those traditions that defined America as different from every other nation in history. Then, the Obama administration came in and replaced the chisels with bulldozers.

To counter that, we offered Mitt Romney. Romney is a fine

man and loves this country, but he obviously wasn't the answer. He offered what amounted to light progressivism. He wanted to keep the good parts of Obamacare. He wanted to blow up the education bubble even further, just as Obama did. He supported NSA spying and even Obama's horrifying claim that he can kill an American citizen on American soil on his own authority.

In spite of these positions, he was deemed too conservative by the electorate. That's why I say the word has no meaning anymore. True conservatives know what it means, but they didn't come out to vote for Romney. They won't come out to vote for another light progressive like Jeb Bush, either. Besides, what good does it do to elect him? We already had light progressivism with his brother. Jeb is even more progressive than George W.

We need a fundamental political alteration of the monopoly game. I've been saying we need a nationalist candidate for years. Real Americans are starving for one. If a truly nationalist candidate ran as a Republican, he would win the nomination and the general election by a landslide. But if we're going to put a nationalist candidate forward, we need to know what he or she would look like.

Nationalism vs. Conservatism

Conservatism has come to mean almost nothing other than "pro-business." Those who call themselves conservatives today have adopted the laissez-faire rhetoric of the old, classical liberals, but they don't really want laissez-faire. They don't propose to dismantle the massive regulatory structure built up by progressives over the past century and allow true laissez-faire competition.

Instead, they seek to tweak regulations, create loopholes, and bestow targeted tax cuts to allow their corporate donors (i.e., masters) to make bigger profits while remaining insulated from new competition by the remaining regulations and taxes.

The problem is these corporations are not American anymore. They are multinational entities with no incentive to be loyal to any particular nation unless they are given one. The Republican Party and most of those within it who identify as conservative don't propose to do that. That's why they backed NAFTA twenty years ago and back the Trans-Pacific Partnership (TPP) today. As far as they're concerned, what is good for big business is an end in and of itself.

This is why the Reagan approach didn't work. Reagan was another fundamentally decent leader and much more authentically conservative than anyone we've seen since. But he was missing that one element that might have made his system successful: true nationalism. Reagan rejected the idiotic socialist policies that had dominated American policy for decades and was successful in reviving economic growth. He just didn't incorporate the kind of nationalist polices that would have prevented the wholesale sellout that occurred under Clinton, with Republican support.

Don't get me wrong. I wholeheartedly believe in a free market economy in which each individual keeps the fruits of his labor and competition determines the winners and losers. But I also recognize, as true conservatives have throughout American history, that the entire world is not a free market. That was why traditional conservatives gave the federal government the power to regulate trade. It wasn't so the government could stick its nose into the minute details of every business in America. It was to defend and preserve the conditions within which Americans could interact freely with each other and remain competitive with the rest of the world.

If the world economy consisted of 190 or so countries just like the United States, a laissez-faire approach on the world stage would be just fine. Perhaps someday that will be true. But here in the real world today, there are not 190 USAs. There is only one which provides the personal and economic liberty that has made America so prosperous. America's uniqueness is what has led to a standard of living unrivaled in the annals of recorded history, with opportunity found nowhere else in the world.

That's why it is not realistic to expect American workers to compete with Chinese workers kept in a state of poverty by political oppression, currency manipulation, and state capitalism. The only way for them to do that would be to accept the low standard of living that goes along with those conditions in China. That's what the progressives argue conservatives want. It's hard to disagree with them when the Republican Party wholeheartedly supports our internationalist president on trade deals like the TPP.

Traditional conservatives were also nationalists. From Alexander Hamilton to Henry Clay to Abraham Lincoln, conservatives have always staunchly believed in economic policies that were best for *America*. When the Republican Party was born, its platform included *higher* taxes. Lincoln was a former Whig who believed in high tariffs to protect American business from longer-established foreign competition.

Lincoln and the Republicans also believed the government had a responsibility to provide the infrastructure necessary for a modern economy to flourish. He wanted to subsidize roads, railroads, and other infrastructure. Contrast that with the Republican reaction to the Amtrak disaster earlier this year.

All they were concerned about was using the tragedy for political gain. From listening to them, you'd think they don't believe the government should even build roads. That's not traditional conservatism, and it's certainly not nationalism.

A nationalist candidate would recognize there is a very specific role for the government. It is not to centrally plan or control every aspect of economic activity, as the progressives believe. It is not to redistribute wealth. But it is to maintain an environment in which a market economy can operate and provide the public goods needed to maximize the efficiency of that economy. It is to protect we the people from foreign powers buying and selling our infrastructure, transporting our manufacturing base, and dumping cheap goods on us to drive small- and medium-sized business into bankruptcy.

After the Amtrak wreck, Republicans immediately negated the fact that the infrastructure of this country is crumbling, despite trillions spent on stimulus. Where did those trillions go? Certainly not into new Hoover Dams, Golden Gate Bridges, Lincoln Tunnels, Empire State Buildings, or even highways.

The taxpayer money collected to rebuild America was stolen. That's just corruption, not necessarily progressivism. True nationalist conservatives shouldn't be arguing that we don't need any government infrastructure. We need honest government like the kind that built the America we're now letting fall into disrepair.

Nationalist Immigration

Regardless of which party has been in power, illegal aliens have flooded over our border. I've talked about why the progressives have allowed this. It's part of their agenda. They want to transform America from a constitutional republic based on English common-law traditions, Judeo-Christian values, and Western European customs into a secular social democracy based on atheism, multiculturalism, and Marxist economic principles.

That Mexican immigrants are more socially conservative and devoted to God, family, and a strong work ethic might be one reason why the Obama administration is bringing in far more Muslims, Asians, and Caribbean Islanders than he is Hispanics. While all immigrants, including Hispanics, tend to vote Democrat, Muslim immigrants are far less likely to assimilate into American culture than Hispanics.

As we've seen, Muslim refugees in particular have completely refused to assimilate, forming self-contained Muslim communities like Little Mogadishu in Minnesota, in which potential sleeper cells are constantly being formed.

None of this would come as a shock to most conservative voters, even if they hadn't read this book. What they don't understand is why the Republican Party, even when they held the White House, Senate, and House of Representatives for six straight years, failed to even slow down the flood of illegal immigrants. Knowing why the progressives are desperate to get them in and eventually give them the vote, knowing that even legal immigrants vote Democrat, why would they not act in their self-interest and stop it?

The answer is the same as for why they support a lopsided trade deal. They're not a nationalist party. They are simply a pro-business party, and low-skilled immigrants provide a source of cheap labor for their corporate supporters. They are so bought and sold by these special interests that they will actually stand by and watch their own demographic destruction before doing anything that might shave a penny off next year's corporate profits.

This is why Larry Ellison, one of the world's richest men, supports Marco Rubio, a shallow man willing to open the floodgates to as many H1-B visas as possible, permitting Ellison, Zuckerberg, and Gates to bring in more foreign tech workers just to lower their labor costs.

I have no particular attachment to the Republican Party, outside of their usefulness in stopping the Progressive-Islamists. Unfortunately, they are going to take all of us down with them by not resisting the single greatest threat to our borders, language, and culture: indiscriminate, unregulated immigration.

So, what would a nationalist immigration policy look like? It certainly wouldn't be closed borders forever. Immigration is not an all-or-nothing proposition. Neither am I arguing for a lower number of immigrants, per se. It's more about who is allowed to enter the United States and why. Immigration policies today bring in people based upon what America can do for them. A nationalist immigration policy would completely reverse this approach and make decisions on whom to admit based on what they can do for America.

Does that mean we never take in refugees, or those seeking a better life in America than is available in their home country? Absolutely not. When you think about it, *nobody* seeks to immigrate unless the opportunities here are better than at home. But there is a finite number of people who can be admitted into the country in any given year, regardless of how efficiently the government agencies work.

That means there are choices to make on who to admit and who we cannot admit, at least for now. We've had a radically liberal immigration policy for decades. We may need drastically opposite measures before we get back to normal.

Nationalist Liberals

I often ask friends if they believe there is any chance to work within the Democratic Party. Unsurprisingly, the overwhelming majority of answers amount to a resounding "No!"

I understand why well-meaning patriots feel this way. Certainly, there is not much chance to work with the leading Democratic *politicians*. They subscribe to an ideology diametrically opposed to everything we stand for. Trying to enlist them to help save our borders, language, and culture would be like trying to transform lions into vegetarians. It's just not going to happen.

Democratic voters are another story. Certainly, there is a large percentage of Democratic voters who are so dependent upon the government or so anti-American that they will never join our cause. They are committed to achieving everything we are committed to stopping. But I don't believe they are the majority. Rather, they are an active, vocal minority whose radical beliefs get the airplay, while the majority of Democratic voters are simply voting for what they believe is the lesser of two evils, just as we are.

I believe a nationalist movement would attract what is either a majority or a significant minority of Democratic voters who are not socialists and who do not seek to destroy society and remake it in a progressive image. I believe this group of Democrats who identify as "liberal" simply do not see in the Republican Party as it exists today a recognition of the individual's responsibility to society that is so vital a part of a nationalist movement. I don't blame them. I don't see it, either.

This group simply places more emphasis on the individual's responsibility to community and nation than on economic freedom. Given the choice between the "conservative" movement as they understand it today and the progressives, they side with the latter, who at least acknowledge some public responsibility.

I believe a nationalist movement would attract large numbers of this group. They are blue-collar Democrats who aren't interested in socialism or forced multiculturalism. They just don't want to live in an America where they are completely sold out to multinational corporations who have no obligation to the nation they are helping to build.

They want to live in the kind of America their parents and grandparents grew up in, where there is economic freedom, opportunity, and personal liberty, tempered by a duty to preserve the nation that makes all of that possible. Once they understand the nationalist platform, I believe many of them will join us without hesitation.

Nationalist Foreign Policy

When George W. Bush invaded Afghanistan, he had overwhelming support from the public, regardless of political affiliation. America had been attacked, and no one denied the need to defend our security and defeat the forces behind 9/11.

It was only when Bush apparently abandoned that mission and pursued his disastrous invasion of Iraq that rank-and-file Democrats turned against him. It was largely the Iraq War that cost Bush and the Republicans Congress in 2006 and the

White House in 2008. To this day, Republicans refuse to admit the Iraq War was a mistake, merely because it was prosecuted by a Republican, even though the rest of the world, including almost half of Republican voters, know it.[1]

I was against the Iraq War from the beginning, for the same reason true conservatives and most rank-and-file Democrats were. It did not defend the security of the United States against anyone who threatened it. Whatever secondary reasons there may have been for invading Iraq beneath the ridiculous "weapons of mass destruction" theory, none of them justified sending our troops to war or the sacrifice of blood and treasure that resulted.

Yet today, most Americans would support military action in Iraq against ISIS, and they disapprove of President Obama's handling of the Islamic State.[2] Why the completely opposite opinions on military action in the same country? Because the American people perceive a real threat from ISIS today that they did not perceive from Saddam Hussein in 2003.

I believe history will show the people were wise on both accounts. If we had a government that truly represented them, we would likely have avoided the mistake of invading Iraq in 2003 and the mistake of letting ISIS continue to grow its power in 2015.

The truth is the Republican Party has become far too eager to go to war for its own sake. I don't think it's any accident that this benefits the big business of defense contractors. The Republicans want to go to war over everything, all the time. The American people want war limited to defending our security.

Meanwhile, the progressives have sent our troops into conflicts like Somalia and Serbia, either to support the

Islamofascists or on humanitarian missions. At the time of this writing, the Obama administration has "signaled that it was prepared to expand military cooperation in the fight against Boko Haram."[3]

It's no coincidence that America's Progressive-Islamist administration would suddenly want to fight the ISIS affiliate Boko Haram in Nigeria the minute the conservative, free-market-oriented People's Democratic Party and its Christian president lost an election to the progressive party of Muslim Muhamad Buhari, Nigeria's former military dictator. Until this election, the administration had expressed little interest in the Nigerians' plight.

Regardless, this fight has nothing to do with the national security of the United States nor the stability of the world. The peaceful transfer of power was the first in Nigeria in decades and represents a step forward in stability, if not in the best interests of the Nigerian people. That's their problem. American taxpayers are not financially responsible for it and sending our troops into such quagmires, should it come to that, further weakens our military.

Most Americans, whether they vote Republican or Democrat, want our military to be used only when it is necessary for our national defense. They don't want to sacrifice lives or treasure to right every wrong in the world or promote democracy in Third World backwaters, whose inhabitants burn our flag. When the military is deployed, they want them given the tools and strategy they need to win decisively and come back home.

In other words, they want a nationalist approach to foreign policy.

40 Actions to Save America

In terms of specific actions, I could probably think of thousands that would spring from a nationalist movement to save this country. I've proposed many over the years. Some were time sensitive; some can still be accomplished. I have other ideas that are brand new. Here are the top forty that come to my mind as most urgent in 2015–2016.

Notice that not all of these have to do with the federal government. Some should be accomplished at the state or local levels. Some should be accomplished outside of any governments at all. There is much we can do in the private sector with the choices we make and the power we have over those who want to influence those choices.

1. **Start a Nationalist Party.** We need a true two-party system. Right now, we have a one-party system. It's a charade, a shell game with no peas under either shell. As we have seen with Boehner and McConnell, we have an oligarchy running America. We voted in conservatives and they were put at the back of the bus. *Conservative* has become meaningless. A Nationalist Party would attract disaffected members from both parties and tip the balance of power back to the people.

2. **Close the borders completely for seven years.** We have had unprecedented immigration into this country, not just in terms of numbers, but of foreign and even hostile cultures. We need time to assimilate the immigrants we have, just as we did the waves of immigrants at the beginning of the

last century. At the end of seven years, evaluate our capacity for normalizing immigration, with nationalist priorities as I've described.

3. **Deport all illegal aliens in American prisons.** That would be up to one-third of the prison population, which exceeds two million prisoners. This is not an expense American taxpayers should be bearing, especially in a down economy.

4. **Repeal the "Anchor Babies" law.** Right now, an illegal alien who crosses our border and gives birth has automatically bestowed citizenship on her offspring. This gives an incentive for illegal immigration, not to mention endangering the mother and baby.

5. **Make English the official language of the United States.** Mandate English for all legal and political transactions, including ballots. If you can't read English, you can't vote, period. Require all government employees to be able to speak, read, and write English fluently.

6. **Require government-issued identification to vote.** This seems like a no-brainer. It doesn't guarantee the voter is a citizen, but it at least confirms he or she is alive. Dead voters overwhelmingly vote progressive.

7. **Reintroduce civics classes to elementary and secondary schools.** We need to teach our children the history and meaning of America's founding fathers, founding documents, and founding principles. This knowledge should also be required on all citizenship tests.

8. **Restore to active duty all military officers purged by Obama.** Offer them a generous bonus as an incentive to return.

9. **Restore physical standards in the military.** If women are going to participate in combat, they are going to have to be able to meet the same physical standards as men. We cannot weaken our military for the sake of progressive politics. Lower standards cost lives on the battlefield.

10. **Restructure military spending.** We need to adequately equip the soldiers who are defending our civilization and stop wasting defense dollars in Germany and South Korea. Pull our troops out of those countries and redeploy them on our southern border. This will help control illegal immigration and ensure that soldiers are patronizing American retailers and businesses instead of foreign ones. Use some of the savings to increase the pay and upgrade the equipment of soldiers on the front lines of the war on radical Islam.

11. **Cut the rest of government significantly.** While our military is struggling, the rest of the meddling federal government is living higher than ever. Cut all nonmilitary spending in each department by 4 percent per year over the next presidential term, for a total reduction of 16 percent by 2021.

12. **Repair our relations with Russia.** Russia should be an ally in the war against radical Islam and a partner in the world economy. The United States should propose an agreement that has Russia cease any aggression outside its borders in return for assurance that the U.S. and Europe will stay out of the affairs of nations bordering Russia.

13. **Sign a mutual defense treaty with Israel.** The United States has no formal treaty with Israel at present. The U.S. would pledge its protection if Israel were attacked by a foreign power in return for Israel guaranteeing the safety of American shipping and trade with its own resources in the region.

14. **End all foreign aid, including to Israel.** The U.S. currently gives $3 billion in annual military aid to Israel and five times that amount to Middle Eastern nations, most of which want to destroy Israel. We can't afford this, nor would we need to bribe other nations not to attack Israel with a formal mutual defense treaty in place.

15. **Recognize radical Islam as the enemy.** We aren't fighting a war on terrorism. Terrorism is a minor problem outside of what is perpetrated by radical Islam. Let's formally recognize the enemy, who doesn't just fight on the battlefield and in terrorist acts, but seeks to infiltrate the West and destroy its borders, language, and culture.

16. **Allow profiling in security investigations.** While the TSA is harassing a Welsh-German grandmother from Indiana, radical Islamists walk onto airplanes without identification and try to blow them up. This is the insane result of banning profiling in security work. The security risks to American citizens come from radical Islamists. They have openly declared their intentions. Let's start our investigations on terrorist plots there and stop harassing innocent Americans.

17. **Demand Congress declare war against ISIS and destroy them.** ISIS claims to be a formal state. They control

territory, have declared war on the United States, and have killed American citizens. This is a no-brainer. Declare war and win it decisively. The rules of engagement should go no further than what is required by the Geneva Conventions.

18. **Close all tax loopholes for Hollywood.** Hollywood has become a fountain of anti-Americanism and has tax incentives to keep churning out the garbage it has been creating. Close them. Let them survive without the government's help.

19. **Fund all climate science research to include the skeptics.** This branch of science has become completely politicized. The reason so many scientists are willing to go along with this preposterous theory is they are dependent upon government money. Balance the funding and we'll see a sudden uptick in skepticism about the real effects of man's activities on climate.

20. **Withdraw from the Trans-Pacific Partnership, if possible.** We don't know the terms of Obama's secret trade deal. If there is a way to withdraw honorably under its terms, the next president should get out of it.

21. **Withdraw from NAFTA.** It has benefited no one but multinational corporations. In addition to killing American manufacturing, it has also destroyed the small farm industry in Mexico, giving further incentive for illegal immigration.[4]

22. **Narrow the Federal Reserve's mandate to a strong dollar and stable prices.** Right now, the central bank is also charged with maximizing employment, managing long-term interest rates, and regulating banks. It's doing none of its jobs

well. Its mandate to maximize employment requires it to inflate the currency, which contradicts its mandate to keep prices stable. As we aren't getting real employment growth anyway, we have nothing to lose.

23. **End the H-1B visa program.** We have STEM workers unemployed and ready to start tomorrow. We don't need to bring in temporary help from other countries. Big business will have to pay the market rate here in the United States.

24. **Institute a flat tax.** Right now, almost half of U.S. citizens pay no income tax at all, while the other half pays progressively more as they become more productive. This is unfair and *counterproductive*, by definition. A 15 percent flat tax on everyone means everyone pays their "fair share," as the progressives love to say. It also eliminates myriad loopholes for all sorts of special interests, including corporate America and Hollywood.

25. **Reinstate the Glass-Steagall Act.** This 1933 law prohibited commercial banks from also operating as investment banks. Its repeal in 1999 was a key factor in the housing meltdown. Here's one regulation that actually helped. Restore it.

26. **Reinstate the Wall Street "Uptick Rule."** This rule required short sales to be made on an "uptick," or at a price higher than the last traded price when the last movement was upward. It sounds technical, but it basically prevents speculators from driving stock prices down purely for short-term gain. Wall Street provides a valuable service when it capitalizes new businesses, creating jobs and wealth. This rule helped keep it

focused on that, instead of functioning as a rigged casino for speculators.

27. **Privatize the regulation of Wall Street.** There is a role for government regulation and a role for the market. Clearly, Congress is never going to regulate the source of its campaign contributions. Create a financial clearinghouse for the oversight of financial derivative debt instruments. Together with prohibitions on bailouts, this would introduce market discipline to the legalized gambling.

28. **Institute tort reform.** Frivolous lawsuits and ridiculously disproportionate awards also drive up medical expenses. States should cap medical liability at $250,000 per claim. This is one thing my home state of California did right and it worked.

29. **Eliminate government employee pensions.** The pension is an outdated concept that never really worked. Virtually no one in the private sector is guaranteed a pension by their employer. Why should government employees receive them? Existing pensions must be renegotiated to reflect economic reality.

30. **End affirmative action.** We've had a black president, black cabinet members from both parties, a black chairman of the Joint Chiefs of Staff, black CEOs of Fortune 100 corporations, and black billionaires. None of these achieved their success through affirmative action. Affirmative action is racism defined, as it assumes people of color need special privileges to make it. Clearly, black Americans have proved they don't. It's time to kill it.

31. **Defund federal unemployment benefits.** Unemployment benefits should be provided by private insurers in state markets. Just as we don't want states to prohibit interstate competition in medical insurance, we don't want the federal government subsidizing unemployment. It encourages people not to work. At the time of this writing, we had a record number of job openings in America.[5] We need to incentivize people to get back to work.

32. **Limit welfare benefits.** Limit welfare benefits to three years and end the incentive for welfare moms to have more babies by capping the subsidies per child. We need to reverse the perverse incentive for people to have more children when they can't support the ones they already have.

33. **End bulk collection of data by the NSA.** The NSA was collecting data on every American. The USA Freedom Act reformed this practice, but it didn't go far enough. We are wasting time and resources on innocent Americans. We know who the enemy is. Get warrants on radical Islamists and stop spying on the rest of us.

34. **Make all state universities and colleges "free speech zones."** Our colleges and universities have become brainwashing centers for the progressive left, where no dissenting speech is permitted. Not only does it further the Progressive-Islamist agenda, it stifles creativity and critical thinking. Tax dollars should not be subsidizing subversion.

35. **Defend freedom of speech against radical Islam.** Americans should feel as secure in their right to criticize

Islam as they are in their right to criticize any other religion. Oppose government infringement of this right, and when the news media supports it, boycott their broadcasts. They need our viewership, but we no longer need them.

36. **Restore freedom of religion in the military.** Stop persecuting qualified officers and soldiers for their religious beliefs. End the war on Christianity in the military.

37. **Defend religious freedom in business.** Regardless of gay marriage laws, individuals should not be compelled to violate their conscience on matters of religion. Support religious freedom restoration acts at the state level.

38. **Restore religious freedom in schools.** The First Amendment guarantees freedom *of* religion, not freedom *from* religion. No religion should be officially promoted in schools, but students and teachers should be free to talk about their religious beliefs without imposing them on others.

39. **Defend freedom of the press.** Oppose any intimidation of the press for unfavorable reporting on the government, regardless of which party is in power. Reward media that challenges the government with your business. Boycott media that bends to the pressure and propagandizes for the government.

40. **Oppose military exercises in our cities and towns.** We have the most powerful military in the history of the world, all of Obama's efforts to weaken it notwithstanding. We do not need them training in our midst, especially doing covert operations in which red states are characterized as hostile. We

should refuse our consent to the participation operations like Jade Helm 15 require.

I chose to put defense of our liberties at the end of the list because it is the last thing I want you to remember. Let's not forget that freedom is the most precious jewel in the crown of our culture. It is more important than prosperity or power. Without freedom, there can be no real virtue and no enjoyment of prosperity.

This list is only a beginning. It is a jumping-off point from which to launch a nationalist movement to restore the America that was the light of the world and build an even better one for the future.

Epilogue: Don't Give Up Hope

The trouble with those who care is that caring in the face of times like these can drive them insane. I know our fight can seem hopeless at times, but it isn't. I truly believe good will win in the end.

One of the best reasons for hope is the millions of college students out there who love their country despite all the forces trying to corrupt them. I ran a contest on my radio program earlier this year asking young people to write an essay called "What Does It Mean to Be an American?" Of the 1,700 essays submitted, the five best essayists will each receive a $20,000 scholarship to the college of their choice.

The winning essays can be found on my website (http://www.michaelsavage.wnd.com/2015/07/here-are-the-winning-essays-in-the-savage-scholarship-contest/). Reading them will give you hope. They certainly did so for me.

Notes

Chapter 1: Government Zero

1. "Lord Sacks: 'If we stand together against religious persecution, we win.'" *Jewish News Online*, June 22, 2015. http://www.jewishnews.co.uk/lord-sacks-full-speech-at-the-uk-israel-shared-strategic-challenges-conference/.

2. Ibid.

3. Thomas Paine. *Common Sense*. In *Paine Collected Writings*. Literary Classics of the United States, New York, 1955, pp. 6–7.

4. Jason Hart. "Top US Public Employee Union AFSCME Gave $65M in 2014, Mostly to Democrats, Progressive Groups." *Fox News Politics*, April 5, 2015. http://www.foxnews.com/politics/2015/04/05/afscme-country-no1-public-employees-union-gave-65m-in-2014-mostly-to-democrats/?intcmp=latestnews.

5. Anne Gearen. "Clinton Is Banking on the Obama Coalition to Win." *Washington Post*, May 17, 2015. http://www.washingtonpost.com/politics/running-to-the-left-hillary-clinton-is-banking-on-the-obama-coalition-to-win/2015/05/17/33b7844a-fb28-11e4-9ef4-1bb7ce3b3fb7_story.html.

6. Greg Sargent. "Morning Plum: Jeb Bush Rips Republicans for 'Bending with the Wind' on Immigration." *Plum Line* (blog), *Washington Post*, May 28, 2015. http://www.washingtonpost.com/blogs/plum-line/wp/2015/05/28/morning-plum-jeb-bush-rips-republicans-for-bending-with-the-wind-on-immigration/.

7. Ben Kamisar. "Jeb Bush Marks Cinco de Mayo with Spanish Video." *Ballot Box* (blog), *Hill*, May 5, 2015. http://thehill.com/blogs/ballot-box/presidential-races/241055-jeb-bush-marks-cinco-de-mayo-with-spanish-video.

8. Andrew Rosenthal. "John Boehner's Back." *Taking Note* (blog), *New York Times*, January 6, 2015. http://takingnote.blogs.nytimes.com/2015/01/06/john-boehners-back/.

9. Kimberly Leonard. "Supreme Court Upholds Obamacare Subsidies." *U.S. News and World Report*, June 25, 2015. http://www.usnews.com/

news/articles/2015/06/25/supreme-court-upholds-obamacare-subsidies-in -king-v-burwell.

10. Michael F. Cannon. "ObamaCare Architect Jonathan Gruber: 'If You're a State and You Don't Set Up an Exchange, That Means Your Citizens Don't Get Their Tax Credits'" [Updated]." *Forbes*, July 25, 2014. http:// www.forbes.com/sites/michaelcannon/2014/07/25/obamacare-architect -jonathan-gruber-if-youre-a-state-and-you-dont-set-up-an-exchange-that -means-your-citizens-dont-get-their-tax-credits/.

11. *Obergefell et al. v. Hodges, Director, Ohio Department of Health, et al.* Scalia in Dissent, p. 4.

12. White House. Office of the Press Secretary. "Remarks by the President at the United States Coast Guard Academy Commencement." May 20, 2015. https://www.whitehouse.gov/the-press-office/2015/05/20/remarks -president-united-states-coast-guard-academy-commencement.

13. Samuel Adams. "To James Warren (October 24, 1780)." Democratic Thinker. https://democraticthinker.wordpress.com/2011/08/01/samuel -adams%E2%80%94to-james-warren-october-24-1780/.

14. Janet Hook. "Liberals Make Big Comeback in 2015, Poll Analysis Finds." *Washington Wire* (blog), *Wall Street Journal*, June 7, 2015. http:// blogs.wsj.com/washwire/2015/06/07/liberals-make-big-comeback-in-2015 -poll-analysis-finds/.

Chapter 2: Zero Leadership

1. Ali Elkin. "Obama's Selma Speech Lauded As One of His Best." Bloomberg Politics, March 8, 2015. http://www.bloomberg.com/politics/ articles/2015-03-08/obama-s-selma-address-lauded-as-one-of-his-best.

2. Quoted in ibid.

3. Quoted in Maya Rhodan. "Transcript: Read the Full Text of President Barack Obama's Speech in Selma." *Time*, March 7, 2015. http://time .com/3736357/barack-obama-selma-speech-transcript/.

4. Andrew Marszal. "George W Bush Cropped Out of New York Times Front Cover Image of Selma March." *Telegraph* (UK), March 9, 2015. http://www.telegraph.co.uk/news/worldnews/northamerica/usa/11458490/ George-W-Bush-cropped-out-of-New-York-Times-front-cover-image-of -Selma-march.html.

5. Cicero, Marcus Tullius. *De Officiis*, Book II, p. 73. http://www .constitution.org/rom/de_officiis.htm.

6. Ibid.

7. Douglas Ernst. "De Blasio Has 'Blood on the Hands' After NYPD Shooting, Says Union President." *Washington Times*, December 21, 2014.

http://www.washingtontimes.com/news/2014/dec/21/de-blasio-has
-blood-hands-after-nypd-shooting-says/.

8. Ibid.

9. Ed Payne. "More Americans Volunteering to Help ISIS." CNN, March 5, 2015. http://www.cnn.com/2015/03/05/us/isis-us-arrests/.

10. "The Complete Transcript of Netanyahu's Address to Congress." *Post Politics* (blog), *Washington Post*, March 3, 2015. http://www.washington post.com/blogs/post-politics/wp/2015/03/03/full-text-netanyahus-address -to-congress/.

11. "Winston Churchill: Address to the Congress of the United States (December 26, 1941)." Jewish Virtual Library. http://www.jewishvirtual library.org/jsource/ww2/churchill122641.html.

12. Associated Press. "Tens of Thousands Attend Anti-Netanyahu Rally in Tel Aviv." *Huffington Post*, March 7, 2015. http://www.huffingtonpost .com/2015/03/07/anti-netanyahu-rally_n_6823346.html.

13. Steven Edwards. "Senate Panel Probing Possible Obama Administration Ties to Anti-Netanyahu Effort." *Fox News Politics*, March 15, 2015. http://www.foxnews.com/politics/2015/03/15/senate-committee-probes -whether-obama-administration-funded-effort-to-oust/.

14. Victoria Taft. "Retired Colonel Sums Up in 5 Words the Mean Girls– Like Reaction of Democrats to Netanyahu Speech." *IJ Review*, March 4, 2015. http://www.ijreview.com/2015/03/263246-retired-colonel-reactoiin/.

15. "The Complete Transcript of Netanyahu's Address to Congress."

16. Garance Franke-Ruta. "Is Elizabeth Warren Native American or What?" *Atlantic*, May 20, 2012. http://www.theatlantic.com/politics/ archive/2012/05/is-elizabeth-warren-native-american-or-what/257415/.

17. Ibid.

18. Michael Smerconish. "'You Didn't Build That!' in Context." *Huffington Post*, July 30, 2012. http://www.huffingtonpost.com/michael-smerconish/ you-didnt-build-that-in-c_b_1721794.html.

19. Steve Peoples. "AP Sues State Department, Seeking Access to Clinton Records." Associated Press, March 11, 2015. http://www.ap.org/ Content/AP-In-The-News/2015/AP-sues-State-Department-seeking -access-to-Clinton-records.

Chapter 3: Zero Strategy Against ISIS

1. Catherine Herridge, Jennifer Griffin, and the Associated Press. "Showing Our Hand? US Military Official Outlines Plan to Retake Iraqi City of Mosul." *Fox News Politics*, February 20, 2015. http://www.foxnews.com/ politics/2015/02/20/us-military-outlines-plan-to-retake-iraqi-city-mosul/.

2. Ibid.

3. Bridget Johnson. "Ramadi Falls, More U.S. Weapons Seized: See the Gains ISIS Made in Just Two Days." PJ Tatler, PJ Media, May 17, 2015. http://pjmedia.com/tatler/2015/05/17/ramadi-falls-more-u-s-weapons -seized-see-the-gains-isis-made-in-just-two-days/.

4. Zoe Brennan and Paul Orengoh. "The Real Reason President Obama Loathes the British…His Grandfather Was Tortured in a High -Security Kenyan Prison." *Daily Mail* (UK), June 19, 2010. http://www .dailymail.co.uk/news/article-1287828/Revealed-Why-President-Obama -loathes-British.html.

5. "Jordan's King Abdullah: Battling ISIS Is 'Our Third World War.'" *CBS News*, December 5, 2015. http://washington.cbslocal.com/2014/12/05/ jordans-king-abdullah-battling-isis-is-our-third-world-war/.

6. Jonathan Karl. "White House Says Shooting at Kosher Market in Paris Was 'Random.'" *ABC News*, February 10, 2015. http://abcnews .go.com/Politics/white-house-shooting-kosher-market-paris-random/ story?id=28871389.

Chapter 4: Zero Military

1. Todd Starnes. "Former SEALs Chaplain Could Be Kicked Out of Navy for Christian Beliefs." *Fox News Opinion*, March 9, 2015. http://www .foxnews.com/opinion/2015/03/09/former-seals-chaplain-could-be-kicked -out-navy-for-christian-beliefs/.

2. Ibid.

3. Evan Perez and Shimon Prokupecz. "Menendez Claims Innocence After Indictment." *CNN Politics*, April 2, 2015. http://www.cnn.com/ 2015/04/01/politics/robert-menendez-corruption-charges/.

4. Rowan Scarborough. "Army's Withdrawal of Officer's Silver Star Sparks Ire of Congress." *Washington Times*, March 15, 2015. http://www .washingtontimes.com/news/2015/mar/15/armys-withdrawal-of-officers -silver-star-sparks-ir/?page=all.

5. Ibid.

6. Sig Christenson. "Air Force General Lost Job over Ethnic Slur." *San Antonio Express-News*, May 4, 2015. http://www.mysanantonio.com/news/ local/article/Air-Force-general-lost-job-over-ethnic-slur-6241570.php.

7. Ibid.

8. Eric Tucker. "Former Blackwater Guards Face Sentencing in Iraq Case." Associated Press, April 12, 2015. http://www.militarytimes.com/story/ military/crime/2015/04/12/former-blackwater-guards-face-sentencing-in -iraq-case/25671413/.

9. Jim Acosta and Kevin Liptak. "For White House, Bergdahl Charges Come After Loud Defense." *CNN Politics*, March 25, 2015. http://www.cnn.com/2015/03/25/politics/bergdahl-white-house/.

10. Allen West, "VIDEO Bombshell: First Words of Bergdahl's Father at White House Were Arabic." Allen B. West, June 2, 2015. http://allenbwest.com/2014/06/bombshell-first-words-bergdahls-father-white-house-arabic/.

11. Rowan Scarborough. "See the Air Force Secretary's Jaw-Dropping Reaction to Flight with Thunderbirds." *Washington Times*, June 28, 2014. http://www.washingtontimes.com/news/2014/jun/28/air-force-secretary-gets-sick-flying-thunderbirds/.

12. "Deborah Lee James." U.S. Air Force. http://www.af.mil/AboutUs/Biographies/Display/tabid/225/Article/467806/deborah-lee-james.aspx.

13. Stephen Losey. "Air Force Secretary's Diversity Plan Will Mean Quotas, Critics Say." *Air Force Times*, March 9, 2015. http://www.airforcetimes.com/story/military/careers/air-force/2015/03/09/air-force-secretary-deborah-lee-james-opportunities-women-minorities-and-enlisted-airmen/24505205/.

14. Ibid.

15. Rowan Scarborough. "Obama's Islamic State Strategy Sparks Doubt, Resentment Among Pentagon Officials." *Washington Times*, May 26, 2015. http://www.washingtontimes.com/news/2015/may/26/obama-islamic-state-strategy-sparks-doubt-resentme/.

16. Bryant Jordan. "No Women Pass Marines Infantry Officer School by Experiment's End." Military.com, April 10, 2015. http://www.military.com/daily-news/2015/04/10/no-women-pass-marines-infantry-officer-school-by-experiments-end.html.

17. Tom Vanden Brook. "Army Says Diversity Training Sent Wrong Signal." *USA Today*, April 3, 2015. http://www.usatoday.com/story/news/nation/2015/04/03/army-diversity-training/25250733/.

18. Todd Starnes. "Pentagon Training Manual: White Males Have Unfair Advantages." *Fox News Opinion*, October 31, 2013. http://www.foxnews.com/opinion/2013/10/31/pentagon-training-manual-white-males-have-unfair-advantages/.

19. Craig Whitlock. "Pentagon Loses Track of $500 Million in Weapons, Equipment Given to Yemen." *Washington Post*, March 17, 2015. http://www.washingtonpost.com/world/national-security/pentagon-loses-sight-of-500-million-in-counterterrorism-aid-given-to-yemen/2015/03/17/f4ca25ce-cbf9-11e4-8a46-b1dc9be5a8ff_story.html?hpid=z1.

20. Loveday Morris. "Photo: Were Iranian Soldiers Fighting in Tikrit?" *WorldViews* (blog), *Washington Post*, April 2, 2015. http://www.washingtonpost.com/blogs/worldviews/wp/2015/04/02/photo-were-iranian-soldiers-fighting-in-tikrit/.

21. "Transcript: President Obama's Full NPR Interview on Iran Nuclear Deal." NPR. April 7, 2015. http://www.npr.org/2015/04/07/397933577/transcript-president-obamas-full-npr-interview-on-iran-nuclear-deal.

22. Josh Lederman and Jim Kuhnhenn. "Obama, Castro Hold Historic Meeting, Vow to Turn the Page." My Way. April 11, 2015. http://apnews.myway.com/article/20150411/summit-united_states-cuba-0c013d6ff7.html.

23. Aaron Klein. "Obama Issues Dire Predictions for Saudis." World Net Daily, April 8, 2015. http://www.wnd.com/2015/04/obama-issues-dire-prediction-for-saudis/.

24. Ibid.

25. "Fact Sheet from State Department: Parameters of Plan on Iran Nuclear Program." Washington Post, April 2, 2015. http://apps.washingtonpost.com/g/documents/world/fact-sheet-from-state-department-parameters-of-plan-on-iran-nuclear-program/1507/.

26. "Iran to Inject Gas into IR8 on 1st Day of Implementing Final N. Deal." FARS News Agency, April 7, 2015. http://english.farsnews.com/newstext.aspx?nn=13940118000331.

27. Reuters. "Iran's Khamenei Says Neither Rejects, Accepts Nuclear Deal, Details Key." Yahoo! News, April 9, 2015. http://news.yahoo.com/irans-khamenei-says-neither-rejects-accepts-nuclear-deal-101644472.html.

28. Dave Boyer. "White House Tweet Pokes Fun at Israel on Iran Nuke Deal." Washington Times, April 9, 2015. http://www.washingtontimes.com/news/2015/apr/9/white-house-tweet-pokes-fun-israel-iran-nuke-deal/.

29. Czarina Nicole O. Ong. "Russia Does [sic] Persecute Homosexuals, Say President Putin." Christian Today, December 6, 2014. http://www.christiantoday.com.au/article/russia.does.persecute.homosexuals.say.president.putin/18327.htm.

30. "Pres Obama on Fareed Zakaria GPS." CNN Press Room (blog), CNN, February 1, 2015. http://cnnpressroom.blogs.cnn.com/2015/02/01/pres-obama-on-fareed-zakaria-gps-cnn-exclusive/.

31. Richard A. Gabriel. "Jihad: War to the Knife." Military History, September 2014; published online at History.net, July 2, 2014. http://www.historynet.com/jihad-war-to-the-knife.htm.

32. F. Michael Maloof. "FBI Has Opened ISIS Cases in 49 U.S. States." World Net Daily, February 8, 2015. http://www.wnd.com/2015/02/fbi-has-opened-isis-cases-in-49-u-s-states/.

33. "Adm. Lyons: "Islam Is the Political Movement Masquerading As a Religion" (video). Before It's News, April 9, 2015. http://beforeitsnews.com/opinion-conservative/2015/04/adm-lyons-islam-is-the-political-movement-masquerading-as-a-religion-2993912.html.

Chapter 5: Zero Education

1. U.S. Department of Education. Institute of Education Sciences. National Center for Education Statistics. "Reading Literacy: Average Scores." Table R2. http://nces.ed.gov/surveys/pisa/pisa2012/pisa2012highlights_5a.asp.

2. Associated Press. "U.S. Education Spending Tops Global List, Study Shows." *CBS News*, June 25, 2013. http://www.cbsnews.com/news/us-education-spending-tops-global-list-study-shows/.

3. Thomas Sowell. "The Survival of the Left." In *The Thomas Sowell Reader*. Basic Books, New York, 2011. Available online at Google, http://books.google.com/books?id=Nfd2KKqZbNYC&printsec=frontcover&source=gbs_ge_summary_r&cad=0#v=onepage&q&f=false.

4. U.S. General Services Administration. Office of Citizen Services and Innovative Technologies. USA.gov. "Science." Kids.gov. http://kids.usa.gov/teachers/lesson-plans/science/index.shtml.

5. K. Michelle Moran. "Children's Opera Plants Seeds of Environmentalism." *C and G Newspapers*, April 15, 2015. http://www.candgnews.com/news/children%E2%80%99s-opera-plants-seeds-environmentalism-82768.

6. Heather Clark. "Barsanti Pre-K Students Model Designs in Recycled Fashion Show." *Fort Campbell Courier*, May 7, 2015. http://www.fortcampbellcourier.com/news/article_763a5062-f502-11e4-a5b9-430cdfc614f8.html.

7. Ibid.

8. Todd Starnes. "One Nation Under Allah: Fury After School Recites Pledge in Arabic." *Fox News Opinion*, March 20, 2015. http://www.foxnews.com/opinion/2015/03/20/one-nation-under-allah-fury-after-school-recites-pledge-in-arabic/.

9. Ibid.

10. Leo Hohmann. "School Snubs Christianity in 'Be Muslim' Assignment." *World Net Daily*, April 16, 2015. http://www.wnd.com/2015/04/pretend-to-be-muslim-assignment-had-no-christian-equivalent/#IVLAZsjqeFb8bc7L.99.

11. Eric Owens. "High School Senior Vying to Be Next Sandra Fluke Pulls Out Free Condom Plan." *Daily Caller*, January 17, 2015. http://dailycaller.com/2015/01/17/high-school-senior-vying-to-be-next-sandra-fluke-pulls-out-free-condom-plan/.

12. "Students Continue Fight to Get Condoms in Schools." WCJB-TV, April 8, 2015. http://www.wcjb.com/local-news/2015/04/students-continue-fight-get-condoms-schools.

13. Stephanie Bechara. "Condoms Will Be Officially Available in Alachua County Schools, Parents Will Have Choice to Opt-Out." WCJB-TV.

April 8, 2015. http://www.wcjb.com/local-news/2015/04/condoms-will-be
-officially-available-alachua-county-schools-parents-will-have.

14. Christopher Wilde. "Please, for Sake of Teens, Bring Condoms Back
to Alachua County High Schools." *Independent Florida Alligator*, April 22,
2015. http://www.alligator.org/opinion/columns/article_01b1c694-e8aa
-11e4-b7ce-27f3501f352e.html.

15. Bechara. "Condoms Will Be Officially Available in Alachua County
Schools."

16. Susan Berry. "Teacher: White 'Privilege' Makes Common Core
Necessary." *Breitbart News*, May 22, 2014. http://www.breitbart.com/big
-government/2014/05/22/teacher-common-core-necessary-because-as-a
-white-male-i-ve-been-given-a-lot-of-privilege-i-didn-t-earn/.

17. "The Derryfield School in Manchester, New Hampshire." USA
School Info. http://www.usaschoolinfo.com/school/the-derryfield-school
-manchester-new-hampshire.109307/enrollment.

18. Leslie Brody. "Thousands of Students Expected to Opt Out of N.Y.
State Tests." *Wall Street Journal*, April 14, 2015. http://www.wsj.com/articles/
thousands-of-students-expected-to-opt-out-of-n-y-state-tests-1429016387.

19. Valerie Strauss. "Why the Movement to Opt Out of Common Core
Tests Is a Big Deal." *Answer Sheet* (blog), *Washington Post*, May 3, 2015.
http://www.washingtonpost.com/blogs/answer-sheet/wp/2015/05/03/why
-the-movement-to-opt-out-of-common-core-tests-is-a-big-deal/.

20. Frederick M. Hess. "Opt-Out Parents Have a Point." *Knowledge Bank*
(blog), *U.S. News and World Report*, May 5, 2015. http://www.usnews.com/
opinion/knowledge-bank/2015/05/05/parents-opting-out-of-common
-core-tests-have-a-point.

21. Richard Brodsky. "Richard Brodsky: Opting Out of Tests Part of
the Citizen Revolt in New York." *Albany Times Union*, May 4, 2015. http://
www.timesunion.com/tuplus-opinion/article/Opting-out-of-tests-part-of
-the-citizen-revolt-in-6239846.php.

22. Janet Lorin. "Fed: People With Old Student Loans Are Struggling to Pay Them Back." Bloomberg Business, April 16, 2015. http://
www.bloomberg.com/news/articles/2015-04-16/student-loan-repayment
-worsens-for-long-term-debtors-fed-says.

23. "What Level of Default Rate Is Typical for the Credit Services
Industry?" Investopedia. http://www.investopedia.com/ask/answers/
030515/what-level-default-rate-typical-credit-services-industry.asp.

24. U.S. Department of Education. Institute of Education Sciences.
National Center for Education Statistics. Fast Facts. "Most Popular Majors."
https://nces.ed.gov/fastfacts/display.asp?id=37.

25. Tyler Durden. "Presenting the Best (and Worst) College Majors." ZeroHedge, May 7, 2015. http://www.zerohedge.com/news/2015-05-07/ presenting-best-and-worst-college-majors.

Chapter 6: Zero Culture

1. Sharon Bernstein. "California Triples Tax Breaks for Film Production." Reuters, September 18, 2014. http://www.reuters.com/article/ 2014/09/18/us-usa-film-california-idUSKBN0HD2DO20140918.

2. Todd Starnes. "University of Michigan Controversy over 'American Sniper' Screening." Fox News Opinion, April 9, 2015. http://www.foxnews .com/opinion/2015/04/08/students-force-university-to-cancel-screening -american-sniper/.

3. Matt Wilstein. "Harvey Weinstein Reveals Details of Anti-NRA Film, 'Won't Make Any More Movies Glamorizing Guns.'" Mediaite, January 17, 2014. http://www.mediaite.com/tv/harvey-weinstein -reveals-details-of-anti-nra-film-wont-make-any-more-movies-glamorizing -guns/.

4. "Harvey Weinstein." Internet Movie Database. http://www.imdb .com/name/nm0005544/?ref_=fn_al_nm_1.

5. "Sean Penn to Melt Down Guns for Sculpture, Dubs Collection 'Cowardly Killing Machines.'" Breitbart News, January 14, 2014. http:// www.breitbart.com/big-hollywood/2014/01/14/sean-penn-gun-statue/.

6. Maureen Dowd. "Obama's Big Screen Test." New York Times, February 21, 2007. http://select.nytimes.com/2007/02/21/opinion/21dowd.html.

7. Richard Verrier and Daniel Miller. "Divided No Longer, Hollywood Poised to Put Big Money Behind Hillary Clinton." Los Angeles Times, April 15, 2015. http://www.latimes.com/entertainment/envelope/cotown/ la-et-ct-clinton-presidential-race-hollywood-support-20150415-story .html#page=1.

8. T.M.P. "Sands of Iwo Jima (1949)" (review). New York Times, December 31, 1949. http://www.nytimes.com/movie/review?res=9502EFD61E3E E03BBC4950DFB4678382659EDE.

9. Robert L. Benson. "The Venona Story." National Security Agency. Center for Cryptologic History. https://www.nsa.gov/about/_files/crypto logic_heritage/publications/coldwar/venona_story.pdf.

10. Luchina Fisher. "Kanye West Tops Time's List of 100 Most Influential People." ABC News, April 16, 2015. http://abcnews.go.com/Entertainment/ kanye-west-tops-times-list-100-influential-people/story?id=30365137.

11. "Former Gator Aaron Hernandez Guilty of Murder, Gets Life in Prison." Orlando Sentinel, April 15, 2015. http://www.orlandosentinel

.com/sports/florida-gators/os-gator-aaron-hernandez-guilty-murder
-life-in-prison-20150415-story.html#page=1.

12. "Ravens' Ray Rice Indicted." ESPN, March 28, 2014. http://espn
.go.com/nfl/story/_/id/10684250/ray-rice-baltimore-ravens-indicted
-aggravated-assault.

13. Katie Sanders. "Bill Clinton: 'I Had the Lowest Net Worth of
Any American President in the 20th Century.'" PolitiFact, *Tampa Bay
Times*, June 29, 2014. http://www.politifact.com/punditfact/statements
/2014/jun/29/bill-clinton/bill-clinton-i-had-lowest-net-worth-any
-american-p/.

14. Isabel Vincent. "Charity Watchdog: Clinton Foundation a 'Slush
Fund.'" *New York Post*, April 26, 2015. http://nypost.com/2015/04/26/charity
-watchdog-clinton-foundation-a-slush-fund/.

15. Drew Desilver. "High-Income Americans Pay Most Income Taxes,
But Enough to Be 'Fair'?" Pew Research Center, March 24, 2015. http://
www.pewresearch.org/fact-tank/2015/03/24/high-income-americans-pay
-most-income-taxes-but-enough-to-be-fair/.

16. John Nolte. "Starbucks CEO Howard Schultz Imposes His Racial
Hang-Ups on America." *Breitbart News*, March 21, 2015. http://www.breit
bart.com/big-government/2015/03/21/starbucks-ceo-howard-schultz
-imposes-his-racial-hang-ups-on-america/.

17. Niraj Chokshi. "The Astonishing State-by-State Rise in Food
Stamp Reliance." *GovBeat* (blog), *Washington Post*, March 3, 2015. http://
www.washingtonpost.com/blogs/govbeat/wp/2015/03/03/food-stamp
-reliance-is-up-in-every-single-state-since-2000/.

18. Jessica C. Smith and Carla Medalia. "Health Insurance Coverage in
the United States: 2013." U.S. Census Bureau, September 2014. http://www
.census.gov/content/dam/Census/library/publications/2014/demo/p60
-250.pdf.

19. "Women's Studies Prof: Islamophobia Meme Is 'the New McCarthyism.'" *Breitbart News*, October 11, 2014. http://www.breitbart.com/
video/2014/10/11/womens-studies-prof-islamophobia-meme-is-the-new
-mccarthyism/.

20. Lauren Zupkus. "Bill Maher and Ben Affleck Have a Fierce Debate
over Radical Islam." *Huffington Post*, October 4, 2014. http://www.huff
ingtonpost.com/2014/10/04/bill-maher-ben-affleck-debate_n_5931832
.html?ir=Comedy.

21. Dale Hansen. "Bill Maher Is Unusually Conservative on Islam." *The
Blog* (blog), *Huffington Post*, October 9, 2014. http://www.huffingtonpost
.com/dale-hansen/bill-maher-is-unusually-c_b_5958996.html.

Chapter 7: Zero Immigration

1. Ryan Lovelace. "U.S. Immigrant Population Hits All-Time High: 41.3 Million People." The Corner, *National Review*, September 25, 2014. http://www.nationalreview.com/corner/388813/us-immigrant-population -hits-all-time-high-413-million-people-ryan-lovelace.

2. Steven A. Camarota and Karen Zeigler. "Projecting the 2012 Hispanic Vote." Center for Immigration Studies, August 2012. http://cis .org/projecting-2012-hispanic-vote-nationally-battleground-states.

3. Alex Swoyer. "Concerns of Muslim Immigration Surge into Western World Come into Focus." *Breitbart News*, May 7, 2015. http://www.breit bart.com/big-government/2015/05/07/concerns-of-muslim-immigration -surge-into-western-world-come-into-focus/.

4. Leo Hohmann. "Congressman Demands Answers on Influx of Syrian Refugees." *World Net Daily*, April 14, 2015. http://www.wnd.com/2015/04/ congressman-demands-answers-on-influx-of-syrian-refugees/.

5. Leo Hohmann. "Feds Hammered for Secrecy on Muslim Refugees." *World Net Daily*, June 3, 2015. http://www.wnd.com/2015/06/feds -hammered-for-secrecy-on-muslim-refugees/.

6. Leo Hohmann. "Syrian Refugee Program Called 'Back Door for Jihadists.'" *World Net Daily*, February 13, 2015. http://www.wnd.com/ 2015/02/syrian-refugee-program-called-back-door-for-jihadists/.

7. Samuel Smith. "Obama Doesn't Identify 147 Victims in Kenya Massacre as 'Christians' or Jihadi Group as 'Islamic.'" CP Politics, *Christian Post*, April 7, 2015. http://www.christianpost.com/news/obama -doesnt-identify-147-victims-in-kenya-massacre-as-christians-or-jihadi -group-as-islamic-137091/.

8. Rich Lowry. "Glossing over Evil: Just Who Killed Who in Kenya?" *New York Post*, April 6, 2015. http://nypost.com/2015/04/06/glossing-over -evil-just-who-killed-who-in-kenya/.

9. Nina Shea. "West Ignores Islamists' Aim to Annihilate Christians." *Philadelphia Inquirer*, April 12, 2015. http://www.philly.com/philly/opinion/ 20150412_West_ignores_Islamists_aim_to_annihilate_Christians.html.

10. "Refugees." *Holocaust Encyclopedia*. United States Holocaust Memorial Museum. http://www.ushmm.org/wlc/en/article.php?ModuleId=10005139.

11. Rafael Medoff. "What FDR Said About Jews in Private." *Los Angeles Times*, April 7, 2013. http://articles.latimes.com/2013/apr/07/opinion/la-oe -medoff-roosevelt-holocaust-20130407.

12. John Bacon. "Ohio Man Accused of Planning U.S. Terror Strike." *USA Today*, April 16, 2015. http://www.usatoday.com/story/news/nation/ 2015/04/16/ohio-indicted-islamic-state-terrorism/25879443/.

13. Michael Cutler. "How DHS Ineptitude Facilitates Terrorist Operations." *FrontPage Mag*, April 20, 2015. http://www.frontpagemag.com/2015/michael-cutler/how-dhs-ineptitude-facilitates-terrorist-operations/.

14. Josh Levs and Paul Vercammen. "Arrests of ISIS Supporters in Minnesota Shed Light on Recruiting, U.S. Says." CNN, April 20, 2015. http://www.cnn.com/2015/04/20/us/fbi-terrorism-probe/.

15. Paul McEnroe. "2 Minneapolis Men Charged with Attempting to Aid Terrorists." *Minneapolis Star Tribune*, November 26, 2014. http://www.startribune.com/local/minneapolis/283857371.html.

16. Leo Hohmann. "U.S. Government 'Breeding Terrorists'—in Minnesota." *World Net Daily*, September 2, 2014. http://www.wnd.com/2014/09/u-s-government-breeding-terrorists-in-minnesota/.

17. U.S. Department of Health and Human Services. Administration for Children and Families. Office of Refugee Resettlement. "ORR Funded Programs Key Contacts." October 24, 2014. http://www.acf.hhs.gov/programs/orr/resource/orr-funded-programs-key-contacts.

18. Stephen Dinan. "Illegal Immigrants Released from Custody Committed 1,000 New Crimes." *Washington Times*, January 30, 2015. http://www.washingtontimes.com/news/2015/jan/30/illegal-immigrants-released-custody-committed-1000/.

19. Steve Almasy, Pamela Brown, and Augie Martin. "Suspect in Killing of San Francisco Woman Had Been Deported Five Times." CNN, July 4, 2015. http://www.cnn.com/2015/07/03/us/san-francisco-killing-suspect-immigrant-deported/.

20. Ibid.

21. Debra J. Saunders. "San Francisco: Sanctuary City for Whom?" *SFGate*, July 4, 2015. http://blog.sfgate.com/djsaunders/2015/07/04/san-francisco-sanctuary-city-for-whom/.

22. Alex Wigglesworth. "Police: Bensalem Child Luring Suspect Exposed Himself, Urinated, Crashed Car Twice." *Philly.com*, April 19, 2015. http://www.philly.com/philly/news/breaking/Police_Bensalem_child_luring_suspect_exposed_himself_urinated_crashed_car_.html?c=r.

23. Stephen Dinan. "Illegals' Crimes Expose Broken Immigration System As Next Border Surge Looms." *Washington Times*, April 13, 2015. http://www.washingtontimes.com/news/2015/apr/13/illegal-immigrants-crimes-expose-broken-immigratio/?page=all.

24. Pam Key. "Border Control Agent: Diseases Coming In We Haven't Seen in Decades." *Breitbart News*, July 14, 2014. http://www.breitbart.com/video/2014/07/14/border-control-agent-diseases-coming-in-we-havent-seen-in-decades/.

25. Navideh Forghani. "Undocumented Immigrants Bringing Diseases Across Border?" ABC15 Arizona, June 6, 2014. http://www.abc15.com/news/national/immigrants-bringing-diseases-across-border.

26. Todd Starnes. "Immigration Crisis: Tuberculosis Spreading at Camps." *Fox News Opinion*, July 7, 2014, http://www.foxnews.com/opinion/2014/07/07/immigration-crisis-tuberculosis-spreading-at-camps/.

27. Natalie Villacorta. "CDC Confirms Respiratory Illness in Children in Missouri, Illinois, More Testing Underway." *Politico*, September 8, 2014. http://www.politico.com/story/2014/09/midwest-respiratory-illness-missouri-illinois-110711.html.

28. Henry Davis. "Uncommon Respiratory Virus May Have Hit Buffalo-Area Children." *Buffalo News*, September 10, 2014. http://www.buffalonews.com/city-region/medical/uncommon-respiratory-virus-may-have-hit-buffalo-area-children-20140910.

29. U.S. Department of Health and Human Services. Centers for Disease Control and Prevention (CDC). "Acute Neurologic Illness with Focal Limb Weakness of Unknown Etiology in Children." September 26, 2014. http://emergency.cdc.gov/han/han00370.asp.

30. U.S. Department of Health and Human Services. Centers for Disease Control and Prevention (CDC). "Summary of Findings: Investigation of Acute Flaccid Myelitis in U.S. Children, 2014–15." April 21, 2015. http://www.cdc.gov/ncird/investigation/viral/2014-15/investigation.html.

31. Jerome R. Corsi. "CDC Denies Enterovirus Link to Illegal-Alien Kids." *World Net Daily*, October 15, 2014. http://www.wnd.com/2014/10/cdc-speaks-on-enterovirus-link-to-illegal-alien-kids/#yHQyYYlBo3o0iBUo.99.

32. Maggie Fox. "Disney Measles Outbreak Came from Overseas, CDC Says." *NBC News*, February 4, 2015. http://www.nbcnews.com/storyline/measles-outbreak/disney-measles-outbreak-came-overseas-cdc-says-n296441.

33. Tony Lee. "CA Illegal Immigrant at DMV: 'Nobody's Passing' Written Test." *Breitbart News*, January 3, 2015. http://www.breitbart.com/big-government/2015/01/03/ca-illegal-immigrant-at-dmv-nobodys-passing-written-test/.

34. James G. Gimpel. "Immigration's Impact on Republican Political Prospects, 1980 to 2012." Center for Immigration Studies, April 2014. http://cis.org/immigration-impacts-on-republican-prospects-1980-2012.

35. Jerome R. Corsi. "Congressmen: Obama Using 'Cloward-Piven Maneuver.'" *World Net Daily*, June 11, 2014. http://www.wnd.com/2014/06/congressmen-obama-using-cloward-piven-maneuver/.

36. Ibid.

37. "Lynn officials: Illegal immigrant children are stressing city services" Crystal Haynes My Fox Boston. http://www.myfoxboston.com/

story/26016031/lynn-officials-illegal-immigrant-children-are-stressing-city
-services.

38. Jim Hoft. "FEDS TO OPEN $50 MILLION RESORT FOR ILLEGAL CHILDREN–Complete With Tennis Courts, Sauna & Pools (Updated)." The Gateway Pundit, July 16, 2014. http://www.thegateway pundit.com/2014/07/feds-to-open-50-million-resort-hotel-for-illegal -children-complete-with-tennis-courts-sauna-pools/.

39. Solicitation Number: BERKS-RFI Escort Services for Unaccompanied Alien Children FedBizOpps.gov. https://www.fbo.gov/index?s=oppo rtunity&mode=form&id=c6d7c0050b912fbc917a46d6709d38bd&tab=core &tabmode=list&=.

40. Mica Rosenberg. "For some companies, influx of migrant children into U.S. means business." Reuters, August 1, 2015. http://www.reuters.com/ article/2014/08/01/us-usa-immigration-contracts-insight -idUSKBN0G13A320140801.

41. GEO Group Management Team. http://www.geogroup.com/ management_team.

42. GEO Group Board of Directors. http://www.geogroup.com/ board_of_directors.

43. Tarini Parti. "'Dark money': ALEC wants image makeover." Politico, July 30, 2015. http://www.politico.com/story/2015/07/alec-koch-brothers -dark-money-anonymous-donation-120784.html.

Chapter 8: Zero Religion

1. John Rook. "Rabbi Seeks to Dispel Myths About Pius XII." Cheshire Herald, June 19, 2010. http://www.cheshireherald.com/node/2695.

2. "The Papacy: For God's Sake." Economist, December 11, 2004, pp. 82–83.

3. Russell Chamberlin. The Bad Popes. Sutton Publishing, Gloucestershire, UK, 2003, pp. 955–963.

4. Jan Hus. De Ecclesia: The Church. Charles Scribner and Sons, New York, 1915, p. 179.

5. "Pope and Politics." Time, September 22, 1924. http://content.time .com/time/magazine/article/0,9171,719174,00.html.

6. Pope Francis, Evangelii Gaudium. Libereria Editrice Vaticana, Rome, 2013, paragraph 204. http://w2.vatican.va/content/francesco/en/ apost_exhortations/documents/papa-francesco_esortazione-ap_20131124 _evangelii-gaudium.html#The_economy_and_the_distribution_of_income.

7. Steve Phillips. Lenin and the Russian Revolution. Heinemann, Oxford, UK, 2000, p. 58.

8. "Putin Speaks at Davos." *Wall Street Journal*, January 28, 2009.

9. Quoted in "Pope Francis Appeals to Americas Summit for Better Distribution of Riches." Merco Press, April 12, 2015. http://en.mercopress.com/2015/04/12/pope-francis-appeals-to-americas-summit-for-better-distribution-of-riches.

10. J.P.P. "How Did the Global Poverty Rate Halve in 20 Years?" *Economist*, June 2, 2013. http://www.economist.com/blogs/economist-explains/2013/06/economist-explains-0.

11. B.C. "The Pope's Divisions." *Economist*, June 20, 2014. http://www.economist.com/blogs/erasmus/2014/06/francis-capitalism-and-war.

12. Bosco Peters. "Pope Renounces Infallibility." Liturgy, April 1, 2013. http://liturgy.co.nz/pope-renounces-infallibility.

13. "First Vatican Council (1869–1870)," chapter 4, paragraph 9. Eternal Word Television Network. http://www.ewtn.com/library/COUNCILS/V1.htm#6.

14. Vatican. Press Office of the Holy See. "Communiqué of the Secretariat of State." December 17, 2014. http://press.vatican.va/content/salastampa/it/bollettino/pubblico/2014/12/17/0968/02096.html#Traduzione%20in%20lingua%20inglese.

15. Cuban Dissidents Detained in Havana Hours Before Planned Protest." *Fox News Latino*, December 31, 2014. http://latino.foxnews.com/latino/politics/2014/12/31/cuban-dissidents-detained-in-havana-hours-before-planned-protest/.

16. Michelle Malkin. "Race-Baiter Democrat Rep. Diane Watson Praises Cuban Health System, Castro & Guevara Who 'Kicked Out the Wealthy.'" Michelle Malkin (website), August 28, 2009. http://michellemalkin.com/2009/08/28/race-baiter-democrat-rep-diane-watson-praises-cuban-health-system-castro-guevara-who-kicked-out-the-wealthy/.

17. "Mao Cheerleader?" (video). *Fox News*, April 30, 2011. http://video.foxnews.com/v/3942582/mao-cheerleader/?#sp=show-clips.

18. Elizabeth Dias. "Pope Francis Speaks Out on *Charlie Hebdo*: 'One Cannot Make Fun of Faith.'" *Time*, January 15, 2015.

19. Thomas Jefferson. "Notes on Virginia, Query XVII." In *Jefferson: Writings*. Literary Classics of the United States, New York, 1984, p. 285.

20. "Pope's Address to Popular Movements" (Vatican City, October 29, 2014). Zenit.org. http://www.zenit.org/en/articles/pope-s-address-to-popular-movements.

21. Thomas Reese. "Does Pope Francis Have a Master's Degree in Chemistry?" *National Catholic Reporter*, June 3, 2015. http://ncronline.org/blogs/ncr-today/does-pope-francis-have-masters-degree-chemistry.

22. Associated Press. "Pope on Climate Change: Man Has 'Slapped Nature in the Face.'" *New York Times*, January 15, 2015. http://www.nytimes.com/aponline/2015/01/15/world/asia/ap-as-rel-pope-asia-climate-.html?_r=0.

23. Arthur B. Robinson, Noah E. Robinson, and Willie Soon. "Environmental Effects of Increased Atmospheric Carbon Dioxide." Oregon Institute of Science and Medicine. http://www.oism.org/pproject/s33p36.htm.

24. Jared Diamond. *Collapse: How Societies Choose to Fail or Succeed*. Penguin, New York, 2005, p. 266.

25. Robinson, Robinson, and Soon. "Environmental Effects of Increased Atmospheric Carbon Dioxide."

26. Manfred Mudelsee. "The Phase Relations Among Atmospheric CO_2 Content, Temperature and Global Ice Volume over the Past 420 ka." *Quaternary Science Reviews* 20 (2001):583–589.

27. P. W. Adams. "*Ugh* Catholic Cardinal Pushes 'Sustainable Development'; Says Gov's Role to Reduce Gap Between Privileged and Majority." Progressives Today, May 22, 2015. http://www.progressivestoday.com/ugh-catholic-cardinal-pushes-sustainable-development-says-govs-role-to-reduce-gap-between-privileged-and-majority/.

28. Ryan Mac. "Richer Than Romney: Al Gore Scores on Sale of Current TV." *Forbes*, January 4, 2013. http://www.forbes.com/sites/ryanmac/2013/01/04/richer-than-romney-al-gore-scores-on-sale-of-current-tv/.

29. Jake Tapper. "Al Gore's 'Inconvenient Truth'?—A $30,000 Utility Bill." *ABC News*, February 26, 2007. http://abcnews.go.com/Politics/GlobalWarming/story?id=2906888.

30. Ben Wyatt. "Paranoia, Parquet Floors and Pool Tables: Welcome to the Sochi Home of Stalin." CNN, June 3, 2014. http://www.cnn.com/2014/02/12/world/sochi-olympics-joseph-stalin-dacha/.

31. David McCullough. *John Adams*. Simon & Schuster Paperbacks, New York, 2008, p. 441.

32. Pope Francis. *Laudato Si: On Care for Our Common Home*. Libereria Editrice Vaticana, Rome, May 24, 2015. http://w2.vatican.va/content/francesco/en/encyclicals/documents/papa-francesco_20150524_enciclica-laudato-si.html.

33. Ibid.

34. Ibid.

35. William M. Briggs. "The Scientific Pantheist Who Advises Pope Francis." The Stream, June 22, 2015. https://stream.org/scientific-pantheist-who-advises-pope-francis/.

36. Ibid.

37. *Laudato Si*, paragraph 60.

38. Ibid., paragraph 233.

39. Ibid., paragraph 50.

40. Ibid., paragraph 189.

41. Ibid., paragraph 193.

Chapter 9: Zero Science

1. Bjorn Stevens. "Rethinking the Lower Bound on Aerosol Radiative Forcing." *Journal of Climate* 28 (June 2015):4794–4819. http://journals.ametsoc.org/doi/abs/10.1175/JCLI-D-14-00656.1.

2. Michael Bastasch. "Scientists Say New Study Is a 'Death Blow' to Global Warming Hysteria." *Daily Caller*, March 31, 2015. http://dailycaller.com/2015/03/31/scientists-say-new-study-is-a-death-blow-to-global-warming-hysteria/.

3. The White House. "Climate Change." https://www.whitehouse.gov/energy/climate-change.

4. Quoted in Jonathan Pearlman. "Australia PM Adviser Says Climate Change Is 'UN-Led Ruse to Establish New World Order.'" *Telegraph* (UK), May 8, 2015. http://www.telegraph.co.uk/news/worldnews/australiaandthepacific/australia/11591193/Australia-PM-advisor-says-climate-change-a-UN-led-ruse.html.

5. "Lysenkoism." Rational Wiki. http://rationalwiki.org/wiki/Lysenkoism#cite_note-0.

6. David Joravsky. *The Lysenko Affair*. University of Chicago Press, Chicago, 1970, pp. 308–309.

7. Michael Asher. "Princeton Physicist Calls Global Warming Science 'Mistaken.'" Daily Tech, December 23, 2008. http://www.dailytech.com/Princeton+Physicist+Calls+Global+Warming+Science+Mistaken/article13773.htm.

8. Adam Weinstein. "Arrest Climate-Change Deniers." Gawker, March 28, 2014. http://gawker.com/arrest-climate-change-deniers-1553719888.

9. Paul Homewood. "Massive Tampering with Temperatures in South America." *Not a Lot of People Know That* (blog), January 20, 2015. https://notalotofpeopleknowthat.wordpress.com/2015/01/20/massive-tampering-with-temperatures-in-south-america/.

10. Maxim Lott. "Distorted Data? Feds Close 600 Weather Stations Amid Criticism They're Situated To Report Warming." *Fox News*, August 13, 2013. http://www.foxnews.com/science/2013/08/13/weather-station-closures-flaws-in-temperature-record/.

11. Ibid.

12. "Cretaceous Period: Life." University of California Museum of Paleontology. http://www.ucmp.berkeley.edu/mesozoic/cretaceous/cretlife.html.

13. Dave Hoopman. "The Faithful Heretic." *Wisconsin Energy Cooperative News*, May 2007. http://www.wecnmagazine.com/2007issues/may/may07.html.

14. Ibid.

15. Global Warming Petition Project (official website). http://www.petition project.org/.

16. Manfred Mudelsee. "The Phase Relations Among Atmospheric CO_2 Content, Temperature and Global Ice Volume over the Past 420 ka." *Quaternary Science Reviews* 20 (2001):583–589.

17. Joe Martino. "420,000 Years of Data Suggests Global Warming Is Not Entirely Manmade." Collective Evolution (CE). http://www.collective -evolution.com/2013/02/08/420000-years-of-data-suggestss-global -warming-is-not-man-made/.

18. Michael Bastasch. "Antarctic Sea Ice Did the Exact Opposite of What Models Predicted." *Daily Caller*, March 2, 2015. http://dailycaller .com/2015/03/02/antarctic-sea-ice-did-the-exact-opposite-of-what-models -predicted/.

19. Christopher Booker. "The Fiddling with Temperature Data Is the Biggest Science Scandal Ever." *Telegraph* (UK), February 7, 2015. http:// www.telegraph.co.uk/news/earth/environment/globalwarming/11395516/ The-fiddling-with-temperature-data-is-the-biggest-science-scandal-ever .html.

20. Ibid.

21. Homewood. "Massive Tampering with Temperatures in South America."

22. Joseph D'Aleo and Anthony Watts. *"Surface Temperature Records: Policy Drive Deception?"* SPPI Original Paper, August 27, 2010. Science and Public Policy Institute. http://scienceandpublicpolicy.org/images/stories/ papers/originals/surface_temp.pdf.

23. Ibid., pp. 24–25.

24. Quoted in John Hinderaker. "NOAA Caught Rewriting US Temperature History (Again)." Powerline, May 5, 2015. http://www.powerline blog.com/archives/2015/05/noaa-caught-rewriting-us-temperature-history -again.php.

25. "Record Antarctic Sea Ice a Logistic Problem for Scientists." *Yahoo! News*, May 12, 2015. http://news.yahoo.com/record-antarctic-sea-ice -logistic-problem-scientists-071717226.html.

26. James Taylor. "Updated NASA Data: Global Warming Not Causing Any Polar Ice Retreat." *Forbes*, May 19, 2015. http://www.forbes.com/sites/jamestaylor/2015/05/19/updated-nasa-data-polar-ice-not-receding-after-all/.

27. Ibid.

28. Ezra Klein. "Obama: The Vox Conversation, Part 1: Domestic Policy." *Vox*, January 2015. http://www.vox.com/a/barack-obama-interview-vox-conversation/obama-domestic-policy-transcript.

Chapter 10: Zero Business Sense

1. "Thank you, Janet Yellen! Stocks Surge After Fed." CNN Money, March 18, 2015. http://money.cnn.com/2015/03/18/investing/stocks-markets-surge-federal-reserve-statement/.

2. National Archives. Federal Register. "Executive Order 12631—Working Group on Financial Markets." March 18, 1988. http://www.archives.gov/federal-register/codification/executive-order/12631.html.

3. Jim Clifton. "The Big Lie: 5.6% Unemployment." Gallup, February 3, 2015. http://www.gallup.com/opinion/chairman/181469/big-lie-unemployment.aspx.

4. "Alternate Unemployment Charts." May 8, 2015. John Williams' Shadow Government Statistics. http://www.shadowstats.com/alternate_data/unemployment-charts.

5. Perianne Boring. "If You Want to Know the Real Rate of Inflation, Don't Bother with the CPI." *Forbes*, February 3, 2014. http://www.forbes.com/sites/perianneboring/2014/02/03/if-you-want-to-know-the-real-rate-of-inflation-dont-bother-with-the-cpi/.

6. Peter J. Wallison and Edward J. Pinto. "A Government-Mandated Housing Bubble." *Forbes*, February 16, 2009. http://www.forbes.com/2009/02/13/housing-bubble-subprime-opinions-contributors_0216_peter_wallison_edward_pinto.html.

7. The White House. "Setting the Record Straight: Six Years of Unheeded Warnings for GSE Reform." October 9, 2008. http://georgewbush-whitehouse.archives.gov/news/releases/2008/10/20081009-10.html.

8. Ed Morrissey. "Harvard study: Dodd-Frank Actually Made 'Too Big to Fail' Even Bigger." Hot Air, February 12, 2015. http://hotair.com/archives/2015/02/12/harvard-study-dodd-frank-actually-made-too-big-to-fail-even-bigger/.

9. Max Ehrenfreund. "Remember Solyndra? Those Loans Are Making Money." *Wonkblog* (blog), *Washington Post*, November 13, 2014. http://

www.washingtonpost.com/blogs/wonkblog/wp/2014/11/13/wonkbook
-remember-solyndra-those-loans-are-making-money/.

10. Michael Bastasch. "GAO: DOE's Green Energy Loans Won't Make a Profit." *Daily Caller*, April 28, 2015. http://dailycaller.com/2015/04/27/gao-does-green-energy-loans-wont-make-a-profit/.

11. Jack Ewing. "European Central Bank Expands Mandate As It Struggles to Keep Zone Intact." *New York Times*, May 24, 2015. http://www.nytimes.com/2015/05/25/business/international/european-central-bank-expands-mandate-as-it-struggles-to-keep-zone-intact.html?_r=0.

12. Peter Morici. "The Poverty of Obama's Foreign Policy." *Newsmax*, May 18, 2015. http://www.newsmax.com/PeterMorici/obama-foreign-policy-history/2015/05/18/id/645172/.

13. Kitco. "24-Hour Spot Chart—Gold." http://www.kitco.com/charts/livegold.html.

14. Lawrence Kudlow. "Waxing Dollar Lifts Hopes for a Boom, Despite Gloomsayers." *New York Sun*, March 13, 2015. http://www.nysun.com/national/waxing-dollar-emerges-as-hope-for-an-economic/89090/.

15. Kara Rowland and the Associated Press. "Reid Throws Brakes on Obama Trade Push." *Fox News Politics*, May 5, 2015. http://www.foxnews.com/politics/2015/05/05/reid-throws-brakes-on-obama-trade-push/.

16. Edward-Isaac Dovere. "Extreme Secrecy Eroding Support for Obama's Trade Pact." *Politico in Europe*, May 4, 2015. http://www.politico.com/story/2015/05/secrecy-eroding-support-for-trade-pact-critics-say-117581.html.

17. Rowland and the Associated Press. "Reid Throws Brakes on Obama Trade Push."

18. Lisa Mascaro and Don Lee. "Obama Suffers Big Loss As Trade Bill Is Defeated at Hands of Democrats." *Los Angeles Times*, June 12, 2015. http://www.latimes.com/nation/la-na-house-vote-fast-track-20150612-story.html#page=1.

19. Cristina Marcos and Vicki Needham. "House Approves Fast-Track 218–208, Sending Bill to Senate." *Hill*, June 18, 2015. http://thehill.com/business-a-lobbying/245417-house-approves-fast-track-218-208-sending-bill-to-senate.

20. Alexander Bolton. "Senate Approves Fast-Track, Sending Trade Bill to White House." *Hill*, June 24, 2015. http://thehill.com/homenews/senate/246035-senate-approves-fast-track-sending-trade-bill-to-white-house.

21. U.S. Department of Commerce. Bureau of Economic Analysis. "March 2015 Trade Gap is $51.4 Billion." May 5, 2015. http://blog.bea.gov/category/trade-deficit/.

22. Jim Acosta. "Obama's Cars Claim in Trade Deal Running on Empty?" *CNN Politics*, May 6, 2015. http://www.cnn.com/2015/05/06/politics/obama-tpp-trans-pacific-partnership-cars-japan/.

23. Paul Bedard. "New Trade Warning: International 'Tribunal' Could Junk U.S. Laws to Help Foreign Firms." *Washington Examiner*, May 7, 2015. http://www.washingtonexaminer.com/new-trade-warning-international-tribunal-could-junk-u.s.-laws-to-help-foreign-firms/article/2564133.

24. Alex Swoyer. "Revealed: The Secret Immigration Chapter in Obama's Trade Agreement." *Breitbart News*, June 10, 2015. http://www.breitbart.com/big-government/2015/06/10/revealed-the-secret-immigration-chapter-in-obamas-trade-agreement/.

25. Ibid.

26. Paul Kane. "Obama Wins Trade Victory in the Senate." *Washington Post*, May 22, 2015. http://www.washingtonpost.com/politics/obama-wins-trade-victory-in-the-senate/2015/05/22/1cb6958e-00c7-11e5-8b6c-0dcce21e223d_story.html.

27. Shan Li and Matt Morrison. "Edison's Plans to Cut Jobs, Hire Foreign Workers Is Assailed." *Los Angeles Times*, February 10, 2015. http://www.latimes.com/business/la-fi-edison-layoffs-20150211-story.html.

28. Ibid.

29. Lily-Hayes Kaufman. "In Defense of the H-1B Visa." *Forbes*, March 22, 2009. http://www.forbes.com/2009/03/22/H-1b-visa-mba-america-tarp-opinions-contributors-universities.html.

30. Adelle Nazarian. "Exclusive: Union Official Says 'Corporate Greed' Behind Push for H-1B Visas." *Breitbart News*, March 16, 2015. http://www.breitbart.com/big-government/2015/03/16/exclusive-union-official-says-corporate-greed-behind-push-for-h-1b-visas/.

31. Robert N. Charette. "The STEM Crisis Is a Myth." IEEE Spectrum, August 30, 2013. http://spectrum.ieee.org/at-work/education/the-stem-crisis-is-a-myth.

Chapter 11: Zero Liberty

1. Chuck Ross. "Breaking: Shooting in Texas Outside of Muslim Cartoon Event Attended by Geert Wilders." *Daily Caller*, May 3, 2015. http://dailycaller.com/2015/05/03/breaking-shooting-in-texas-outside-of-muslim-cartoon-event-attended-by-geert-wilders/.

2. "O'Reilly on Pamela Geller Mohammed Drawing Contest: 'Insulting The Entire Muslim World Is Stupid'" (video). Real Clear Politics Video, May 6, 2015. http://www.realclearpolitics.com/video/2015/05/06/oreilly_on_pamela_geller_mohammed_drawing_contest_insulting_the_entire_muslim_world_is_stupid.html.

3. Josh Feldman. "O'Reilly Tackles Texas Shooting: 'Insulting the Entire Muslim World Is Stupid.'" Mediaite, May 5, 2015. http://www

.mediaite.com/tv/oreilly-tackles-texas-shooting-insulting-the-entire-muslim-world-is-stupid/.

4. Penny Starr. "Domestic Terror Attack on Family Research Council in New Exhibit at National Crime Museum." *CNS News*, March 20, 2015. http://cnsnews.com/news/article/penny-starr/domestic-terror-attack-family-research-council-new-exhibit-national-crime.

5. "NBC Terrorism Analyst: Mohammed Drawing Event Attackers Were 'Nutcases'; Plenty of Christians 'Have Done the Exact Same Thing'" (video and transcript). Real Clear Politics Video, May 4, 2015. http://www.realclearpolitics.com/video/2015/05/04/nbc_terrorism_analyst_evan_kohlmann_mohammed_drawing_event_attackers_were_nutcases_christians_jews_exact_same_thing.html.

6. Ibid.

7. Todd Starnes. "WH Silent over Demands to Denounce 'Piss Christ' Artwork." Fox News Radio. September 21, 2012. http://radio.foxnews.com/toddstarnes/top-stories/wh-silent-over-demands-to-denounce-piss-christ-artwork.html.

8. Patrick Poole. "Kansas City Mosque That Wanted to Ban Free Speech Will Hold Funeral for TX Jihadist Nadir Soofi." PJ Tatler, PJ Media, May 6, 2015. http://pjmedia.com/tatler/2015/05/06/kansas-city-mosque-that-wanted-to-ban-free-speech-will-hold-funeral-for-texas-jihadist-shooter-nadir-soofi/.

9. Ibid.

10. Ibid.

11. Ibid.

12. Randy DeSoto. "ISIS Makes Terrifying Threat to US, Names These States, Gives Time Frame." Western Journalism, May 7, 2015. http://www.westernjournalism.com/isis-claims-to-have-71-trained-soldiers-in-targeted-u-s-states/.

13. Todd J. Gillman. "White House on Garland Attack: No Act of Expression Justifies Violence, Even If It's Offensive." *The Dallas Morning News*, May 4, 2015. http://trailblazersblog.dallasnews.com/2015/05/white-house-on-garland-attack-no-act-of-expression-justifies-violence-even-if-its-offensive.html/

14. The White House. Office of the Press Secretary. "Press Briefing by Press Secretary Josh Earnest, 5/5/2015." May 5, 2015. https://www.whitehouse.gov/the-press-office/2015/05/05/press-briefing-press-secretary-josh-earnest-552015.

15. Ayaan Hirsi Ali. "Why Islam Needs a Reformation." *Wall Street Journal*, March 20, 2015. http://www.wsj.com/articles/a-reformation-for-islam-1426859626.

16. Carla Power. "What Ayaan Hirsi Ali Doesn't Get About Islam." *Time*, April 17, 2015. http://time.com/3825345/what-ayaan-hirsi-ali-doesnt-get-about-islam/.

17. Haroon Moghul. "Ayaan Hirsi Ali Is Hurting Islam: Why Her Radical Reformation Is in Desperate Need of Reform." *Salon*, April 21, 2015. http://www.salon.com/2015/04/21/ayaan_hirsi_ali_is_hurting_islam_why_her_radical_reformation_is_in_desperate_need_of_reform_partner/.

18. "Exclusive—Ayaan Hirsi Ali Extended Interview" (video). *The Daily Show with Jon Stewart*. Comedy Central, March 23, 2015. http://thedaily show.cc.com/extended-interviews/gndgo0/exclusive-ayaan-hirsi-ali-extended-interview.

19. Josh Gerstein, Tarini Parti, Hadas Gold, and Dylan Byers. "Clinton Foundation Donors Include Dozens of Media Organizations, Individuals." *Politico*, May 15, 2015. http://www.politico.com/blogs/media/2015/05/clinton-foundation-donors-include-dozens-of-media-207228.html.

20. Peter Schweizer. "Stephanopoulos, ABC Have Not Fully Disclosed Clinton Ties: Schweizer." *USA Today*, May 18, 2015. http://www.usatoday.com/story/opinion/2015/05/16/stephanopoulos-abc-clinton-schweizer-foundation-hillary-column/27436475/.

21. John Nolte. "Obama Rips Fox: 'We're Going to Have to Change How the Media Reports.'" *Breitbart News*, May 12, 2015. http://www.breitbart.com/big-journalism/2015/05/12/obama-rips-fox-were-going-to-have-to-change-how-the-media-reports/.

22. "Not How They Roll: Pentagon Asks Media to Scrap Old Footage of ISIS Columns." Fox News, May 15, 2015. http://www.foxnews.com/world/2015/05/15/pentagon-asks-media-to-can-old-footage-isis-columns/.

23. U.S. Army Special Operations Command. "Request to Conduct Realistic Military Training (RMT) Jade Helm 15." Available at https://docs.google.com/file/d/0B3axduuybL0jdjZQUjhsSmJsZTA/edit.

24. Alex Newman. "Establishment Press Discredits Itself with 'Jade Helm' Deceit." *New American*, May 7, 2015. http://www.thenewamerican.com/usnews/politics/item/20827-establishment-press-discredits-itself-with-jade-helm-deceit.

25. Paul Joseph Watson. "Walmart Death Camps for Martial Law Takeover? (Debunked)." Infowars, April 22, 2015. http://www.infowars.com/walmart-death-camps-for-martial-law-takeover-debunked/.

26. Ray Stern. "'Jade Helm 15' Operation in Arizona by U.S. Army Worries Wackos." *Phoenix New Times*, April 28, 2015. http://www.phoenix newtimes.com/news/jade-helm-15-operation-in-arizona-by-us-army-worries-wackos-7287578.

Chapter 12: Zero Police

1. The White House. Office of the Press Secretary. "Remarks by the President on Community Policing." May 18, 2015. https://www.whitehouse.gov/the-press-office/2015/05/18/remarks-president-community-policing.

2. Louis P. Lochner. "States' Rights Scrapped Under Hitler Leadership." *Reading Eagle*, May 24, 1933. https://news.google.com/newspapers?nid=1955&dat=19330524&id=g45fAAAAIBAJ&sjid=d2QNAAAAIBAJ&pg=5737,3958913&hl=en.

3. Perry Chiaramonte. "'War on Police': Line-of-Duty Deaths Rise Amid Racially-Charged Rhetoric, Anti-Cop Climate." *Fox News*, May 17, 2015. http://www.foxnews.com/us/2015/05/17/war-on-police-line-duty-deaths-rise-amid-racially-charged-rhetoric-anti-cop/.

4. American Council on Public Safety. Press release. May 18, 2015.

5. Officer Down Memorial Page. https://www.odmp.org/search/year?year=2015.

6. Andy Banker. "Worries About 'Ferguson Effect' After Police Killed on Duty Jumps 90%." Fox 2 News Now, May 12, 2015. http://fox2now.com/2015/05/12/danger-in-the-line-of-duty/.

7. Associated Press. "The Latest in Cleveland: Holiday Arraignments for Protesters." *Yahoo! News*, May 24, 2015. http://news.yahoo.com/latest-cleveland-cafe-patrons-were-pepper-sprayed-135604010.html;_ylt=A0LEVw0rqp1VvFsAYhpXNyoA;_ylu=X3oDMTExcjZhcGFzBGNvbG8DYmYxBHBvcwMxBHZ0aWQDVUlDMV8xBHNlYwNzcg--.

8. Charlie Savage and Jonathan Weisman. "N.S.A. Collection of Bulk Call Data Is Ruled Illegal." *New York Times*, May 7, 2015. http://www.nytimes.com/2015/05/08/us/nsa-phone-records-collection-ruled-illegal-by-appeals-court.html?_r=0.

9. Stephen Dinan. "Patriot Act Phone Snooping Likely to Expire After McConnell Gambit Backfires." *Washington Times*, May 24, 2015. http://www.washingtontimes.com/news/2015/may/24/patriot-act-nsa-phone-snooping-likely-to-expire-af/.

Chapter 13: Saving a Nation with Nationalism

1. Carrie Dann. "Not Worth It: Huge Majority Regret Iraq War, Exclusive Poll Shows." *NBC News*, June 24, 2014. http://www.nbcnews.com/storyline/iraq-turmoil/not-worth-it-huge-majority-regret-iraq-war-exclusive-poll-n139686.

2. David McCabe. "Poll: Most Support Vote for War Against ISIS." *Briefing Room* (blog), *Hill*, February 16, 2015. http://thehill.com/

blogs/blog-briefing-room/232911-poll-most-support-vote-for-war-against
-isis.

3. Michael R. Gordon. "U.S. Signals Willingness to Expand Military
Cooperation with Nigeria." *New York Times*, May 29, 2015. http://www
.nytimes.com/2015/05/30/world/africa/us-signals-willingness-to-widen
-role-in-fighting-boko-haram-in-nigeria.html?_r=0.

4. Dustin Ensinger. "Illegal Immigration and NAFTA." Economy
in Crisis, February 5, 2011. http://economyincrisis.org/content/illegal
-immigration-and-nafta.

5. Andrew Soergel. "Record Number of Job Openings in April, Says
Labor Department." *U.S. News and World Report*, June 9, 2015. http://
www.usnews.com/news/articles/2015/06/09/record-number-of-job
-openings-in-april-according-to-labor-departments-jolts-report.

Index